MW01323947

$urviving Your Business Debt

A financial survival guidebook for business owners, financial managers, and CFOs

Kenneth Easton

PublishingWorks
Exeter, New Hampshire

To order additional copies of this title contact your local bookstore or log onto the below web site. The author may be contacted at the following E-Mail address: info@survivingyourbusinessdebt.com.

Website: www.survivingyourbusinessdebt.com or The Easton Group, P. O. Box 16053, Hoocksett, NH 03106

Published by: PublishingWorks, Inc., 60 Winter Street, Exeter, NH 03833. 603-778-9883.

Marketing & Sales by: Revolution Booksellers, 60 Winter Street, Exeter, NH 03833. 800-REV-6603.

Designed by Kat Mack
Copy editing by Kate Petrella

ISBN-13: 978-1-933002-50-7
Printed in Canada
LCCN: 2007929397

$URVIVING YOUR BUSINESS DEBT

DEDICATION

To my beloved wife
Brenda

Who's been through it all.

and our devoted children
Catherine, Thomas, and Carolyn

Our gifts from God

Thank you for your love, your prayers, and your patience
as well as your repeated editing of the book text.

Especially thanks for your confidence as I approached
and completed this book.

TABLE OF CONTENTS

ACKNOWLEDGMENTS

The author would like to thank the hundreds—no, thousands—of borrowers, their professional associates, and the accountants, attorneys, and business consultants with whom I have interacted over my thirty-eight years of business finance. The diversity of financial challenges, as well as the exposure to an array of industries, made every day of my career a challenge. Such continuing experiences added to my cumulative knowledge, making my services to subsequent borrowers more valuable.

Likewise, my professional and personal relationships with my peers, including commercial lenders both in commercial banking and commercial finance companies, senior management of lending institutions, commercial attorneys, and commercial loan brokers, enabled my consistent professional growth from day one, as did hundreds of hours of training.

Especially I would like to thank Mr. Richard Mount, President of MidCap Business Credit, for his confidence in a recently discharged Marine going to night school as he taught me the commercial finance business (before we had computers). A mentor and good friend over the years and, from time to time, a business associate on a financing opportunity, he has always been a patient teacher and a prudent adviser. Always someone to make time to listen to business problems, he never failed to provide reasonable, and frequently unique, solutions. Thank you, Richard.

Certainly Mr. Lewis Spiller, now retired from the commercial finance industry, with whom I spent many years at G. E. Capital and Textron Financial Corporation, is a multi-talented professional. He was always a champion of the needs of his borrowers. Contributing his expertise to editing the factoring portion of the book was much valued. Lewis and I are more than professional associates—we are good friends. It was a pleasure spending many years of my working life with Lewis. And I wouldn't forget—go Georgia Bulldogs!

I would also like to thank my "LLC" attorney, Mr. Jay Maiona of New Hampshire. Not only did he help establish my LLC but edited many of the legal aspects of this book. His help in deals just prior to my retirement was always timely and dedicated. Also, I would be remiss not to acknowledge the frequent professional and personal help from the late Attorney Sanford Rosenberg and Attorney Robert Satten of Connecticut. Without the Uniform Commercial Code and legal professionals such as those acknowledged here, business finance would have been much more difficult—if not impossible.

Other memorable and valued industry associations included Richard W. Madrish, Robert E. Koe, and David Dear of G. E. Capital Corporation; B. Jay Carter of Textron Financial Corporation; Dan Burd of Systran Financial Corporation; Joe Quagenti of LSQ Funding; Stephen K. Mackowitz and Ken Benson of the Digital Federal Credit Union; George Riordan of The Connecticut National Bank; John Pardy of The

Connecticut Bank and Trust Company; and many others. It is noted that the names of some of the aforementioned financial institutions have since changed.

To all of my former bosses, employees, fellow lenders, professional associates, and business borrowers, a sincere thank you for participating in, and adding immensely to, a long and fulfilling career.

AUTHOR'S NOTE TO READERS

There are a number of different approaches to consider as you set about reading $urviving Your Business Debt. You may read each chapter in the order presented. Chapter flows present the practical development of the commercial loan relationship, from the loan application, credit approval, and closing through daily usage of the loan(s) provided, and on to problem developments, strategies and tactics to defuse difficulties, worst-case scenarios, identifying and attracting replacement lenders, and financial relationship management techniques. If the reader is not dealing with pressing situations at the moment, this continuing development scenario provides an overall "flow" to the entire process.

The reader may also select specific chapters, or topics within a chapter, to address a current situation. If targeting a specific concern, it would still be wise to cover all chapters, as ideas may be developed elsewhere that could further benefit the current situation. Frequently, there are references in one chapter to related specifics in another. The Index may also be of help.

The Author is not an attorney and nothing in this book should be construed as legal or other professional advice. Each situation is unique so the Borrower should engage competent (business oriented) legal counsel to provide specific advice, especially in those situations which are, or may become, critical to business survival, jeopardize the borrowing relationship, potentially affect the personal assets of the Borrower or loan guarantors. The Borrower should value his attorney's counsel as the information, strategies and tactics contained within this book are considered. The importance to the Borrower of such legal assistance is both recommended and emphasized throughout this book. Likewise, other qualified professionals such as accountants and reputable business consultants may additionally be relied upon.

Throughout this book the capitalized term "Lender" is used. It may be used to identify either an individual in a lending capacity or an institution. Institutions include a commercial or savings bank, a credit union, a commercial finance company, or the many classifications of alternative lenders. These are discussed within this book. Likewise, the capitalized term "Borrower" may represent an individual entrepreneur or commercial business borrowing entity that, as part of its financial strategy, utilizes and leverages borrowed funds to provide or enhance business capital and/or cash-flow requirements.

INTRODUCTION

Why the Book?

As I worked with hundreds of business Borrowers in a variety of credit and loan situations, it became quickly apparent that the Lender almost always had business finance knowledge and resources superior to those available to the average business Borrower. This is of course not unusual, but the scales often seemed weighted against the business Borrower. Lender resources are designed to be of support to Lenders during their process of loan qualification and administration. Such processes are not necessarily intended to be of benefit to Borrowers or to address the Borrower's best interests.

Inexperienced or overzealous Lenders may inappropriately control or manipulate the Borrower in order to achieve results advantageous to a Lender. Lenders may also fail to inform Borrowers as to possible alternative strategies and tactics that may improve a Borrower's situation. It is, of course, recognized that these Lenders are not employed as business consultants.

Lenders are supported by comprehensive policy manuals, Senior Lender associates with years in the lending business, and the reality that they may, directly or indirectly, be controlling the "life blood" of business Borrowers—cash flow. As in any universe of specialists, there will be some Lenders that are simply incompetent or inefficient. Positions occupied by such Lenders may ultimately be damaging to their Borrowers.

Business Borrowers frequently have no such resources on their side of the desk. While a good portion of these small- and medium-size businesses do maintain an accountant or attorney relationship, these professionals may not be seen but one or twice a year. The larger businesses may have the availability of seasoned financial consultants. While such outside professionals frequently work wonders for a business, incurred costs can be daunting to the smaller business.

The reason I wrote $urviving Your Business Debt is to enable business Borrowers to understand, evaluate, and effectively deal with the many difficult, even perilous business situations. These may be brought on either directly by the Borrower or by inexperienced, uninformed, overzealous, or disinterested Lenders. Many business Borrowers will at some time find themselves subject to the stressful business finance situations described. However, with the information contained within this book, Borrowers can be both forewarned and forearmed. They will be able to employ the strategies and tactics provided to save their business, their fortune, and—not least important—their peace of mind.

PROLOGUE

"You're right - I remember it as a great day."

The scenario below is played out many times. Not only by the individual entrepreneur, within small and medium size businesses, but also within the financial lives of even the most sophisticated business borrowers.

I may have lost sleep the night before, wondering how I was going to allocate the new funds the bank was lending to my company. It was quite simple: pay off selected key suppliers, repay some of my bank's older debt, and support future cash flow requirements. The bank seemed happy to re-structure and increase my existing loan. Of course, I looked forward taking some of this "extra cash" to pay for an overdue vacation. And I really did need the new club membership to catch the attention of new business contacts— quite expensive, but you have to spend money to make money, right?

But now things have changed, and in such a short time too. My financial forecasts looked good to the bank and my employees were all high on the company. Sure the forecasts were "blue skying" it a bit, but I heard that the economy, especially within my industry, was improving. That would take up any slack. Of course, I could blame any shortfall on an "economic downturn."

I really didn't see this coming. Sales were down. Must be a cycle. I had to stretch payables a bit to meet cash flow needs and receivables were a bit slow, even though I increased discounts. So what's new? Everyone has that problem, don't they? While I did have a few different lending officers, they all said they had confidence in my company. There really was no reason for me to be concerned.

My bank loan interest rates and fees just kept increasing. The bank complained about my risk rating and then their letters started coming.

The account was transferred from the commercial loan department to the bank's loan workout group, but the bank called it "special assets." Oh, I was special all right. And I should have told my Partner, and my wife, about the situation a bit sooner.

Suddenly, or so it seemed, the bank wanted their total loan repaid immediately. What kind of sense does that make? Even my lawyer and accountant didn't know anything about this. I didn't communicate with them much. I really didn't want to worry them (or pay their fees) and good luck getting a new lender in 30 days with my troubled company!

After a few weeks the bank made a move towards actually seizing the business assets I had pledged as collateral. They even placed a lien on my personal residence. I didn't think that was fair. The bank closed my business checking accounts and the cash was applied to my loan, plus the bank's expenses. The employee's payroll funds were in jeopardy as well. This was really getting out of hand. I don't know how long I can take this.

Why didn't I see this coming?

What could I have done to avoid this?

Why didn't the Lender help?

Does anyone care?

CHAPTER 1

YOUR LENDER'S REASONABLE EXPECTATIONS

"You've got to be kidding—I didn't sign something like that!"

"But that's not what I thought would happen."

"No way did I intend my home to be your collateral!"

"My Board did not know this was a loan covenant."

Know What You Signed (A Primer)

For the reader steeped in business financing, the information presented within Chapter 1 may appear to be substantially fundamental. It is intended to be. Such a reader may wish to continue on to Chapter 2—but then again, you may miss something!

The fact that you purchased this book may indicate that you have the basic knowledge of the availability of business borrowings from commercial banks and recognize the larger world of alternative lenders. You want to know more!

You may have been subject to the serious, even life-changing, consequences of having an unresponsive or overzealous Lender, a flawed loan structure, or little advice as to how to handle a critical borrowing situation. This book is designed to clarify and remedy these challenging situations.

The Borrower should, throughout this book's suggestions and recommendations, work with his legal counsel or other professionals to ensure compliance with appropriate laws and regulations and understand the ramifications of the tactics and strategies proposed.

However, let's not ignore some of the basics as to loan documentation and loan structures to which you may have *already* become obligated. There may also be Guarantors supporting your business loan: family, friends, or other business or government entities, which also have potential exposures relating to your borrowing relationship.

This chapter is not intended to be an exhaustive study of legal documentation or Lenders' internal operations but rather a brief overview, ensuring that the author and the reader commence on common ground.

Throughout the book, the terms "Borrower" and "his" and "you," and "Lender," "his," and "its," are used interchangeably depending on the situation or impact desired.

The Borrower initially signed (or will sign) a Promissory Note ("the Note"). This is a legally enforceable document acknowledging the debt and promising to repay a certain amount of money that was previously loaned, at a certain interest rate, at a predetermined time. This Note is also the *primary evidence* of a Borrower's debt to a Lender. Depending upon the size of the business, the size of the loan, and other considerations, it may be a relatively brief document or a multipage document with supporting schedules and exhibits. The detailed terms and conditions of the loan may be further expressed within a Loan & Security Agreement, discussed later in this chapter.

Let's review the most basic types of Notes a commercial Borrower may encounter:

- The Term (or installment) Note
- The Demand Note
- A Combination or Time Note
- The Mortgage Note

Term Notes: Within the structure of a Term Note there are specific considerations:

1. Specific maturity (payment) date.
2. Provisions for periodic principal and interest payments.
3. May be periodic *interest only* payments with a single final loan payment of all principal. Payment of a remaining loan principal due at maturity is frequently called a "balloon" payment.
4. The Note may further reference other supporting borrowing relationships and/or security agreements.
5. Where two or more secured Notes are to the same borrower, collateral may be different on each Note (but not necessarily so), and the Notes may be referred to as "cross collateralized"—*all collateral supports all Notes.*
6. There are other documentation components that may be relevant, such as a security agreement(s), guarantee(s), subordination agreement(s), and so on. These will be discussed in later chapters.

Demand Notes: These may be a bit more onerous for the Borrower. That is, more onerous than is an installment or term note. This "demand" feature allows your Note to be "called" by the Lender when the Borrower is in loan default—or at other times as provided for within the loan agreement. Payment in full is usually required when the loan is "called" by a Lender. On a Demand Note there is no maturity date. However, some informal understanding may exist between the Borrower and Lender as to when the Demand Note is reasonably due. While this may be comforting, don't bank on it. "Demand" can quite simply mean "We want it now!"

> If such an informal understanding exists between the Borrower and the Lender, get it in writing within a letter agreement—signed by the Lender, on the Lender's letterhead—because times, situations, and lending officers change.

Basic differences between a Demand Note and Term Note are:

1. There usually is no principal repayment due during the life of a Demand Note (interest will be due as agreed). An exception to this may be in the case of an asset-based lending relationship; the loan may be written on a demand basis, but loan principal payments are made in the form of the Borrower's accounts-receivable collections.
2. Payment is usually due in full once the Demand Note is "called."

Some similarities between Demand and Term Notes are:

1. Interest is usually paid to the Lender on a monthly or quarterly basis.
2. Notes may be secured or unsecured, and Notes may also be related to other supporting loans, collateral and/or security agreements, which may additionally identify the loan's terms and conditions.
3. Guarantees and subordinated debt may represent further Note considerations.

Combination Notes: Unusual—but they do exist. In this case a "demand" condition is documented, although a term loan repayment structure is actually in force. Certain

Borrower conditions may activate the combination Term and Demand feature. If this happens, it indicates that the Lender is uncomfortable with the Borrower and is "hedging his bets." He wants to be able to call the loan at any time but would like some principal reduction at the same time. This "Term Loan" could be called even if a Borrower's term payment status is current. Lenders are usually cautioned by their legal counsel in this situation, in which Lenders are trying to have the best of both worlds. The loan is best structured either as a Demand or Term Note. Any other "arrangements" *could be documented* through a separate Letter Agreement signed by both parties.

Mortgage Notes: This Note is secured by a properly recorded mortgage on land and/or real estate. The amount of the Note is stipulated, and repayment provisions are indicated. A Mortgage Note may relate to one or more properties. As in the other notes, guarantees (individual or governmental) may be an important element of loan structuring. Loan documentation may additionally include real estate appraisals, environmental assessments, and various searches.

A Final Note on Notes: The Borrower *must* have a **signed and dated copy** of the Note in his possession. "Signed" means the Borrower's and Lender's signature, and all guarantors and witnesses' signatures–*in the original.* While the Lender does retain the "original" of the loan documents, the Borrower should have *originally signed* copies as well. I know—it may look like there are two originals floating around, but there really are not. The loan closing attorney knows which is the real "original" and which is the Borrower's originally signed "copy." Frequently, Notary signatures, seals, or stamps must also be in evidence. Keep your "original copy" in a safe place but keep a "working copy" close by for reference.

The Borrower should be attentive to the following, a portion of which may be found in the loan's supporting documentation:

- The amount of the Note—is it correct, and do you agree?

- If the Borrower negotiated such, are closing costs included in the Note?
- The date of the Note; confirm.
- The maturity date; confirm.
- Is the interest rate as agreed?
- Are the payment arrangements as agreed?
- Is the collateral properly identified?
- Is there a prepayment penalty?

Assuming that your loan is already in effect: Do you (or can you) pay off the loan at maturity? If not—are you planning to renew?

Not much chance of renewal? We will discuss your alternatives. It may *not* be advisable to indicate to your Lender, at this time, a potential inability to pay off the loan. See Chapters 6—7.

What about all of the other attached loan documents? Really, in this book, there are only a few we would want to consider at this time:

The Loan and Security Agreement: This agreement is significantly longer than the Note document and details both the Lender's *and* the Borrower's responsibilities during the term of the borrowing relationship. Most all secured or revolving credit loans would have such an agreement as a part of the overall lending agreement. These are the highlights:

- Identifies Lender and Borrower
- Provides Definitions: Terms used within the Agreement
- Details Borrower's Covenants (see next paragraph)
- Details Lender's responsibilities
- Agreement to pay loan as promised
- Collateral maintenance and reporting requirements
- In some cases, allows Lender to inspect/audit collateral
- Provides for periodic financial information to be sent to Lender
- Details regarding other loan terms and conditions

Borrower's Covenants (promises you make to the Lender): There are really two general types of covenants the Borrower makes to a Lender: *financial* and *non-financial*. The explanation of each covenant may go into much detail or, in some cases, be quite brief. While the non-financial covenants may seem quite general, the financial covenants are quite specific. Covenants may later be modified with the Lender's permission; this may require re-documentation of the loan and involve costs to the borrower. More on covenants later on in this chapter.

The UCC1 or UCC Financing Statement: While this document is usually one of the shortest documents within a loan package, it can be one of the most important. Without the UCC1 being filed properly at a state or municipal location (there are different state-by-state requirements), the Lender may have jeopardized his priority position. To ensure what is called a Lender's "perfection" of a claim, and his priority status among other Lenders (determined by date and time of filing), a Lender *must* file correctly within the provisions of the Uniform Commercial Code ("UCC"). This filing is public notice of the Lender's claim against a Borrower's assets (collateral is generally identified). As a matter of note, this is one of the sources that credit agencies utilize (office of the secretary of state) to determine the identity of Lenders and a loan's supporting collateral. They may then place this information within a business credit report.

REALITY CHECK

A Borrower should check the UCC records at least twice annually to see what debt is recorded against his company. Do this by calling the secretary of state's office and asking for the UCC Division. There usually is a specific process to follow, at minimal cost. **Do not fail** to do this—there may be incorrect debt information reflected against your company. If there is incorrect information, either you or your attorney should contact the Lender in question to request a UCC Release. If the Lender fails to release (be sure to recheck to see if the correction has been completed), there may be certain penalties due to the Borrower from the Lender. Also, as long as the incorrect information appears in the state records, the Borrower's financial position is improperly reflected to anyone searching the UCC records. PS: Your commercial attorney may know UCC service firms that will accomplish such searches for a fee. It's wise to take care of this—ASAP!

Sometimes state UCC offices are so backed up recording information that new debt may not be reflected for some time. Also, once the debt is paid off, the Lender must *release* this filing to ensure that public records are up-to-date. This is not always accomplished on a timely basis due to a state office backup of work or the Lender's failure to file the releasing UCC document. A Borrower may be unduly burdened by a credit agency reporting a business debt when, in fact, the loan has been paid off. UCC filings do have a finite life and can expire unless renewed.

TIMELY PAYMENT OF PRINCIPAL AND INTEREST

At the commencement of a borrowing relationship, there is little doubt that the Borrower expects to pay the Lender's principal and interest bills on time—even a bit before the due date. Why wouldn't you? The Lender expects the same thing. But life happens . . .

There may be times when you are unable to make a payment on your loan, for any of a multitude of reasons. At this time we will not discuss the options regarding what to do at these times. Such survival tactics are discussed in Chapter 6.

At the beginning of a new borrowing relationship, elements of the commercial loan closing frequently result in more closing costs than had been planned. In some loan structures, the *net loan proceeds* (closing costs deducted from anticipated loan proceeds) are then seriously impacted. The Borrower may have given a pre-approval deposit to the Lender to cover the costs of appraisals, special audits of books and records, environmental site assessments, or attorney fees, but the actual costs incurred by the Lender for such requirements may wind up being considerably more than estimated. Too, if there is a drawn-out credit approval process or legal documentation concerns, the Lender's legal fees may exceed earlier estimates.

Initial loan proceeds are generally used to pay:

1. **Your former Lender:** your new Lender will want a *first position* on supporting collateral, so the former debt (principal, interest, costs, and pre-payment penalties (if any) must be paid at loan closing.

2. **Prepaid interest**, depending on the loan structure agreed upon. This amount could reach almost the total of one full month of interest. Close the loan as close to the end of a month as possible, preferably on the last business day of the month. If the loan is closed during the first week of a month, the Borrower could have almost an entire month's interest due at closing, because in most instances, interest is calculated and paid up through the next month end.
3. Costs related to appraisals, special audits, and/or environmental site assessments (net of deposits already received by the Lender).
4. Attorney fees and costs.
5. Title insurance when applicable.
6. Lender credit investigation costs; background checks.
7. Flood searches, UCC searches, and so on.
8. Loan broker fees (usually 1%–2% of the overall approved credit facility [the loan]—not the amount initially loaned). The Borrower may also handle this payment outside of the loan closing.

All of the preceding items (plus others too numerous to mention) may reduce net loan proceeds to the Borrower. Reduction of loan funds could seriously jeopardize the borrower's cash flow for a month or two from the time of closing.

REALITY CHECK

An early cash flow strategy. Put in the extra work to identify all closing costs. If these costs are going to be much more than you initially expected, tell your Lender that, in order to reduce the impact of closing costs on your orderly cash flow over the next couple of months, "interest only" payments for that period (one to three months) are requested. This is also a plus for your Lender because he will receive the interest payments as agreed; only the principal payments are held up for a short period. Communicate this before the loan closing—not after. Otherwise, it will appear that you do not have a handle on your cash-flow forecasting.

Lenders like to have all assurances that loan payments will be made on time. They may ask the Borrower if it is all right to charge the company's operating account for the payment due monthly (or whatever period is involved). If a Borrower has a significant amount of "free" cash flow, this automatic charging may pose no problem. However, for seasonal reasons, or a tendency toward slow receivable collections, cash on deposit from time to time may not cover such automatic payments. *The Borrower should seek to initiate his own payments to the Lender.* This could avoid overdraft charges, insufficient funds fees, and delinquency credit reporting by the Lender.

REALITY CHECK

Another cash flow strategy. By having the Lender charge your account monthly, you lose absolute control over your cash. You never know what the future may bring; the Borrower must protect his cash flow. Also, loan payment terms usually permit a grace period of 5–15 days from the loan payment due date to make the payment. Again, the availability of those funds for another two weeks may make an important difference in an unexpected obligation (possibly for a supplier?). However, if you do not make payments on a timely basis, you will be charged late charges. It's all in the discipline of cash control. Can you do it?

While we are on the subject of Lender charges and procedures impacting cash flow, let's think about the Lender's position in all of this. Remember that above all, Lenders are in business to make a profit.

It has been said that the average business in the United States is earning an excellent profit—for its Lender. The truth of this statement, of course, depends on the specific situation.

The Lender is expected to develop profitability from its loan portfolio. If this were not possible, the money would be loaned elsewhere—or loaned to a Borrower from whom a reasonable return could be realized.

At the same time, some Lenders (considering their exorbitant fees, noncompetitive rates, and inappropriate loan terms and conditions) may seriously affect the Borrower's cash flow and, in some cases, the Borrower's chances of financial survival.

Some ways a Lender develops returns on loaned funds are:

- Interest rates (fixed or variable), including interest rate benchmarks and utilization of different indices
- Loan closing fees (usually 1%–2% of the approved facility)
- Audit fees (in the case of asset-based lending)
- Commitment fees (usually due upon issuance of a Lender's

commitment letter)

- Good faith deposits (to prove Borrower is serious before a Lender commences working on the credit request and utilizing its resources)
- Operating account minimum balances (enables earnings on deposited funds)
- Facilities fees (much the same as commitment fees)
- Credit line non-usage fee (Borrower is *not* using entire approved credit line, and is then charged for that portion not used, usually at a rate of ¼%–½%)
- Application Fee (usually $100–$500, usually submitted with application)
- Loan origination fee (similar to an application fee or a good faith deposit—another "catchall" fee income designation)
- Collection days (Borrower's submitted loan payments are held one or more days before application against the loan; thus, the loan balance is higher for a few more days, and the Lender earns more interest)
- Prepayment penalties (Borrower should be careful in considering paying off the loan early, which can incur hefty penalties; see Chapter 5)
- Forbearance fees, which may be charged when difficult loan relationships are developing (for example, loan defaults). The Lender may charge a forbearance fee for not doing anything for a period of time; depending upon the size of the loan and the perceived risk, the fee may be a considerable amount. More on this in Chapter 5.

> Do not accept lender fees at face value. Investigate and challenge—more than not, it will be worth your while.

When considering the pressure on banks to maximize returns, and the increasing emphasis on developing fee income, does it really make more "cents" for a Lender to make small loans or larger loans? Generally, it may cost a Lender less to maintain one large loan than ten small ones.

However, thanks to U. S. government, state, and municipal loan and loan guarantee programs, Lenders may, in many ways, remove a good deal of the additional risk usually associated with smaller loans. With such help, as well as unique and beneficial fee structures, these smaller loans can still be profitable to the multiple Lenders that could be involved. Still, many small businesses are burdened with interest and other loan costs that could almost cripple such a Borrower. It is more important than ever for the small business borrower to know what the "deal" is and understand his borrowing alternatives.

HONEST Communications—NO SURPRISES

Certainly your Lender doesn't want any surprises during your lending relationship—and you don't need any from your Lender.

This means that you will be (you absolutely *must* be) an "Honest Abe"—not some of the time, but *all* of the time.

When a difficult situation exists, it may be temping to bend the truth, or not file a withholding tax report, or put too much "blue sky" within your financial forecasts. **Don't do it!** You don't need the grief that could follow. More people than just the owner of a business will suffer should charges of dishonesty become substantiated. Keep in mind the loan Guarantors, who may be your partners and your family.

If you're having difficulty making payments, remember that things could get worse if you resort to dishonesty. Records could be subpoenaed. A court hearing may discover prior falsehoods. Your case could be seriously prejudiced (by discovery of added dishonesty) before a judge or jury.

In the normal course of events, let your Lender know when:

- Your loan payment will be late.
- You did not make your deposit of withholding taxes.
- Cash flow was diverted from debt or other requirements as payment(s) to a key supplier that could no longer be deferred.
- A subcontractor threatens to put a lien against assets.

A professional and seasoned Lender generally seeks to be a business "partner." While a delinquency or cash flow situation may be devastating to you, remember that this is the lender's routine business and to him it may really be "no big deal." The Lender has seen such difficulties many times before, and he may offer suggestions, as may your accountant and attorney.

The individual lending officer has certain "authorities" (and his boss has a few more) that enable him to:

- Adjust payment due dates: Move the delinquent payment(s) to the end of a loan term, thus freeing up the current loan payment(s) for the company's use.
- Simply change the loan due date to another convenient time during the month. However, the Borrower is not usually forgiven any interest.
- Allow a bank account "overdraft" for 30 days (or whatever) to allow for collection of receivables or other repair of cash flow.
- Re-document the loan so as to more realistically address terms and conditions affecting the Borrower's current situation.
- Make additional "emergency" loans to the Borrower as may be needed (usually up to 10% of the already approved credit facility).

Such assistance may generally be offered to those Borrowers who have demonstrated integrity and fair dealings with the Lender. These actions may only take a phone call, or possibly a week or more to re-document the loan.

> The lending officer doesn't "have to" *do* anything.
> Why should he? It's really all on you!

Reliable Financials—how to get them!

It is of *major* importance to provide timely and reliable financial reports. Loan covenants detail the types of reports are that required, and their due dates. Lenders may give Borrowers and their accountants 30 to 90 days (or more in the case of year-end financials) to complete such tasks.

Generally, the monthly or quarterly financials required may be prepared internally by your bookkeeper (sometimes with accountant guidance). Your accountant will prepare your year-end financial statement, or annual report, and taxes. In some cases the accountant will prepare only the year-end tax return. *A Lender will usually want to be brought up-to-date more frequently than annually.*

There are generally a few components of the term "financial statements":

- **Balance Sheet:** Assets, liabilities, and net worth (expressed as capital or owner's equity), reflected at a precise point in time. The net worth section may be expanded upon to reflect stockholder distributions, changes in retained earnings, and the like.
- **Income Statement (or Profit and Loss Statement):** Revenues, cost of goods sold, gross profit, expenses, net profit, taxes, and profit after taxes are reflected. There may be separate exhibits further detailing elements of the operations.
- **Cash Flow Statement:** Your beginning cash for the period is impacted by all of the "ins and outs" during the business period. This usually includes income or losses, borrowed or paid-back funds, capital expenditures, and certain changes in asset balances, finally arriving at the closing cash balance as reflected at the end of the period.
- **Notes:** An important element within the financial statement is the Notes section. This section, at the end of the financial statements, clarifies the internal accounting procedures; type of depreciation used; detail of leases and company debt; debt subordinated to a Lender; officer loans; certain shareholder (owner's) dealings; and so on. It may even address important events that may have occurred, or may occur *following* the reporting period (disclosure is essential). The accountant usually prepares this section.

Your Lender may require specific reports periodically, or everything at one time. Reports are usually "as of" a monthly, quarterly, semiannual or fiscal year-end period. Your Lender may wish to see your first-quarter results (i.e., "Three Months Ended March 31, 200x"). The loan covenant may give you until April 30, or later, to complete this quarterly statement and deliver it to the Lender.

Provide comparative income statements to your Lender, which compare this year's period results to last year's same-period results. Quarterly, or even monthly, submissions of this nature reflect the Borrower's good faith. This way, variances from last year, or from the same month last year, are readily identified by both the Borrower and the Lender (especially by you in advance!). Comparisons may already be reflected within the current Income Statement—not usually within the Balance Sheet section. Such analyses, when completed by the Borrower, indicate that the Borrower is well informed. You should do this for your own good. These analyses and submissions demonstrate that the Borrower is on top of issues. Do this *whether or not required* by loan covenants. When these issues are again brought up, you will have a good handle on the reasons and mitigating circumstances surrounding these items.

You must review any variances carefully prior to presenting (or sending) the reports to your Lender. Whether asked to or not, include your narrative explaining positive variances as well as negative ones. Don't forget to highlight the good stuff!

By doing this, you will have all the answers researched and supported—before the Lender asks!—and you will be telling the Lender that you are a cooperative and knowledgeable Borrower.

How much reliance should be placed on your financial statements?

It depends on the situation. There are generally three kinds of financial statements that you can use:

Compilation: This is usually the least expensive, and some say, the least creditable. A compilation may be prepared internally within the reporting company, by the bookkeeper or internal accountant. A certified public accountant (CPA) is not usually involved. But if a CPA does assist with a compilation, he or she may simply place the data provided in a logical format—there may or may not be supporting Notes or schedules. The CPA expresses no opinion as to accuracy, as he or she did not "test" or prove any of the Borrower's information. In this respect, compilations are different from the other two types of financial statements explained here. Compilations frequently are used for monthly or quarterly periods or within a business where there are not significant borrowed funds involved.

Reviewed: Reviewed statements are moderately expensive. They are quite creditable for the small- to medium-size businesses with less than $1,000,000 in borrowed funds. The CPA reviews most items. Notes are attached addressing accounting procedures, inventory information, debt and lease schedules, and other relevant events or processes. Additional special schedules may also be attached, detailing specific aspects of the business performance. Reviewed statements are usually acceptable for quarterly and year-end financial reporting—again, for the medium-size business.

Audited (or "Certified"): This format is the most expensive and enjoys top creditability among Lenders or other public parties (to include information required from public companies). Lenders may seek audited statements for Borrowers with outstanding loans in excess of $1,000,000. Acquisitions or buyout situations would usually require a history (at least three years) of audited statements. It would stand to reason that if a Borrower is planning to sell his business (or is planning to go "public" or otherwise offer stock in the company), audited statements should be in place for the past few years.

The numbers presented within an audited presentation will have much more validity, as all material items are tested by the CPA. This includes, but is not limited to, verification of accounts receivable, accounts payable, inventory amounts and costing, depreciation, company debt, and the like. Material Notes and additional supporting schedules are presented.

Also an "opinion" is expressed by the CPA within an audited statement. This is to the effect that numbers presented fairly represent the condition of a company as of a specific date. There are "qualified" opinions as well; exceptions may be stated. But the audited statement is prepared by an independent CPA, and that's what outsiders are seeking. The CPA stands behind the numbers presented. While most CPAs carry errors and omissions insurance, their reputation really is what backs up the strength of their certified financial statements. Because of the great extent of testing required for certification, give the CPA adequate notice if you want audited financial statements. Six months' notice would not be too early. Note: For such certifications, the CPA must be independent of the company.

A discussion with your accountant could further assist in deciding which financial statement type is a best for you, considering your current situation and future strategy.

Real Experiences!

You would think that purchasing an improved parcel of real estate involving a three-unit commercial building would be a routine transaction. All three spaces were currently under long-term leases: a convenience store, a post office, and one residential apartment. It should have gone even more smoothly, as the Buyer/Borrower was the owner-manager of the store for the past few years. He was familiar with the tenants and their cash flow (payments came through the store), and knew his market. He signed a Purchase & Sale Agreement (P&S) with the real estate Seller. He assumed that getting the money for the purchase price would be easy. The price was $800,000, and the Buyer felt he could put down about $160,000. The closing date was 30 days from the P&S Agreement date. He went to a Lender and they briefly discussed the deal. It looked like a loan could be arranged with certain personal or governmental guarantees supporting the deal. The Lender asked for certain routine documents required to validate the store's earnings, etc. Documents required included two years of the business's year-end financial statements, accompanied by federal tax returns. The Borrower said "No problem," and returned to his store. After not hearing from the Borrower for three weeks, the Lender called. The Borrower indicated that his accountant had to finish last year's financial statement and then file the tax return. Another three weeks passed. Finally the Borrower called and said he had not had any financial statements prepared for the past three years. Tax returns also were not filed for the same periods. He was going to have an accountant (did he really have one before?) go back and prepare financial statements for the missing years. Another week passed, and he called the Lender and said the accountant wanted too much money to do this, and he was dropping his loan request. The Lender asked the Borrower, "Didn't you know you had to file business tax returns?" The Borrower replied, "I put all of the store's money back into the business. I thought that if I did that I did not have to file." As far as the financial statements were concerned, he said, "I knew what I was making, I didn't need an accountant to tell me." Needless to say, his P&S expired, and a few months later the business was sold to another party.

REALITY CHECK

If you see the need for substantial commercial loan borrowings during the next few years, or additional equity partners need to be brought in, or a future sale of the company is possible— commence planning for audited financial statements now.

You'll save a lot of grief later on (lack of preparation time), and may be able to spread out initial costs over a period of time (as equal monthly payments).

You'll then be ready for almost anything!

Regardless of the size of the business or the financial performance, annual financial statements and tax returns should be prepared and filed, preferably by an accountant. If a business is going to need an important loan in the future, is considering attracting partners, is planning to sell securities, or even is thinking about selling out in a few years, an accountant's financial statement (at least a "reviewed" statement) should be available for the past two or three years. Opportunities and reversals happen unexpectedly. If you haven't arranged for appropriate financial statements—do it now! **Reliable financial statements will never come back to haunt you.**

Note: You may have to switch CPAs to get the type of financial statements that you want. Certain smaller "shops" are limited in what they wish to do, and may not accept transitioning an existing client to an audited status. If this is the case, the existing accountant, or your Lender, may provide you with names of CPA firms that they feel are reputable.

Commitment to Forecasted Performance

Financial forecasts (otherwise known as "projections") prepared by the Borrower assist the Lender in determining the Borrower's ability to service (pay) the debt under varying scenarios. Also, forecasts assist the Lender in setting certain financial ratios and covenants.

The Lender routinely asks the Borrower for *financial forecasts*—usually prepared for at least one year in advance (columns by month) and, in some cases, a second year (columns by quarter). Such forecasts utilize the elements (and format) of an Income Statement. Certain items, such as depreciation and taxes, are sometimes left out. Inasmuch as a key determination within a forecast is to determine the amount of cash flow, before and after debt service, elements of depreciation expense, taxes, and interest expense may be included following the operating aspects of performance. There can be many nuances in cash-flow determination, so working with your accountant in preparing such forecasts is worthwhile.

Revenue predictions can be determined from orders projected to be "in house" at appropriate (or seasonal) periods or through percentage extrapolations from prior year's actual revenues. Because much depends upon the "reasonable" accuracy of forecasts, it may be prudent to place this qualifier box in the corner of each page of forecasts:

Forecasts are subject to 5%–15% variances due to conditions beyond our control.

This acknowledges the fact that the Borrower is not infallible and he is letting all know, up front, that variances will, of course, occur. If orders are canceled, national situations or industry downturns occur, or production problems affect productivity—you are covered.

This does not mean that the *Borrower is not accountable for poor results*—but an up-front qualifier was provided to the Lender as to reasonable variances.

REALITY CHECK

Forecasts are not commitments but rather reasonable estimates based on the world as we now know it. Don't get locked into forecasts being an exact science. Remember to consider using a variance qualifier box. Your accountant may assist you in determining reasonable variance percentages—or in deciding whether you should utilize the phrase at all.

Assumptions, which support your forecasted line items, are an important part of the forecast presentation. Your Lender realizes that you don't have a crystal ball. It is customary, as an attachment to your forecast, to include an assumptions schedule. This establishes, either in narrative or number format, your logic or thinking behind establishment of forecasted numbers. It's possible that you do not need to explain each line of a forecast. Consider adding a statement such as this at the beginning of the assumptions schedule: "All recurring general and administrative ("G&A") expenses are being increased 5%." Other assumptions may be appropriate: "Sales are expected to increase by 16% in 20xx due to new lines carried (provide detail); "New customers are anticipated due to the company's entering into new markets (provide detail)"; or "An overall 2% price increase will be implemented in xxxx."

In the more sophisticated forecasts, a "sensitivity" approach may be required, in which you provide your Lender with three forecast scenarios:

1. **Best Case:** All things come together as you had hoped.
2. **Most Likely Case:** Reduced growth with increased expenses.
3. **Worst Case:** The bottom falls out; low sales, expenses increase materially. Objective: Demonstrate that you can survive!

Later your Lender will compare your submitted forecasts to the financial statements reflecting your actual results. Inasmuch as you have initially analyzed your assumptions, you are now prepared to justify or explain variances to actual results. Of course, highlight company successes—do not overly dwell on negatives. Forecasts are also a Lender's tool whereby financial covenants may be developed, so don't get carried away on best-case scenario forecasts!

When the Borrower is not in compliance with a financial covenant, he may be in *loan default*. It is the Lender's election whether or not to declare a Borrower's default. This could be an occasion for your Lender to "call" your loan, or restrict or discontinue credit—or he may simply disregard the covenant violation, not declaring a loan default. We will discuss this situation more fully later.

When business changes arise, the Borrower may revise forecasts before being required to do so by the Lender.

LOAN COVENANT COMPLIANCE

Generally, in addition to a Note, a Borrower is operating under a Lender's Loan & Security Agreement. This document, among other things, indicates certain legal promises (covenants) made to the Lender.

Covenants *may* be violated, *but not without Lender's permission.*

Non-Financial Covenants (The following is only a sampling of covenants possible):

- Maintain books and records pertaining to the company and bank collateral in such detail, form, and scope as is satisfactory to the Lender.
- Provide the Lender with timely company information.
- Permit inspection by Lender of Borrower's books, records, and collateral when reasonably requested.
- Borrower will hold title to all assets pledged as collateral. There will be no further collateral pledges without Lender's permission.
- Borrower will protect Lender's collateral.
- Restrictions on borrowing elsewhere without Lender's permission.
- Maintain and pay for required insurance (to include coverage on Lender's collateral).
- Do not merge, consolidate with, or acquire an interest in other business entities.
- Do not make loans, advances, or extensions of credit to any other persons, affiliates, stockholders, officers, or employees,

other than reasonable advances for travel in the ordinary course of business.
- Borrower must notify the Lender when the Borrower is in loan default.

Financial Covenants (The following is only a sampling of covenants possible):

- Pay the debt as agreed.
- Maintain selected, or all business bank accounts, with the Lender.
- Maintain certain levels of deposits in selected accounts.
- Borrower will not incur additional loans or advances from any other source without Lender's permission.
- Will not sell or dispose of assets (usually within certain dollar amounts) without Lender's permission.
- Certain financial ratios will be maintained. (Samples of these will be detailed; see the next section).
- Pay all taxes and insurance premiums on a timely basis.
- Prepare a specific type of business financial statement, which will be due at specified times. Some may be prepared internally; others, by a certified public accountant acceptable to the Lender.
- Pay no dividends (or make officer or stockholder loans) without Lender's permission.
- Salary restrictions on owners and officers.
- Restrictions on capital expenditures (equipment, fixed assets, and so on).
- Guarantors and business officers may be required to provide annual, or more frequent, personal financial statements, with supporting schedules.
- Officer's / owner's life insurance, in stated amounts, may be required and assigned to the Lender as additional collateral.

FINANCIAL LIQUIDITY RATIOS (LIMITED SAMPLING)

Numbers utilized in computing ratios are usually derived from periodic financial statements provided to the Lender.

Current Ratio: *Current assets divided by current liabilities.* A rough indicator of the ability of a Borrower to service current obligations. The higher the ratio the better positioned the Borrower is to service debt due. This ratio may become suspect considering an inspection of the condition of inventory, the aging of accounts payable and receivables, and so on. A Lender may discount a portion of unqualified current assets in determining this ratio. An example may be expressed as 4.4 (a higher ratio) or may be down to 0.6 (less than $1 of assets to service $1 of liabilities).

Quick Ratio (aka "acid test"): Cash added to accounts receivable divided by current liabilities. This is a refinement of the current ratio in its more conservative manner. This ratio is expressed in the same manner as the current ratio.

Sales /Accounts Receivable Ratio: Net sales divided by accounts receivable. The result measures the accounts receivable turn during a year (or lesser period)—or how long it takes to get paid during a period for a sale. This may be expressed as the number of annual turns 8.1x.

Day's Receivable Outstanding: Sales/accounts receivable ratio divided into 365 days in a year. Using the example above, 365 days divided by 8.1x (turns) equals 45 days of outstanding accounts receivable. Most times it's all in the manner of preference whether "turns" or "days" are utilized.

Cost of Sales/Inventory: Cost of sales divided by inventory. This measurement is used to determine the number of times the inventory turned during a year (or other period).

FINANCIAL LEVERAGE RATIOS (LIMITED SAMPLING)

Debt-to-Worth Ratio: Total liabilities divided by net worth (or tangible new worth). A rough indicator as to the amount of support provided by the net worth against the (total) liabilities of the business. The result may be expressed as 2.6x or 5.3x or 11.1x—however it works out. The lower the ratio, the more desirable the relationship may be to a Lender. Over 7.0x may indicate the need for a more structured type of secured lending. The higher the ratio, the greater the risk assumed by a Lender. A low ratio of 1.1x indicates excellent liability coverage and could be a very desirable credit to a Lender.

Loans in which a Borrower has a high debt-to-worth ratio are referred to as highly leveraged transactions (HLT). These loans are frequently given a higher level of scrutiny (frequently unfavorable) by Lenders. Improved earnings or capitalization may eliminate such a risk assignment.

FINANCIAL COVERAGE RATIOS (LIMITED SAMPLING)

Earnings Before Interest and Taxes (EBIT)/Interest: Earnings from the income statement (usually the line "Operating Income") are divided by total interest expense. Do not include taxes or interest expense when developing the operating income number. Divide interest paid to all sources (not just this Lender) into the operating income to see if the earnings provide coverage to pay these aggregate interest costs. A high ratio such as 6.7x indicates a Borrower's ability to handle the existing interest level, but a low ratio such as 1.2x indicates that caution should be observed—coverage is close. This ratio may further be expanded to read "EBITDA." Here you are further netting depreciation ("D") and amortization ("A") out of the operating income. In reality, many financial statement presentations already reflect depreciation and amortization within the regular operating income section. The Borrower's Loan & Security Agreement will detail the components of this ratio. This ratio is another determination of a Borrower's capacity to assume added debt and/or manage current debt.

Caution #1—Many of the preceding ratio determinations are at one day in time (a Balance Sheet item is as of one specific date). But that date's results could be misleading to a Lender, especially if you have a seasonal business or another unique profile. Also, measurements may also be made as of a six-month or three-month period. Inasmuch as these periods are less than a 365-days formula, adjustments must be made. Ensure that you are aware of the period the Lender is considering for ratio development. Your accountant will be helpful in adjusting formulas for your future use.

Caution #2—The adequacy of your ratios to a Lender may be dependent upon how other businesses within your industry compare with your ratios. There are national services that provide listings of industry ratios, sorted by general business sizes, of which both your Lender and your accountant are aware. It may be wise to ask your Lender for a copy of such an industry guideline (numbers change annually) so you can 1) see how you measure up with other same-size companies, and 2) see that your Lender is using the proper Industry SIC (Standard Industrial Classification) Code for your business. The SIC Code has been updated to the North American Industry Classification System (NAICS) for utilization within federal statistical agencies. (Also see Chapter 7.)

Some additional Lender covenants (benefiting the Borrower) are:

- To advance funds to Borrower under agreed-upon conditions
- Issue periodic loan statements to borrower
- Lenders must be reasonable in their requests
- Lenders must maintain confidentiality of financial transactions as well as the information obtained from the Borrower

REALITY CHECK

Know the covenants (promises) you've made to your Lender. The Lenders are not going to forget! It is important for the Borrower to keep a log recording (or calculating) his compliance requirements. More on this later.

WHEN YOU ARE IN DEFAULT!

Lender's Rights and Remedies: A Lender may declare a default without taking further action (at that time). Or he may declare a default and require the Borrower to take immediate action (or provide a reasonable time frame) whereby remedial actions would be completed. Here are some instances that may trigger a Borrower's default:

- Failure to make payment when due
- Loan covenant default
- Failure to insure collateral
- Unauthorized removal, sale, or disposal of collateral
- Legal seizure of collateral by third parties
- Double pledging of collateral
- Breach of Security Agreement's representations or warranties
- Death or dissolution of Borrower
- Insolvency of Borrower
- Appointment of Receiver
- Assignment for benefit of creditors
- Bankruptcy proceedings
- Lender deemed insecure*

*Lenders may deem themselves insecure for any number of reasons. It may be due to an industry's downturn, the death of an owner, the fact that the Borrower's financial forecasts have been consistently inaccurate, or that actual performance has been disappointing. It is also possible that the Borrower's personal actions, inside or outside of the business, may have the Lender concerned regarding the continued viability of the business or its management.

LENDER'S SECURITY INTEREST IN ASSETS

Throughout these discussions, we are talking about "secured" loans; the Borrower has pledged certain owned assets to the Lender as collateral. Should the Borrower default on the loan, these assets may be liquidated (by the Lender, his agents, or in cooperation with the Borrower) to ensure Lender repayment of principal, interest, and costs.

Within the Loan & Security Agreement, the Borrower has agreed to protect these assets to the best interests of the Lender. To reiterate some items already identified within the covenant section, and to introduce others which may be included, the Lender expects and may have a right to:

- Establish the value (market, auction, knock-down or otherwise) of his collateral
- Determine what collateral is deemed to be "ineligible" and set collateral advance rates
- Ensure that Borrower maintains insurance on pledged assets in agreed-upon amounts with the Lender named as loss payee
- Require that officer's life insurance be within the collateral package
- Establish that Borrower's assets are to be physically protected, sometimes even in an off-site bonded warehouse
- Require that quantities of assigned assets are correctly reported
- Require that quality of assigned assets be maintained
- Receive periodic Borrower reporting as required
- Enter into the Borrower's business property, at reasonable times, and inspect the books, records, and collateral

REALITY CHECK

The Lender must be "reasonable" in its requests for information, certain performance achievements, and constraints imposed upon the Borrower—from the loan closing through the life of the relationship.

The Lender is not there to run your business—that's your responsibility. However, Lender liability lawsuits may develop from what appears to be "unreasonable" actions taken by the Lender. Discuss such concerns with your commercial attorney.

Finally, your loan is in place and all seems well. But—a fact of life is that nothing stays the same. Performance deteriorates, collateral becomes less valuable, people disappoint, and expectations are sometimes unreasonable—on both sides.

Read on to see what you're going to do about it!

CHAPTER 2

RECOGNIZING THE DANGER SIGNALS

"I can't seem to get my Lending Officer on the phone anymore."

"I really don't think the Lender has a clue as to what we're doing."

"We need help—where the heck is he?"

"He wants what? . . . or we will be in default!"

Inexperience or Frequent Changes of Lending Officers

> *Cash flow* is the *life blood of your business*.
> Does the *majority* of cash flow come from your Lender(s)?
> A deteriorating borrowing relationship can play havoc on financial management.

Lending Officers (LOs), like the rest of us, do get tired. Tired of their job, their boss, and even of the *Borrowers within their loan portfolio*. Within the lending industry there is a name for the latter—"Borrower fatigue."

An LO may, at any one time, handle from ten to fifty commercial loan customers (individual business lending relationships). The number depends on the size and complexity of the relationships. Of course, LOs often appreciate and favor certain choice borrowers. These are most often loans in which Borrowers are sophisticated in the techniques of dealing with Lenders, always on time with requirements, and usually have the larger loan and deposit relationships with the institution.

In truth, the bulk of loan relationships is nonspecific, of little challenge, and requires little maintenance. And a good deal of the rest, as far as some LOs are concerned, can be anywhere from a distracting nuisance to a difficulty to be avoided.

In the perception of some LOs, these more distracting and difficult relationships take too much of their time. Such Borrowers are not sophisticated enough to grasp the needs and the responsibilities of an LO. And then there are the Borrowers that never seem satisfied; always threatening to leave the bank, and calling the LO's boss when the LO is not (immediately) receptive to their needs. And yes, some LOs will go out of their way to avoid communicating with these difficult or demanding customers. These accounts, to the LO, are always a problem and bring nothing but difficulties. But what about these Borrowers—are they forever locked into a less than effective relationship?

In the normal course of events, LOs do get promoted (or fired), necessitating the assignment of new LOs to existing Borrowers. The more experienced and proficient Loan Officers do not long remain on the "lending platform" (acting as direct lenders) but may rise to management responsibilities or leave the Lending institution for a better position. From a Borrower's point of view, this is perceived as the "revolving-door syndrome."

Real Experiences!

It's not always the lending institution that makes the difference—sometimes it's *all* about a Lending Officer. Case in point: A Southeastern manufacturer of automobile parts went to a large alternative Lender and obtained an asset-based revolving line of credit of $2,000,000. The Loan Officer made a concerted effort to know the industry. He also consciously developed a close relationship with the three business partners. After four years, the Loan Officer left the institution and accepted a position with another alternative Lender—one offering factoring. The Borrower, over the next year, produced disappointing results for his first Lender. The Lender began making unreasonable collateral demands and the Borrower's risk rating was downgraded.

The Borrower called up his former Lending Officer seeking his help through his new institution. Being familiar with the prior Lender's policy and procedures, the Lender believed the Borrower when he said that impractical constraints were hampering the company's recovery. A collateral analysis revealed that the Borrower was no longer qualified for a return to asset-based lending but would, on a selective basis, be able to factor many of his larger accounts receivable The Lending Officer, of course, knew the account intimately and assured the credit approval authorities that a positive turnaround was imminent. The Borrower paid off Lender number one and became a factoring client of the second alternative Lender. The Borrower, according to projections, began to flourish. Over the next few years both profits and net worth grew.

You guessed it! Another opportunity opened up for the Lending Officer at yet another alternative Lender; this one a full-service commercial Lender. Due to the growth of this now preferred borrower, the factoring company was unable to provide a larger line of credit supported by an asset-based loan. Needless to say, the Borrower again called his former Lender at his new institution. Within 60 days a material revolving line of credit was closed. The former Loan Officer was, of course, instrumental in the timely credit process and approval. Once in a while, that special Borrower and Loan Officer relationship survives, in spite of the actual Lending institution involved. It is especially valuable and rewarding to both parties to nurture such a relationship in both good and bad times. Sometimes, of course, replacement loan help may not develop—but *reliable advice* from a friend is always valuable.

With new lending officers frequently assigned, the Borrower becomes frustrated—explaining his business over and over, "reselling" his forecasted performance, and providing more business tours and Lender (training) meetings. The Borrower hopes that the new LO will understand, to some extent, his particular industry and that, after the Borrower's training efforts, the LO will be receptive to his needs—and stay on the job for a while.

As a result, and in many cases, the more junior and unseasoned officers are actually dealing on a day-to day basis with much more seasoned business (and possibly needy) Borrowers. The more seasoned lenders, however, are assigned to the "key" (more profitable) accounts, which are at higher borrowing levels and utilize the Lender's sophisticated financial management services. *This is not a level playing field.*

So who handles the larger portfolio of numerous small- and medium-size business loans?

To a borrower's detriment, it's:

- The LO just out of credit training
- The inexperienced LO
- The LO with no clout with the credit committee
- The LO eager to please superiors on "loan control"

It is frequently with this enthusiastic, eager, inexperienced LO that a seasoned Borrower, or a Borrower in trouble, must cope.

The Borrower's dealings with a "beginner" LO could result in the following *relationship deficiencies*:

- Strategic financial counseling may be absent.
- Techniques of innovative loan structuring may not even be known.
- Problem-solving abilities are not supported by hands-on experience.
- This junior LO may not have the "ear" of the credit committee.
- No supporting clout with Lender's senior management.

In this scenario, two things can happen:

1. You'll become one of those unimpressive Borrowers handled "by the book" (that in itself can be a disaster—no flexibility whatsoever)
2. Get ready for this one—the Borrower must become a mentor to the new LO.

The benefits of the second possibility are obvious. First, it is unlikely that Lender management will provide you with your pick of replacement Lending Officers unless you are already a "preferred" commercial customer of the institution.

If you are stuck with the newly assigned LO—and are *really* concerned with the potential negative results to your company—*go proactive*!

Treat the new LO *as if he were already* a seasoned officer—utilizing the relationship management techniques discussed in Chapter 10.

REALITY CHECK

It is very important to utilize all applicable aspects of the relationship management techniques presented in Chapter 10—*at all Lender management levels.* You are going to make the LO an expert on your company, even almost a part of your management team, keeping him informed on company and forecasted changes, bringing the LO to industry meetings, and so on. At some point in time, Lender management will see this LO as the only one who really knows your industry and your needs.

The Borrower's training efforts can result in a dependable Loan Officer as well as a knowledgeable advocate within the Lender's organization—and that's a real plus!

If after all your efforts it still turns out that the relationship (in personality or otherwise) is really a disaster, it never hurts to ask for a change of Lending Officers. To maintain all courtesies, write to the head of the lending group, with a copy to the LO, citing difficulties. Don't threaten to leave the institution (such a move takes planning; see Chapter 7). Make it clear that this is, from your viewpoint, a very disappointing situation, but that you do seek to preserve the overall borrowing relationship.

INABILITY TO ACCESS YOUR LENDING OFFICER

Have you ever felt that the Lender is just too busy for your business or to address your needs?

- No time to return your calls ("in a meeting")
- Defers your questions and concerns to others
- Too busy to constructively critique your needs and /or performance
- Very slow follow-up (or none at all) on "in-process" items
- Too busy to visit your company
- Frequently cancels appointments once made
- Not notified of LO "coverage" provisions when the LO is out of the office, on vacation, is traveling, or is sick

If some of these apply to your situation, it is obvious that your LO:

- Is overloaded with priorities he perceives to be more important than yours
- May have been assigned other "projects" that have become more important than servicing his Borrowers
- Or—*you've failed* in demonstrating the importance of your relationship, your business potential, the value of your account to the Lender, and your new-business referral potential to the Lender (important to LOs).

In all of these cases, it is obvious that you are not getting his attention!

If this is not a critical error now, it certainly will be when you need immediate attention. If this is a serious issue and needs immediate cure, *stop reading now*! Go directly to Chapter 10 and devour the financial relationship management techniques presented there. You should immediately implement these techniques, which can turn around your relationship with your Lender.

UNREASONABLE PERFORMANCE EXPECTATIONS

Performance expectations were initially established at the commencement or the renewal of your credit facility (the loan). Note: the credit facility is the overall amount a company can borrow. The loan is the actual amount that is currently outstanding against that credit facility. The Lender's expectations of your future business performance were initially developed by you, the Borrower, in the form of financial forecasts, assumptions, product and marketing information, and historical and industry considerations. The LO has usually already made his own assessment of the Borrower's management capabilities. Background checks (if required) and credit reports have also been obtained by the Lender as a matter of routine.

Prior to signing your Loan Agreement, you must understand the financial covenants, both as to the reason for them and the process for determining compliance or noncompliance. Usually a Borrower does not recognize the importance of covenants or how a loan default could injure the business. Again, remember that many covenants are based upon the *Borrower's* financial forecasts.

Red Flags (the Lender's covenant tracking systems) alert the Lender when the Borrower is not performing according to expectations. These red flags usually indicate a potential loan covenant violation.

STOP HERE! In the next section we will consider remedies whereby a Borrower can deal with loan covenant violations or other selected loan defaults. Usually this evaluation and possible negotiating processes could be lengthy and costly—but may be avoided altogether. Before continuing, read The "Bail Out" at the end of this chapter.

Certain covenants were reviewed within Chapter 1. Some of those are revisited in this section, and others are introduced here for the purpose of addressing violation solutions. *Check with your accountant and/or legal counsel when considering these options.*

Covenant Violations and Solutions

A violation of the current ratio (current assets divided by current liabilities). If this ratio is not being maintained at 2 to 1, or whatever number is established, it could indicate that a Borrower is buying too much inventory; receivable collections are slow or slowing; accounts payable are higher than anticipated; valuable cash is being used to purchase fixed assets (or for other unplanned expenditures) rather than for daily operating capital.

Solutions: Attract outside cash into the company from independent sources (or internally, as in the case of amounts due from officers; long-term debt) in the form of capital or subordinated debt. Subordinated debt, for purpose of Lender's analysis, is treated as capital. This is because debt that is subordinated cannot be paid back (to creditors, officers, or others) without the Lender's permission (see Chapter 5). Step up receivable collection efforts. In the case of delinquent receivables (over 90 days), consider converting some of these nonperforming current assets to a long-term Note. This action changes the completion of the obligation from a current asset to long-term asset. Likewise, with payables, work out longer term payment arrangements with suppliers. By signing a Note to a vendor, the Borrower's current liability will change into a long-term liability, thus improving the current ratio. Work with your accountant and attorney in developing appropriate Note formats.

A violation of not maintaining a minimum net worth (assets minus liabilities). A dollar amount is usually indicated for minimum net worth, e.g., $100,000 or $500,000. Sometimes this definition is further tightened to indicate *tangible* assets minus *tangible* liabilities. Such specifics would be spelled out within the loan agreement.

Solutions: The most basic correction would be additional contributions of cash equity. Ideally these additional funds (capital) would be from the current owners, or alternatively, from current or new investors. Consider having other Lenders or officers (or even key suppliers, in the worst-case scenario) subordinate their debt to the prime Lender. These subordinations create capital in the eyes of the Lender. Of course, improved earnings could help solve the problem. This could also be the time to consider bringing in a Mezzanine Lender (see Chapter 8).

A violation of the debt-to-worth ratio (liabilities divided by net worth). In this violation, the calculation exceeds the established ratio (e.g., 4.1 instead of covenant of not more than 2.1). Debt may be accumulating too fast (effects of seasonality) or business losses are unfavorably impacting the existing retained earnings (within the net worth section).

Solutions: All of the previously mentioned solutions may effectively address this deficiency. Also, additional debt reduction, other than cash reduction of payables or accelerated debt payments, may be appropriate. Suppliers may take an equity or subordinated debt position in place of all, or a part, of their current accounts payable or Note Payable. It also may be possible to attract additional business ownership, who would contribute additional capital and thus positively affect the company's net worth.

A violation of the accounts receivable collection period. This violation occurs when accounts receivable within 60 days (covenant amount) are stretching to 120 days in age. An aging of all open accounts receivable by account, by month, and by invoice date will indicate the age of all uncollected accounts. Violation of this covenant may indicate poor internal credit and collection policies.

Solutions: Tighten up credit and collection practices. All new accounts must pass a credit check. Call accounts once they've exceed 30, 60, and 90 days. Insist on immediate payment or you'll have to cease or curtail future shipments. Sometimes a discount (such as 2% 10 days, net 30) may accelerate account payments—if the Borrower can afford such a discount. Alternative: "We cannot ship additional product unless a 15% payment is additionally received against your older amount owed on each future order." Or, "Until your account is current, all future orders will be prepaid." There are many variations to this scenario. A Lender may also ask the Borrower to prepare a "Credit Policy Manual" to ensure that the Borrower understands, and implements, essential credit and collection programs.

A violation of inventory turn (cost of sales divided by inventory). The covenant may read, "Inventory will turn not less than 'X' times annually." A violation may indicate an accumulation of slow-moving or obsolete inventory, manufacturing for stock, and carrying too much inventory to support current sales levels. Seasonal businesses would generally calculate this ratio in seasonal increments, such as fall and winter, or by month or quarter to more appropriately address such fluctuations.

Solutions: Sell off excess inventory, donate excess or obsolete inventory, and produce only for specific orders, if realistic. As of this writing, there were certain tax breaks for the donation of certain types of inventory. Consider having your customers purchase the required raw material (or other inventory) for their manufactured product. Note: While the "customer's inventory" is on your premises, the customer still owns it—not you. Thus, your level of inventory is not increased by the customer's delivery of materials. This also works when an order consists of very expensive raw materials or subcomponents and the business does not have the cash, or credit, to support such a large inventory purchase. Also, for the larger orders, the Borrower may wish to consider purchase order financing (see Chapter 8).

Lender charges of covenant violations

First, seek—in writing—the Lender's detailed explanation of the covenant violations. The Borrower should then respond in writing to the Lender, detailing the reasons for such violations. Your accountant should help you with this. You may also *tactfully* allude to the inappropriateness of such a covenant to your business profile (if such is the case). Further, demonstrate how you can (or cannot) remedy the violation(s). When you respond in a letter format, remember that it may be used months down the line against you, so be truthful where outcomes are really in doubt. Your accountant should also review the previously mentioned solution suggestions to ensure that they are practical and reasonable for your specific business. Your accountant should recalculate the ratio violated, *ensuring that the Lender has calculated it correctly.*

Real Experiences!

This particular Borrower was recently at odds with his Lender due to alleged loan covenant violations. The Borrower was taking much time away from his business responsibilities trying to address the Lender's many requirements. The final insult was when the Lender sent down one of its junior lending officers to inform the Borrower of even more violations recently discovered. The lending officer, not familiar with the entire situation, was more than surprised when the Borrower picked him up and banged him against the wall repeatedly, saying, "Joe, it's not you, it's just the bank that you work for!" After an exchange of relevant information (to include how to monitor covenant trends) there was a long period of apologies—from both parties. Not enough can be said for Borrower and Lender covenant communications—even in the more testing of situations.

If your Lender declares a loan default or tightens existing covenants as a result of an alleged violation of loan covenants, go to Chapter 3 to find the information you need. Generally such a situation would be recognized by a Lender when annual financial statements are issued by your accountant and subsequently delivered to your Lender for his review. But remember, in most Loan Agreements, the Borrower is *supposed to tell the Lender* when he is in default. Accordingly, the Borrower is expected to continually "track" his own covenant compliance. This is an excellent idea in that the Borrower will know *ahead of the Lender* when a covenant is about to be in jeopardy—*and he will be ready with answers and solutions.*

UNMANAGEABLE REPORTING REQUIREMENTS

Reporting to a Lender *more frequently than monthly* is neither generally reasonable nor significant. The exception to this would be a case in which asset-based lending is employed (see Chapter 8). Here, a Borrower's reporting of collateral and proceeds (receivable collections) is done on a *daily* basis. These specialized asset-based Lenders (also known as "formula lenders") also can make requested loan advances on a daily basis, depending upon the Borrower's level of "eligible" collateral, approved loan formulas, and outstanding loan balances.

Generally, monthly, quarterly, semiannual, or annual financial statements are satisfactory to a Lender. These are then reviewed by the LO for loan covenant compliance. Complaints from Borrowers concerning frequency of reporting generally revolve around the belief that they do not have the time, systems, or personnel to provide such an abundance of reports—they need to run their business.

Lender demands for more frequent information may be indications of:

- A lack of understanding of the business
- Distrust of previous numbers provided
- Lender's analysis revealing that the situation is deteriorating
- Nonrecognition of Borrower's time and effort required in preparing reports

Once the Lender's specific concerns have been clarified, offer to have a third party (consultant or accountant) review these concerns (which will take at least a week) and get back to the Lender with reasonable solutions. Reporting issues are the types of problems that should be reconciled without major difficulty. Reporting requirements have seldom driven Borrowers to another Lender—*but it has happened.*

FREQUENT LOAN "RESTRUCTURINGS"

Following *initial* loan structuring, which is done at the time of the (initial) credit approval, loan restructurings are usually routinely addressed on an annual basis. The actual timing may be based upon the anniversary date of the credit approval or scheduled for 3–5 months following the Borrower's calendar or fiscal year end (this provides time for the financial statements to be prepared and then sent to and analyzed by the Lender).

A "routine" restructuring may result in:

- Interest rate adjustments (up or down)
- Adjustment to the overall line of credit (increase or decrease)

- Additional adjustments to the general loan terms and conditions
- Tightening (or relaxation) of certain loan covenants
- Addressing Borrower requests

Loan restructurings—*other than periodic reviews*—usually are due to situational reactions by the Lender and are usually to the benefit of the Lender.

These restructurings may be due to:

- Covenant violations
- Unexpected / unidentified losses
- General industry deterioration (perceived or real)
- Risk rating deterioration (see following section)
- Other loan defaults
- Collateral deterioration (perceived or real)
- New Lender exposure(s) identified
- An unusual event has occurred with the Borrower
- Acquisition or merger of Borrower's company
- Death of a principal Borrower or Guarantor
- Loss of trust, or Lender confidence, in the Borrower

Other "internal" Lender reasons:

- Inaccurate internal credit analyses
- Change of Lender's internal credit policies
- Merger or acquisition (institutional)
- Regulator pressures
- Faulty internal loan documentation

The Lender may, in the face of one or more of these situations, require the Borrower to do, *or consider*, any number of remedies to address or forestall a potential loan default. The following list represents only a sampling of alternative requirements a Lender may address:

- Increase business capitalization (cash investment)
- Update appraisals
- Provide additional collateral
- Collateralize a personal guarantee

- Upgrade the type of financial statements provided
- Consider that the Borrower utilize another CPA firm
- Hire a qualified consultant
- Develop an updated business plan

The question that must be addressed by the Borrower, in an attitude as unbiased as possible, is this:

Has the Lender's position actually been weakened, or does the Lender's request appear to be unjustified?

The Lender, of course, seeks additional comfort. *He has determined that his collateral (or loan recovery position) is, or may be, in jeopardy.* Also, should the Borrower comply with the Lender's request, additional costs could quite possibly be incurred by the Borrower.

Gaining Time—a Process

One important element on the Borrower's side is time—time to prepare, to negotiate, and to resolve problems.

> **In the first instance of Lender communication, the Borrower will always involve his legal counsel**—to review *all* outgoing *and* incoming letters, to be present at meetings, and to be involved in the meetings and luncheons discussed in this section.

The Lender *must* notify the Borrower in writing as to covenant violations (the Borrower should always ask for the Lender's concerns *in writing*). Not only will that take more time, but the Lender may then rethink, or modify, his voiced position.

Once the Lender's letter is received and reviewed, notify the Lender (again by letter) of your reaction, rebuttals, and/or justifications. Also include your recommendations. The Lender knows that if he implements a Borrower's recommendation, the Lender may at least get an amended Loan Agreement without a drawn-out and time-consuming dialogue.

Following this exchange of letters, one or two additional meetings should be held, *preferably at the Borrower's site*, to negotiate remaining points. Such meetings are a good time for the Borrower to bring up new concern(s) and request further flexibilities, as appropriate, from the Lender. The Lender is not expecting to address any new issues at this time. My experience is that agreements to preliminary concerns come quicker when the Lender must also focus on unexpected "new" concerns. A tour of the Borrower's facility would also be appropriate at this time, allowing you to restore camaraderie. Follow up each meeting with a letter to the Lender citing your understanding of the agreements reached. The Lender again is expected to respond in writing.

Now back off a bit. It does not hurt to host a luncheon following the apparent final meeting to "stroke" personalities and lower tensions.

Following this final meeting—or luncheon—the Lender will make its necessary decisions, with results turned over to the Lender's attorney to document (legalize) agreements mutually reached. These new documents will be sent to the Borrower and his attorney for their approval and revisions. At this point, the Borrower, or his attorney, can still cross out or "red line" items not agreed upon or added by the Lender. Frequently documents such as these are sent back and forth a few times until a final consensus is reached.

Bottom Line: The Borrower did not cave. He worked and improved his situation—over time!

Considering all of the letter writing, meetings, and document reviews, we're talking a duration of four to six weeks. *It is possible that the situation that made your Lender nervous in the first place has since passed.*

If the Lender's initial requirements were completely unacceptable and could cripple certain aspects of your cash flow, supplier relations, and marketing or production strategies, to the serious detriment of the business, use this valuable four- to six-week lag time to negotiate to your benefit. Even to the extent of:

- Making your "case" to senior Lender management (senior Lender, senior credit officer, or president)
- Seeking municipal, county, state, or federal loan guarantees to have the Lender's loan exposure reduced, thus relaxing its position
- Seeking replacement financing elsewhere

(Chapters 7, 8, and 9)

- Strategizing with your attorney considering legal options

Throughout such negotiations, the Lender may use the term *risk rating.*

RISK RATINGS AND MODIFICATIONS

For the purpose of "internal" credit evaluations, and to provide regulators with consistency in the measurement of the institution's credit risks, a schedule of risk ratings (numbered from 1 to 10—see list that follows) has been established by many lending institutions to measure commercial borrowers. It may be compared, in theory, to a consumer credit score.

Within the process of the initial credit review (and subject to Lender's approval) a risk rating is initially established for each Borrower. Once approved, the risk rating "sticks" unless it is improved (lower number) or the Borrower's position deteriorates (higher number). Changes to this rating usually occur at the annual credit review. *The rating may remain the same—it does not have to be changed.* In the case of loan violations (a missed loan payment or in any case in which the Lender deems himself insecure), a change in the risk rating may occur.

It is interesting to note that an LO may generally downgrade a rating by his signature only, with supporting memorandums sent up the chain and into the Borrower's credit file. However, the LO cannot generally, on his own, improve a risk rating. Upgrading must go through a series of superiors' approvals to make it happen. So—*it is much easier for the LO to lower a risk rating than to improve one*, considering the process. Also, during the Lender's regulatory inspections, the adequacies of assigned ratings are evaluated and adjustments may be recommended.

These risk ratings judgments *travel with the commercial Borrower* (within the institution) during the lending relationship. These ratings are frequently referenced as a "quick" measurement of the credit quality of the Borrower. Due to the established risk rating, a Borrower could be turned down for a business credit card, borrowing for business vehicles, or other financing considerations. Ratings also have a material impact on interest rates and fees charged to the Borrower.

It is imperative that a Borrower knows his risk rating and strives to ensure that he is at the lowest possible number. Ask the Loan Officer for your risk rating.

An example of a risk rating schedule as utilized by many Lenders is shown in the following list, which was derived from a number of samples:

1. Superior:	Risk free
2. Very Strong:	Substantially risk free
3. Strong:	Minimum risk
4. Good:	Better than average risk
5. Satisfactory:	Average risk
6. Acceptable Risk:	Less than average risk
7. Followed Assets:	May be within workout group
8. Substandard:	Potential loss
9. Doubtful:	Serious problems may result in total loss
10. Loss:	Most likely uncollectible

Within each category there usually are, for the guidance of the LO, additional instructions to assist in determining the risk rating selection. To view an entire risk rating schedule, ask your Lender.

The "Bail Out!"

The "loan violation reconciliation process," whether involving covenant violations or other concerns, usually involves great expenditures of time by all parties. There is a way to "bail" on all of these considerations—*if the parties can quickly agree.*

If the whole situation of a covenant violation, and the loan default scenario, is the result of a *one-time set back or anomaly*, a quick resolution may be in order. There is no practical need for extended covenant renegotiations. Such a short-term setback may be due to an order cancellation, product rejections by a large customer, bankruptcy by one customer, an unexpected plant shutdown, loss of a management member, or other *immediate* happenings. The entire covenant altercation may be avoided simply by modifying the existing Loan Agreement by use of a

REALITY CHECK

A quick re-writing of your loan covenants to conform to your existing situation could be an easy "fix" to a potential loan default. This frequently works if there is no long-term setback but rather an identifiable and *short-term* performance anomaly.

Letter Agreement. It may be wise to specify, within the Letter Agreement, the benchmark event that would return the Borrower to the original Lending arrangement. It is suggested that the Borrower work closely with his attorney in negotiating and approving such a Letter Agreement.

There is little sense in incurring the legal expenses in redoing the loan documentation if a "quick fix" Letter Agreement would suffice. The Lender may, however, require updated financial forecasts along with new Borrower financial assumptions to support this scenario.

CHAPTER 3

THE BORROWER IN TROUBLE

"You're kidding—sign over my home?"

"They want a fee to not call our loan!"

"We're being transferred to which loan group?"

Loss Of Trust (YOURS or THEIRS)

In commercial transactions, whether it is with suppliers, customers, associated professionals, or lenders, it is imperative to maintain a strong relationship in which trust is not only implicit but strictly observed. Should *either party* violate this trust, an important relationship may be permanently damaged.

Where a loan transaction is involved, the Lender seeks to have the Loan Agreement address almost every potential loan loss exposure. The reader may remember from Chapter 1 that one of the last stated non-financial covenants that may lead to a loan default is "Lender deemed insecure." That is virtually a Lender's catchall for any unforeseen event.

While most of this chapter covers a Lender's lack of trust toward the Borrower or his company, there also are *times when the Borrower may lose trust in the Lender:*

- Lack of professional knowledge
- Lack of consideration for a Borrower's situation
- Promises made but not kept
- Failure to cover overdrafts as agreed (checks returned to suppliers)
- Stated loan "approvals," per the LO, were *not* in fact truthful and could seriously jeopardize business arrangements (Borrower may have indicated to others that Lender's loan approvals were in place, when actually they were not)
- "Eleventh hour" Lender changes to credit approvals or loan documents when the Borrower has little choice but to accept; Lender is not dealing in good faith
- Lending Officer will report one thing to his superiors, with a conflicting report to the Borrower

When the Borrower loses trust in the Lender—either the individual Loan Officer or the institution as a whole—it is time to aggressively seek a qualified and receptive replacement lending institution. These actions are covered in Chapter 7.

REALITY CHECK

Lender liability issues? Contact your legal counsel for advice. If your lender's actions, or the lack thereof, result in damage to your business, there may be Lender liability.

Do not inform the Lender of this *possible* position; let your counsel evaluate this with you first. Your counsel then would make any bank contact. A knee-jerk reaction on the part of the Borrower could immediately jeopardize the existing borrowing relationship, however difficult, and possibly impact cash flow unfavorably.

Lenders also lose trust in their Borrowers. Such trust, or confidence, may be lost for any of these reasons:

- Financial numbers presented are not dependable
- Collateral values are consistently overstated
- Taxes are not paid on a timely basis; Lender is not notified
- Inaccurate personal financial statements
- Attempting to hide liens placed against the business
- Double pledging of collateral
- Borrower does not return calls
- Borrower does not respond to information requested by Lender
- A consistency of *past due* loan payments of interest and /or principal

This lack of trust is usually only identified in the Lender's attitude toward the Borrower. Lenders are frequently cautioned not to confront Borrowers with "trust accusations." Rather, this would be the time for the Lending Officer (LO) to prepare collateral schedules and update valuations as best he can, to assure his Lending institution of the loan's collateral adequacy. Once collateral support appears satisfactory, the LO may then commence to prepare a demand letter for loan repayment; possibly citing other loan deficiencies rather than the trust issue. Frequently, the receipt of such a letter may be the Borrower's first indication of any Lender dissatisfaction.

Real Experiences!

The loan officer was really surprised that after all of the loan applicant's work, it had come down to this. The company was a large product supplier—though not overly profitable—to the state's transportation industry. All loan application information was provided. The prospective Borrower's accountant had also supplied many of the supporting schedules. Historical tax returns, as well as personal financial statements, were made available. Enough information was available for the Lender to make a decision. Admittedly, it was going to be tough approval—but it did have a 50—50 chance.

Then the company owner blew it. He asked the Loan Officer to check out his warehouse, which is nothing out the ordinary—a tour is the normal thing to do. In the middle of this large warehouse, there was what seemed to be a secured, enclosed room. The owner unlocked and opened the door. It looked like an inventory room for a quiz show. There were refrigerators, huge televisions, chandeliers, computers, and much more. The owner said, "I really need this loan approved. If you see anything here you would like, just say the word and I will have it delivered to your home." The owner's integrity was *immediately* compromised. The Loan Officer felt he could in no way trust the company information already provided. The loan was already disapproved even before the first folder was opened. Moral: No one needs, or seeks, these extra inducements. No one should have to go to these lengths for a loan. There are many sources for appropriate business financing for just about any situation.

A week or so later the loan officer received a call from this previous applicant. Four tickets to a playoff game were available—if the loan officer would reconsider.

Warning: A Lender's lack of trust in the Borrower may well find its way into the *permanent* credit file of the institution and forever "color" a Borrower's risk rating and influence future requests for credit approval.

TIGHTENING OF LOAN COVENANTS

So—what does a Lender do when he perceives he cannot trust a Borrower?

One of the Lender's key tools in protecting himself in a lack-of-trust situation is to *tighten existing loan covenants.* One knows that in tough times loan covenants may be loosened—they usually are—but this is *more* than tough times—*the Borrower now cannot be trusted*!

Remember, this is only the Lender's perception—unless, of course, the Borrower really is not trustworthy. *If the Borrower has been untruthful in business dealings with the Lender, or others, the Borrower should discuss the issues with his legal counsel for direction.*

A Lender will best use this time to put himself in an improved covenant and collateral position *before* he declares a loan default or calls the loan (demands payment).

Here is a short list of some things a Lender may seek to do when a concern as to the viability or trustworthiness of a Borrower is in question:

- Accelerate the review of covenant compliance from annually to quarterly or monthly
- Tighten covenants further
- Amend existing Loan Agreement(s)
- Arrange for monthly meetings to "update" the Lender
- Seek more frequent financial forecasts
- Demand that forecasts be prepared by Borrower's accountant, rather than the Borrower
- Reduce payables (possibly even quicker than already negotiated suppliers)
- Have a third party verify accounts receivable
- Have a third party "audit" the books and records of the Borrower
- Recommend putting selective delinquent receivables in "collection" status
- Seek executed Notes in place of aged open accounts (to the Lender, a Note is a more convincing evidence of debt, especially older debt)
- Write off questionable receivables earlier than planned
- Place selected inventory components in a bonded ware-

house; this represents controlled access monitored by non-Borrower personnel
- Request that certain creditors subordinate their position to the Lender (see Chapter 5)

. . . and the list goes on

Note: The Lender may request that you keep a certain level of cash liquidity in your business bank account. This is a normal request—especially so at the onset of a relationship. Some loan arrangements require the Borrower to keep *all operating and payroll funds* with the Lender's institution. Generally, a commercial bank lender has the "right of offset" against the Borrower's accounts, placing offset proceeds toward the loan, interest due, and certain expenses. This can happen *suddenly and without the Borrower's knowledge*—at least for a few hours.

REALITY CHECK

If placing funds in another institution is *not* a covenant violation, keep some business funds in a bank or other institution *not associated with your current Lender*. It is best to have the approval for such a setup at the very beginning of a relationship. Reasons may be proximity of bank branches to you or your employees, or a long-term previous relationship. You are then protected when a Lender moves suddenly against your bank accounts– all available funds are not lost!

The Lender's dissatisfaction with its relationship with the Borrower is evident in the actions mentioned in the previous list. *The strategic response by the Borrower will be of material importance over the next months.* See Chapters 6 and 7.

CREDIT ENHANCEMENTS SOUGHT

The Lender, feeling much less satisfied with the relationship, most probably has already reduced the risk rating (see the explanation of risk ratings in Chapter 2). As a result of this reduction, he must prove to his superiors that he is "on top" of the Issues and that the Lender's loan recovery is not in jeopardy. Most likely collateral "enhancements," whether really needed or not, could be required for a continuance of the relationship.

Let's take a look at some of the more common credit enhancements.

Personal Guarantees—"Collateralization"

The Borrower (and other majority owners) may have already given the Lender an uncollateralized personal guarantee—frequently known as a "blanket" guarantee. The Lender may now want to make sure certain personal assets (supporting the guarantee) will not be lost to it. The Lender is clearly indicating that it is uneasy with this loan and is "covering all bases." It may seek a first, second, third (or whatever necessary) position in your home, vacation home, land or investment properties, other businesses, and so on. Should there be a limited amount of equity in the home, it may not be worthwhile for the Lender to take a position. However, with significant equity, it would be advantageous for a Lender to obtain a legal position in the property. This action would not permit the Borrower to obtain a junior mortgage on his property for other purposes. The Lender effectively "locks in" the Borrower's equity—for additional Lender's security—if needed.

Sometimes a Borrower may be in a corner and, for all intents and purposes, be *forced* to provide collateralization of a guarantee. A Borrower may, for any number of vital business situations, permit such collateralization until:

- A replacement Lender is found. (Remember, personal guarantee collateralization could still be required by the *new* Lender—or not).
- The Lender later determines that the Borrower is now in an improved position and releases this additional collateral.

Once a guarantee is collateralized, it may be difficult to convince a Lender to later remove this "additional collateral" position. Ensure that benchmarks are in place, and documented, to trigger such releases. (See Chapter 5 for options regarding limited and unlimited personal guarantees.)

Family members may be required to provide guarantees: Sometimes, while one spouse has already has provided his personal guarantee, the other spouse has not. It is not uncommon for the Lender to require (or "request") that the other spouse also provide a personal guarantee for the business debt. There have been numerous instances when the other spouse has refused. This does not necessary jeopardize the Borrower's relationship; the Lender will usually try this if for nothing else than to emphasize the seriousness of the situation. However, if personal assets are substantial, the Lender may be concerned that one spouse may transfer assets to the other, possibly removing them from the Lender's collateral base.

Suppliers or solid customers may provide guarantees: It may be paramount to a receptive supplier (material funds owed to supplier by Borrower) or key customer that the Borrower's business operations are not disturbed in any way. This could be due to contracts already in place, or that a customer's seasonal inventory depends on scheduled shipments of Borrower's product, and so on. A Lender, recognizing this, may suggest that the Borrower approach the supplier or customer, indicating the business problem (hopefully a temporary one) and requesting that the supplier provide a "limited guarantee" to the Lender (see Chapter 5). It is unlikely that such a contact would provide a full guarantee for the entire business debt. However, the supplier or customer may stand behind a *portion* of it—a least the amount that might represent a year's worth of business to him, or 10% of the overall debt, for example. Such a guarantee may come with a time limit; the supplier or customer does not want to be on the hook forever. This type of guarantee could be an inducement for the Lender to back off from a current adverse action.

You can learn more about personal guarantees and their options in Chapter 5. Also see Purchase Order Financing in Chapter 8.

Pledging of additional assets:

In order to strengthen a Lender's position, the Lender may require that additional collateral be pledged. The Borrower may be financing other business assets, such as machinery, equipment, or real estate. Considering the initial down payments and amounts paid on these accounts since their loan inceptions, there is most likely *some equity* now contained within these other financed assets.

The Borrower's prime Lender would seek to take a "second position" in these other assets. The secondary Lender's lien would of course still be "first" in its specific collateral. However, additional equity (built up as payments are made) would now be "owned" by the primary business Lender.

The Borrower's inventory may be removed (or not) and placed under bonded warehouse control: Should a material amount of the Lender's collateral involve inventory, including adaptable components, raw materials, and finished goods, such elements may more accurately be controlled by utilizing a bonded warehouse operation. This is a privately owned service business employed by Lenders to "record and control" movements within the Borrower's inventory. Services are especially valuable to a Lender if it is lending against inventory on a formula basis or if the Lender distrusts a Borrower's inventory reporting. Fees paid to the servicing company are the responsibility of the Borrower.

Such controls are targeted to ensure that the quantities and the inventory valuations reported to the Lender are correct. "Certificates" are issued to the Lender periodically by the bonded warehouse company certifying as to the accuracy of reported inventory data. Inventories are closely controlled by these service companies. Controls are accomplished either at the bonded warehouse location (inventory must be moved from the Borrower's location) or at the Borrower's facility in a designated and secured (fenced off) area. The service company's personnel may be employed or, in some cases, the Borrower's employees may be utilized when inventory remains on the Borrower's premises. Actually, these types of operations are not too unwieldy. Both the Lender *and the Borrower* are assured of accurate numbers.

Relationship transferred to the asset-based lending area: Should the Lender's collateral involve accounts receivable and inventory, the asset-based lending (ABL) department may better control risks for the Lender. Rather than the Lender just taking a "blanket" lien against collateral, supporting collateral is now *evaluated on a daily basis*, and advances (loans) against this collateral are based upon pre-approved loan formulas. In other words, the amount a company can borrow (frequently on a daily basis) is determined by levels of "eligible" receivable and inventory. The word "eligible" means that not all receivables and not all inventory components would be qualified for such borrowings. But it must be remembered that *all accounts receivable and inventory are collateral for the Lender*. There would be a credit limit based on the *total* of all borrowings. **Caution**: ABL lending usually requires daily reporting by the Borrower to the Lender of all sales, collections, credits, debits issued, and so on, as the Lender maintains substantially duplicate records within its ABL operation. Also, customer invoice payments are frequently directed toward a Lender's lockbox rather than the Borrower's company.

Interest Rate Increases

Certainly, raising the interest rate on borrowed funds can be a credit enhancement for the Lender. *Higher interest income mitigates some of the Lender's risk.* A measure of Borrower comfort is appropriate in that there is usually a "cap" interest rate within the Loan Agreement, which will limit the level to which rates can increase (see Chapter 5). In most financial institutions, the Lender will notify the Borrower in writing of its intention to increase the interest rate. The Borrower is frequently required to "sign off" on this letter before the Lender can raise the rate.

The Borrower should discuss interest rate change concerns with his accountant *before* addressing these with the Lender.

If the explanation for the rate increase is not satisfactory to the Borrower, the Borrower should arrange for a meeting with the Lender. Again, there is a favorable element of timing to the Borrower, as it may take a week or so to arrange and/or conclude such a meeting. Whatever compromises the Borrower may have achieved, he should ask for a new interest change letter (not initialed pen changes). His legal counsel will review the new letter before the Borrower signs off. This procedure may not abolish the rate increase, but *the rate increase may at least be deferred*, as the discussion/compromise period has most likely been spread over about four weeks. Consider asking the Lender to have the new rate effective as of the first day of the *next* month—*not* retroactive to the previous month.

Within the initial loan agreement the Borrower has already agreed to either a fixed or variable rate—or some combination. This may also be the time to consider a change in rate indices or the consideration of interest rate "hedges." The size of the Borrower's loan and the sophistication of the Lender may depend on whether such financial products are offered.

There is much more about lender interest rates and fees in Chapter 5.

Unexpected or Updated Appraisal Requirements (M&E, R/E)

A Lender's apprehension over reported collateral values may be resolved to the Lender's satisfaction by updating existing appraisals. Updating normally occurs within the terms of the *original* Loan Agreement—usually every few years, although some Lenders' policies require updated appraisals annually. This is especially so if the appraisal was completed over a year ago, completed by another financial institution, or the volatility of the equipment or real estate markets makes it advisable for a Lender to re-evaluate its collateral valuations.

Appraisals requested by the Lender *beyond the terms* of the original loan agreement are called "unexpected." These unexpected appraisals (unexpected on the part of the Borrower) can be cause for Borrower concern. The Lender may be concerned that the Lender may have to liquidate (sell off, auction, etc.) his collateral to generate funds to pay off the loan. There may also be less onerous reasons for an unexpected appraisal, and it is best to find out what's going on early—especially as the Borrower usually has to pick up the cost of the updated or new appraisal.

These requirements and results don't happen all at once. It usually takes at least one month for a completed appraisal to be received by the Lender from the appraiser. The Lender wants to know today's value!

While it is obvious that the Lender is hoping for improved values, such higher values could also be a plus for the Borrower. With a higher valuation, an increased loan against these assets may be obtainable from a (current or new) Lender.

Loan-to-Value Ratios:

However, if the appraisal comes in at *lower* values than expected, possibly even lower than the *initial* appraisal, the Lender may want the loan to be immediately paid down to a lesser amount. Usually the loan would be paid down to reflect the Loan Agreement's stated loan-to-value ratio. For example, "The loan-to-value will not exceed 80% of the appraised value." If the appraisal comes in at $300,000, the loan then should not exceed $240,000. If, in this case, the new appraisal is $260,000, the loan cannot be over $208,000. If there was a $240,000 loan then outstanding, the Borrower would have to come up with $32,000 in order to be in compliance with the agreed loan-to-value ratio. It may be possible to arrange a separate Term Loan (secured by other collateral or a short Demand Note) with the current Lender to generate proceeds for the loan reduction required.

To reduce the Borrower's appraisal costs, *try to use the same appraiser as used before*. Loan agreements generally provide that the Lender has the choice of appraisers, but usually there is some flexibility. Also, make sure the Borrower gets a "complete" copy of the new appraisal—not just the Lender.

Alternatively, the Lender will attempt to get a least three bids for the appraisal. Absent other concerns, the Lender will select the lowest bidder to do the appraisal. It is the Lender who actually engages the appraiser—not the Borrower—though the Borrower pays the cost. It takes time for the Lender to order these bids from appraisers; just getting a bid may take a week or so. If it is a larger appraisal, the bidding appraiser may want to do a "walk through" prior to committing to a bid price. *Again, this extra time to plan is on the Borrower's side.*

Once an appraiser is selected by the Lender, the engagement is placed on the appraiser's agenda. It usually takes two to four weeks for the appraisal to occur. Allowing a week for the appraiser to prepare the report, the time required has expanded up to four to six weeks from the time bids were sent out to the time the appraisal report is completed.

NOTE: Make sure that the Borrower—*not just the Lender*—gets a complete copy of the new appraisal.

It is also important to find out the *type* of appraisal a Lender requires—it can be a clue to the Borrower as to the Lender's probable intentions.

Machinery & Equipment Appraisals:

Fair Market Value (FMV): A value that a willing buyer would offer a willing seller *without duress* and in the *normal course of business*. This valuation frequently is used in the acquisition mode or for balance sheet purposes.

Orderly Liquidation Value (OLV): Usually a 50% or more discount off of FMV. Sale of equipment by Lender (or Seller of goods) could occur within a 60- to 90-day time frame. Such timing also provides a reasonable opportunity for the auctioneer or seller to advertise to a wide range of potential buyers.

Auction Value ("Knock Down"): Largest discount off of FMV. Referred to as "under the hammer" or "on the block." *Time is of the essence.* Advertising of the sale may not be as extensive, and a bulk sale may be an alternative consideration of the Lender. Whether to hold a piecemeal collateral sale or a sale in bulk is determined by which method would most likely maximize results.

The appraisals described in the previous list require *detailed* asset inspections plus comprehensive machinery and equipment descriptions. Two other appraisal techniques are:

"Desktop" appraisals:

The appraiser completes all of his work from his office without the benefit of viewing the assets. This can be the least expensive of appraisals. Information may be provided directly from the Borrower or based on prior appraisals or equipment schedules. When significant dependence is to be placed upon an accurate valuation, the "desktop" may be the least dependable.

"Walk-through" appraisals are preferred over the "desktop" in that the appraiser is actually within the facility viewing the equipment. This method does not usually provide detailed asset descriptions. The appraiser will value items viewed utilizing his own equipment database and experience resources. It is close to the least expensive type of inspection—the appraiser may spend only a day or so on site.

Frequently, machinery and equipment appraisers will have extensive database resources through which to obtain the most recent equipment values as the result of recent auctions.

Real Estate Appraisal

Basic valuations may seem similar to those indicated in the previous section (Fair Market Value or Auction Value). However, commercial properties, investment properties, and construction and other development properties (as well as land, improved or otherwise) are diverse in their potential income revenues and valuation processes. Real estate appraisals must therefore cover a wide divergence of data to be relevant to a specific property, considering its use, earnings, revenue potential, and the like. Elements of comparable properties, occupancy rates, expenses, lease terms, area market conditions, and environmental considerations are additional and essential components.

Complete Appraisal:

This is referred to as a self-contained report, meaning that all elements are available within the report. This is unlike other reports, in which selected documentation and supporting data may remain within the appraiser's office. This is the most expensive report and is considered desirable by Lenders for higher-valuation properties.

Complete Appraisal / Summary: Obviously, many elements of narration and data input are limited within "summary" format. The Lender's satisfactory experience with certain appraisers enables this less expense and less time-consuming report to be utilized. These appraisals are generally utilized for the small- to moderate-size appraisal requirements.

Lower-Value Properties—In this case, a limited "approach" method may be utilized. Within all commercial property appraisals, one or more of three general valuation approaches are presented: income approach, sales approach, and market approach. Lower-value properties may utilize only one, or possibly two of these approaches, to arrive at a reasonable value.

Drive-by Report:

Generally, for loans under $250,000, complete appraisals are not required. The LO should have a good grasp of local or neighborhood values. A judgment of value is made relative to the LO's experience considering comparable property values and possibly other like properties within his loan portfolio. This may literally be only a "drive-by" or a stop with some limited building inspections conducted by the LO.

Many Lenders prefer commercial real estate appraisers with the professional designation of "MAI" (Member of the Appraisal Institute). For more information on the designation, as well as a listing of MAI appraisers in your area, go to *www.appraisalinstitute.org*.

REALITY CHECK

Don't sign or agree immediately to any of the lender collateral enhancement requests discussed thus far *because you now need time to plan strategies.*

Again, as explained in Chapter 2, *delaying tactics* (time required for a prudent review of the Lender's requests by the Borrower, his lawyer, and consultants) can now serve your best interests as you:

Determine the viability of the Lender's requests with your attorney, accountant, consultant, and affected business and family members.

Utilize the time by working the *replacement* Lender strategies, as may be necessary, provided within Chapter 7.

FORBEARANCE FEES

The Lender has decided that the Borrower is in loan default. The Lender does have the right to declare (put the Borrower on formal notice of a loan default) or not to declare the Borrower in default. To *not* declare the Borrower in default really means that a "pass" (perhaps temporary) is given to the Borrower. There may be extenuating circumstances as to the development of the default but, for whatever reason, default is not an issue at this time. For the Borrower, this can be an acceptable outcome.

However, *if the Lender seeks to declare a loan default*, which is an official act, that decision may affect the Borrower's risk rating and will become a part of the Borrower's credit file. Ramifications may be the Lender's request for credit enhancements, tightening up on the existing loan covenants, giving the Borrower a period of time (30–90 days) to resolve the situation, or even "calling" the loan. If time is provided to the Borrower to clear up a problem, it usually comes at a cost—possibly a forbearance fee.

The forbearance fee is a fee that induces the Lender to stand still and not do anything—although it may have the legal right to take action. The Lender agrees not to exercise its default remedies or rights under the Loan Agreement during the forbearance period. The Lender's fee may be based upon a percentage of the existing loan outstanding, a percentage of the approved credit facility, or may appear to be a somewhat arbitrary amount. I have has seen average forbearance fees from $5,000 to $25,000—some with seemingly *no correlation* to the amount of the debt owed. Usually, there is little reluctance by the Lender to negotiate. Lenders actually are pleasantly surprised when Borrowers accept this fee requirement without question. Of course they are—it's all pure fee income! The Borrower's normal interest payment requirements are usually not interrupted during a forbearance period.

Forbearance fee payments may be negotiated to be paid in installments, or a Demand Note may be signed to defer all or part of the fee for a period of time. Options depend upon the flexibility of the Lender.

The Borrower should be notified in writing by the Lender as to a loan default. In the same letter, or a separate letter, the forbearance fee opportunity is provided by the Lender. The Borrower may wish not to accept a forbearance fee arrangement, but rather proceed with another strategy. *The Borrower is advised to contact his attorney, accountant, and business consultant to discuss the ramifications of these letters and the strategies available.*

REALITY CHECK

The Borrower may find that certain of the Lender's requests may not be entirely realistic or doable within the time frame requested. Often the expense to the company to comply with a request can be way out of line considering a Lender's desired results.

Frequently, an *absolute refusal* by the Borrower on key items will cause the Lender to modify the request to a more reasonable one. The Borrower wants the Lender to think and reconsider. The Borrower will *not* object to anything up front but must take the Lender's request home, consider it, and consult with advisers.

Do not volunteer to provide "extra" collateral to the Lender. Any backup assets the Borrower may have, or may later receive (including other offers of supporting guarantees), must be kept in reserve for the really tough times, should they come.

LOAN TRANSFERRED TO THE WORKOUT DEPARTMENT
(Special Assets Group)

Sorry—there's no doubt now as to the Lender's intention—*the Borrower is on the way out!*

The purposes of a Lender's "workout group" or "special assets group" (one and the same) are:

1. Loan "recovery," with a minimal loss to the Lender of loan principal, interest, and associated expenses.*
2. Ensuring that all loans in a recovery category are handled uniformly according to Lender policy by seasoned Lender personnel especially trained in loan recovery work.
3. Taking difficult lending relationships out of the hands of less experienced lending officers.
4. Less frequently, rehabilitating Borrowers back into an acceptable risk rating and returning them to a conventionally controlled loan portfolio.

*The term "recovery" is used because the Lender may have already "written off" the Borrower's entire loan balance once it is assigned to loan workout. That is not to say that the debt is lost to the Lender—only that for internal record-keeping purposes the loan may not be a performing asset and, as such, does not appear on the asset side of the Lender's balance sheet. So when the loan is paid, to whatever extent, there can be a Lender "recovery."

In the normal course of events, and prior to such assignment to loan workout, the Borrower has probably been subject to as much rehabilitation efforts as he's reasonably going to get from his regular lending officer.

While it may be infrequent that a Borrower recovers from the workout group, the Borrower may still have a chance to salvage this bad situation because:

- He will have a new lending officer
- He will have a seasoned lending officer
- Many Borrower biases may be left with the old lending officer
- He will have a lending officer with some authority

Complementing a workout Lending Officer's authority is the fact that, in some institutions, these officers also receive financial incentive (over and above salary and benefits) for the dollars they "recover" from Borrowers assigned to them. So, while they may not collect the entire loan, interest, and expenses, they do get a bonus on any funds collected or that are involved in a "settlement."

Because of these specialized officers' experience and proven judgment capabilities, they have a wide range of authority. This authority may extend to reducing the amount of recorded debt and compromising accumulating interest charges and/or Lender expenses. Should the Borrower have sources (even from a new Lender) of debt payoff, such payoff may result in a settlement below the balance of the debt going into loan workout. *These officers are more likely to listen to and consider ideas from the Borrower as to how to settle this debt or restructure the entire relationship.*

What may have seemed an *impossible* situation to an inexperienced lending officer may be a "tough but not impossible" situation to an experienced workout officer.

This entire workout scenario is a critical time for the Borrower because:

- Credit line is reduced or terminated
- Additional loan advances may be nonexistent or limited
- Negotiations with new Lenders may be under way (should have been done long ago; see Chapter 7)

- Collateral auction or foreclosure threats are possible by the Lender
- Suppliers and customers are nervous as to the status of the company
- In the more serious of considerations, a member of the Lender's staff may be on site daily at the Borrower's place of business
- Business closure may be imminent

REALITY CHECK

In these kinds of difficult and complex Lender negotiations, the Borrower should always maintain a narrative and chronological log of all meetings, attendees, agendas, meeting content, and outcomes of each. It is possible that such a log would be invaluable in case of future litigation. The Lender maintains such a record within its credit files—but these notes are from the Lender's perception of events. The Borrower must maintain his own independent log.

It's a sad fact that most distressed Borrowers assigned to the loan workout group will not offer such cooperation. *Your positive attitude will be refreshing and you can leverage an agreeable relationship within this workout group.* Phone calls will be answered, more possible solutions to difficulties will be provided, civility will be maintained, and some relaxation in "requirements" may be in evidence.

As further developed within the upcoming chapters, a Borrower's ultimate reconcilement may be:

- Obtaining initial, or additional, guarantees for the existing debt from federal, state, or municipal governments
- A complete loan restructuring within the existing Lender
- Attracting replacement Lender financing
- New equity partner
- Exercise of a buyout offer
- Beneficial sale of the business
- Sale of selected assets to reduced debt

It is inevitable that others will become aware of your difficult situation, and you may have to overcome "bad press" as you take aggressive action to save your company. Even here, follow the relationship management techniques discussed in Chapter 10. In the long run, you can be a "class act"—and this will never come back to haunt you.

I have observed what I believed to be unnecessary business liquidations as well as inspiring success stories. The success stories inevitability resulted from a good attitude, honesty, competent legal representation, and aggressive participation by all parties within the various recovery scenarios.

To repeat what was said earlier: The objective in all of this is to gain time for the Borrower to reconcile his borrowing situation.

We have discussed a number of *delaying opportunities* that provide the Borrower time to regroup, and, if necessary, plan a realistic course of action. The Borrower should not be alone in this; he should utilize his attorney, accountant, and business consultant.

Unfortunately, in some situations, dialogue between the Borrower and Lender breaks down to the extent that only the lawyers talk.

Such *restricted conversations* may be recommended by legal counsel. The plus in such a situation is that a very formal circle of communications is then maintained between the Lender to Lender's counsel, the Lender's counsel to Borrower's counsel, and the Borrower's counsel to the Borrower. These "controlled" communications result in a limited amount of information falling through the cracks. Neither the Borrower nor the Lender is making agreements without the other's knowledge or outside of their legal advisers.

This course of action, of course, is very expensive to the Borrower. He not only must pay his own lawyer, but also the Lender's lawyer as part of the expenses of loan recovery. Also, within the original loan documentation, the Borrower usually has already agreed to pay such expenses incurred by the Lender.

Stress does increase when a collateral liquidation is imminent; personal residences are foreclosed upon and children may have to be pulled out of schools because of lack of personal funds. The emotional stability of the Borrower may be taxed to the utmost because of such closure or liquidating situations. The Lender may not be willing, possibly upon the advice of his counsel, to even meet personally with the Borrower. *In these stressful situations, the Borrower should rely on his legal counsel to handle all communication aspects.*

In all of the situations described in this chapter, resolution of the problems may take a few weeks or up to a few months. Time really is on the Borrower's side.

Elements of compromise and resolution, even including the addressing issue of finding a new Lender(s), may be successfully accomplished in a timely and orderly manner—contributing much to the chances for a successful outcome.

REALITY CHECK

The Borrower will offer full cooperation to the workout lender.

The Borrower will keep his legal counsel and consultants *informed at all times* of all activities, providing them with copics of relevant documentation and communications.

Borrower will not sign any Lender documents without first having his legal counsel's approval.

CHAPTER 4

PITFALLS OUT OF YOUR CONTROL

"What do you mean—my industry's got a problem?"

"We're in Rochester—and I need approval from San Francisco?"

"I'm with a new bank? I didn't want a new bank!"

"The Fed's sold my loan?"

A Perceived Industry Stigma

Many Lenders are reluctant to lend into industries that they view as inherently possessing too much credit risk. These may also include industries that require specialized lenders or unique control procedures:

- Entertainment
- Restaurants
- Fishing
- Lumber
- Agriculture
- Oil exploration
- Leasing companies
- Construction / developers
- Hotels / motels
- Health Care / medical

Also, considering environmental issues, certain business classifications may be suspect by Lenders:

- Chemical
- Plating
- Farming
- Storage facilities
- Paint manufacturing
- Food processing
- Dry cleaners
- Gas stations

Conversely, there are Lenders that specialize and thrive on industries that others would not touch—because these Lenders are experts. More than likely, for each item in the preceding lists, there is a Lender, somewhere, that successfully specializes in that industry. How to find such a Lender? See Chapter 8.

REALITY CHECK

Ensure that the Lender's credit committee does not have an aversion to the Borrower's industry.

The Borrower should do this *before* spending valuable time and resources developing a Lending package for a potentially unresponsive Lender. The local LO may not know of industry-associated losses or problems elsewhere within the Lender's institution, but the credit committee and loan workout department will. How do you find out? *Ask!* Either ask the LO to talk to the head of loan workout or have him ask a more senior LO to discuss this concern with a member of the credit committee. The Borrower does not need to find out at the eleventh hour that the Lender would really rather not lend to the Borrower's industry.

A Borrower's job is to *keep the Lender informed as to the Borrower's industry.* It is important for the LO to understand the industry and thus better understand the concerns and needs of his Borrower. Dissatisfaction voiced by a Lender against the Borrower's performance may, in reality, be an industrywide problem and not necessarily an inherent problem of one Borrower. With current industry information made available to the Lender, he can become proficient in that industry—to the benefit of the Borrower. The Lender will then:

- Have added confidence in the handling of this loan relationship
- Support the Borrower when problems are industry oriented
- Be creditable in his presentations on behalf of the Borrower (annual credit reviews; requests for additional credit)
- Senior Lender management will begin to recognize the LO as *their* expert in the industry

There are a variety of ways to bring your Lender "on board" regarding industry information. The following activities can cost next to nothing or involve a considerable expense. The determining factors as to the extent of activities are the loan size and importance of this particular Lender to the Borrower's business and, of course, the amount of Borrower resources that are available.

1. The most basic activity is to *invite your Lending Officer ("LO") to your business location.* This may be a warehouse, a manufacturing facility, or simply a set of offices. The point is to present a business overview to your LO and, if appropriate, to have the LO visit the manufacturing and/or distribution

process. In addition to a tour, also consider a Lender meeting with the business officers and department managers, who would prepare relatively short presentations about their responsibilities. The senior business officer(s) should provide an overview of the industry and its issues, recent business highlights, and general industry and business forecasts.

2. As available, *provide relevant industry articles* to your LO. A cover note may be added clarifying the point to be made or direction of the article. As the LO seldom reads more than credit reports and financial statements, such articles are a welcome diversion. Not only will the LO develop an industry understanding, but the article will find its way into the Borrower's credit file for further reference.

3. *Subscribe, on behalf of your LO,* to your standard industry or trade publication. Most industries tend to have a national association that publishes a periodic trade magazine. Such publications cover a wealth of industry information such as trends and developments, with some highlighting specific businesses. (Could yours be one of them?) Frequently, Lenders who specialize in lending to a particular industry will advertise within the industry publication in an attempt to attract this specialized loan business. Once the (low-cost) subscription begins, the LO will have a *recurring source of current industry information.* Have renewals directed to the Borrower. The Borrower, of course, should also subscribe to his own industry publication.

4. Most businesses belong to an *industry trade association.* These associations frequently have regional chapters that hold monthly meetings. While the Borrower himself should attend these meetings from time to time, it would be advantageous for the Borrower to invite his Lender, the Lender's superiors, and even the credit analyst—all at once or individually—to attend a meeting. Pick a meeting with an interesting speaker. Considering both the industry information gleaned by the Lender(s) and the networking available to him, the overall relationship could be greatly enhanced. Some Borrowers go further and become officers or directors of these chapters, perhaps even going on to national offices.

Nothing mysterious here—just good business. The LO is developing industry proficiencies, which enables him to be perceived within the Lender's institution as an industry expert. The Lender's credit committee will also be more apt to rely on his industry evaluations and agree to his recommendations.

REALITY CHECK

Commercial business loan requests have been disapproved because of a Lender's previous loan losses, or a simply a bad situation, with another company in the same industry. The Lender may not now have the necessary confidence in other businesses associated with the industry. That's life, and it's not going to change.

Loan Approvals: Who, Where, When?

These days it is not uncommon to find a lending bank within the Borrower's home area controlled by an out-of-state parent. This may be especially so following the acquisition of a local Lender by a larger national Lender.

Unfortunately, the Borrower may not be aware of certain outside controls until a *material* local decision must be made in a short period of time. While the local LO may support approval of a Borrower's request, the distant head office may only consider loans within its *established policy*. Policy *exceptions* requested by the distant LO may not be given much weight.

Also, it is most likely that only limited decision-making authority is given to these "remote line Lenders" (the junior lending officers who service the loans, review credit, and monitor the local loan portfolio). This is not always true, as there may be a local (on-site) senior lender with reasonable credit authority. However, Borrowers frequently find out too late that a second- or third-level approval must be obtained from a distant headquarters office before a critical loan request can be resolved.

An example: Lender's policy dictates that the LO has only $10,000 authority to honor (to pay) checks without funds being available within a Borrower's operating account. The Borrower informs the Lender that money will be deposited tomorrow to cover developing overdrafts. However, it may be local policy that checks made out to suppliers in the amount of $50,000 have already arrived at the Lender's operations center and will be "bounced" and returned unless a decision by a person of authority can be achieved by 3:00 P.M. After that point, checks will be returned unpaid—with appropriate insufficient funds fees charged, of course. That's really a killer, as suppliers may then become of wary of a Borrower's business stability and his ability to pay suppliers on a timely basis.

It is always important for a Borrower to know the level of "authority" with which he is dealing:

- Can loan decisions, temporary advances over the approved credit line, and checking account overdraft decisions be made locally—at the local area Lender's office? *Identify* the person with the most dollar authority.
- Do important, or immediate need, decisions have to go to higher levels of authority—even possibly out of the regional area?

A Borrower should be clear as to what the Lender can do—*without* additional authorities—and plan accordingly. If you don't know your LO's authorities, find out *now*! And if you can, also find out the authorities of your LO's immediate manager (and just where he is located).

BANK MERGERS, ACQUISITIONS, AND CLOSINGS

The merger, acquisition, or closing of the Borrower's Lender should *not* come as a total surprise.

The local financial and legal communities, along with the local, state, or national media, may be addressing such potential institutional changes. The local newspapers and business reviews will be following such activities. The concerns, advantages, or disadvantages depend on which side of the merger or acquisition one is on.

Media stories related to the following may be clues to potential ownership changes within lending institutions:

Bad loans
Successive losses
Shareholder concerns or lawsuits

Difficulties at annual meetings
Management shake-ups
Poor regulatory inspections
Cease and desist orders

It does not necessarily follow that all mergers and acquisitions will present horrific situations for the Borrower. Some of the transitions will work smoothly and without difficulties to existing Borrowers. But there are unique exceptions with serious downside potentials.

In what ways could these scenarios affect the Borrower and his existing Loan Agreement?

- The loan could later be "called" (immediate requirement to pay, usually in full).
- Loan repayment arrangement(s) may be accelerated.
- Deposit accounts may be "frozen" for a period of time (an extreme measure).

In these instances, a *proactive Borrower* must preserve cash flow and his current lending arrangements when everything else within the institution may seem to be in turmoil.

If the Borrower's existing Lender is in a merger with, or is being acquired by, another Lender, the Borrower may observe a deteriorating control situation, which could affect his current lending relationship. His current Lender may suffer in these ways:

- Loss of its decision-making capabilities
- Previously established Loan risk ratings may be re-classified
- Reassignment of existing key Lender personnel
- Certain of the Lender's senior personnel may resign
- New personnel from the acquirer are now in positions of responsibility
- New lender policies are at once imposed upon the Lender being acquired

"Mergers of equals" are hardly ever that simple, as one institution is usually more "equal" than the other. Synergies may result in the reduction of human resources, legal, loan workout, or other departments. Dual-institution lending departments will be consolidated, with *decision-making responsibilities usually remaining with the acquirer.* Policies foreign to the acquired Lender will be quickly implemented, leading some Borrowers to find that they are no longer qualified to borrow from the new Lender.

Your LO (if he's still there) could be tied up for weeks addressing policy revisions or data input. This formerly independent Lending institution will not have any reasonable amount of time to develop *new* business. Furthermore, personnel at all levels will be distracted by personal career choices, such as whether to resign, stay, or "mark time" to see what happens. Some senior officers usually will stay (with much fanfare) to give the aura of supporting new management. Frequently, once new management is successfully in place, former management may depart.

Your Lender is bound by the Loan Agreements you executed. The new Lender must abide by these agreements and they usually cannot be set aside.

However, once the dust has settled, Borrowers who are below a certain risk rating may no longer be acceptable to the Lender. During the first few months of a new Lender taking over, all risk ratings are reviewed and "adjusted" accordingly—*according to the new Lender's policy*. This is how the new Lender "cleans house." This is also the time that a number of Demand (for payment) Letters to unsuspecting Borrowers may be issued.

NOTE: Should your existing Lender be the acquiring Lender, the preceding scenarios are usually reversed, without material consequences. The Borrower notices few changes, because the policies of the dominating Lender (*his existing Lender*) remain in place.

In a Lender closure situation, the lending portfolio (which includes your loan) may be "sold" to another local or national Lender. Again, this in no way negates your existing loan agreement. However, a new Lender usually requires an entirely different "acceptable" credit profile—and a change in your risk rating could unfavorably affect your future borrowing opportunities.

There are always exceptions to the preceding observations, but in general, at the commencement of rumblings about Lender problems or changes, the Borrower should:

- Plan tactics with his accountant and attorney
- Assume the worst-case scenario—being asked to leave by the current Lender. The Lender asks the Borrower to find a replacement Lender
- Select replacement Lender candidates and improve loan terms and conditions (see Chapter 7)
- Develop a cash reserve in another institution (if this would not be a current covenant violation)
- As may be appropriate, prepare letters to key suppliers and/or customers indicating that the Borrower's business may be facing some Lender turmoil, which could continue over the next few months. Emphasize that it is not of the Borrower's making, and stability is expected to be resumed shortly. If possible, enclose supporting media articles reflecting the Lender's difficulties.

To follow your Lender's progress or lack thereof, consider becoming a shareholder, which ensures your receipt of annual and/or quarterly reports. Of course, when you walk into Lender's office, such reports are usually available for the asking. If you wish to research your existing Lender's (bank's) position in the eyes of regulators, there are firms that may enable you to compare your bank lender among its peers. Two of these are Veribanc, at *www.veribank.com*, and BauerFinancial, Inc., at *www.bauerfinancial.com.*

Regulators and Their Impact

When a regulator (FDIC, for example) takes over a lending institution, the Lender's operational procedures may be affected. Loan Agreements are generally honored—*although the timely processing of loan advances and posting of loan payments may be slowed* a few days or a week or more before the new Lender (purchaser) effectively takes over. The Borrower should copy all payment checks, bills, and coupons, as well as requests for loan advances. Such documentation may be valuable when later asking the Lender to reverse fees charged for late payments, overdrafts, and so on. These charges were *not* the Borrower's fault, but rather the fault of the regulator's processing.

The regulator will have set up, or will set up, an office or entity to address all operational aspects of a Lender being closed or monitored. These operations are responsible to see that certain functions of the institution to be closed are carried on without interruption. Sometimes the purchasing bank is in the process of "taking over" before the public is aware of what is happening. Announcements will be made in the media, and to all customers and borrowers of the institution, identifying the new Lender's personnel and changes in document processing.

Should a business borrowing relationship have been handled as agreed, the regulators may not attempt to disturb existing lending arrangements or risk ratings. However, if it is evident that an agreement has not been abided by, the regulators may call thc loan, discontinuc loan advanccs, or give the Borrower time to find another Lender.

Regulators may also "criticize" an institution's management for failure to appropriately assign risk ratings. The basics of risk ratings were discussed in some detail within Chapter 2. Some nontraditional Lenders, which are discussed in Chapter 9, do not use risk rating systems as described.

Regulators may require banks to set up additional capital reserves for any loans on their books that are classified as highly leveraged transactions (HLTs). These loans are usually at the lower tier of the risk rating classifications.

Regulators are protecting the public (to include commercial Borrowers) against Lenders that do not follow the rules. *When regulators "move" on an institution, a Borrower's routine processes may be upset for a short time—but this need not be a catastrophic event.*

REALITY CHECK

The factor that I see as the most prevalent obstacle to a timely loan closing is a recently discovered, unreported, or unresolved *environmental concern.*

Such concerns may be, but are not limited to, hazardous wastes, groundwater problems, pollutants, septic tanks, fuel tanks, chemical issues, radon gas, lead paint and asbestos issues, and the like.

ENVIRONMENTAL CONCERNS

Most Lenders will require that a "determination," a transaction screen, or a Phase I or a Phase II Environmental Site Assessment be completed prior to a loan closing. Also, certain online firms can provide specific environmental transactional information. On-site examinations and tests are accomplished by certified and licensed professionals satisfactory to the Lender. Without a completed and satisfactory environmental report, a *preliminary loan approval* may still be granted. But a *final* approval (and loan closing) usually is subject to a satisfactory environmental inspection(s)—*satisfactory to the Lender.* If the Phase I site inspection results in an unreconciled finding, a Phase II may be then required by the Lender.

It is not my intention to provide an extended dissertation relative to the legal and practical concerns of environmental issues—there are inspection specialists and licensed remedial companies available for that purpose.

However, the following are a few *practical concerns.*

Initially, and usually *prior to loan approval,* environmental issues are reconciled over the weeks and months of a Lender's routine due diligence. Should environmental concerns arise, these are usually reconciled by means of environmental inspections of various types and levels of sophistication. These inspections are usually ordered by the Lender and paid for by the Borrower (frequently in the form of pre-approval Borrower deposits). When deficiencies are reported to the Lender (formal reports are provided to the Lenders from their engaged environmental outside contractors), the Lender has choices to make:

1. Determine that the issues are not material enough to proceed with any remedial actions and proceed to the loan closing.

2. Determine that the issues are material but only to the extent that the Borrower can correct (remediate) the situation prior to the scheduled loan closing. The Borrower may actually be able to correct issues himself or engage a licensed environmental remediation firm to correct issues. Usually a final report by the remediator will be issued to the effect that the property is now within established state or federal guidelines. The Lender may then be able to proceed with the loan closing.

3. If the issues are material, determine that it then must conduct additional inspections. Following a satisfactory level of inspections, the Lender *may* require that certain levels of actual remediation procedures be concluded on the property. Such work may take weeks, months, or in some cases over a year. Borrower costs could be material.

Considering #3 above, the Lender may feel that the time and expense involved for complete and satisfactory remediation would be too costly to the Borrower. Or, the extent of contamination still may not be completely known, thus exposing the Lender to potential environmental issues in the future. Generally, both the property owner (the Borrower) and/or the existing Lender (in certain situations) may be legally liable for remedial or other legal costs resulting from future environmental lawsuits. Considering that the Lender is usually the one with the "deep pockets," and may have the most to lose, the Lender's decision may be simply to not proceed with the loan application.

This can be a shocker to a Borrower who has been working with the Lender over a number of months to close the loan.

> Note: From time to time, certain insurance companies provide Lenders *environmental risk insurance*. The Borrower usually pays for this at loan closing. A checklist is provided to the insurer by the Lender with the appropriate premium then being determined. Such insurance may help defray certain environmental risk concerns of a Lender. This insurance is not always available.

Real Experiences!

Can a large commercial loan close when an environmental hazard is discovered shortly prior to loan closing? In some cases the answer is yes. This California HVAC manufacturing company saw an opportunity to purchase a similar business in New Mexico. While not as profitable as the buying entity, it had an important share of the total southwest market. It was determined by the buying team that current owners (a large conglomerate) were simply "not paying attention." It was also ascertained that the environmental hazard of wastewater dispersion existed through the term of the current owner (the seller).

It was ultimately determined that the seller was responsible for remediation. The bank was willing to make the loan if funds, in an amount to satisfactorily address the estimated remediation costs, were deposited with the bank in an escrow arrangement. A Letter Agreement was drafted and executed by the involved parties.

At the loan closing the Borrower (the buying company) routinely obtained their normal loan proceeds and then paid to the seller the purchase price for the business. The seller of the property has now been paid. The seller then sent a predetermined amount of funds back to the Lender for the purpose of establishing an environmental escrow account.

A licensed remediation company, approved by the buyer and Lender, was hired by the seller. During this process a number of legal and environmental issues were also resolved. Over a number of months the clean up was satisfactorily completed, the remediation company's periodic invoices were paid from the escrow account and finally, after the final remediation company's invoice, the remainder of the escrow fund was returned to the Seller. Creative loan structuring and the use of "Letter Agreements" can be effective tools in the resolution of these problematic situations.

So what to do?

First, there is a "before the fact" issue. It is easy to say you should have known the history, or current regulations, regarding environmental issues on a purchased property. This is something the property purchaser can, and should, determine before the initial closing on the property. The purchaser simply conducts his own environmental study—engaging a professional. The purchase and sale agreement may indicate that the agreement is "subject to" a satisfactory environmental inspection. *It is important that the Borrower work closely with his legal counsel in developing this entire process.* The Borrower most likely should not purchase the property should compelling hazards be in evidence. Should the purchase still be consummated, it may come back in the future to haunt the Borrower.

But it is now—"after the fact." It looks as if the loan closing may be delayed. Or, the worst case for the Borrower, *it may never happen at all.* To now attempt to source another Lender—considering all of the credit work, providing supporting documents, the approval process, and yes, *another* environmental go-around, we're talking another few months.

If the Borrower feels, and the remediation requirements support this, that the costs can be managed and remediation could be accomplished within a time frame extending out to one year, the Lender *may* agree to the strategy that follows.

The Borrower will issue a *Letter Agreement* (*or "Side Letter"*) at the loan closing (on Borrower's letterhead, prepared with the assistance of the Borrower's legal counsel), indicating that:

The Borrower will indemnify the Lender against all costs and/ or lawsuits that may arise from this environmental mitigation or subsequent and similar exposures arising from this environmental exposure.

The Borrower will pay all costs of remediation.

The remediation will be completed *to the Lender's satisfaction* no later than (date).

Estimated costs of remediation will be placed in an escrow account with the Lender. Draws against this account by the Borrower will be made in a predetermined fashion and utilized against periodic billings for remediation. *This method will assure the Lender (and the Borrower) that funds will be available to pay for remediation.*

In order to develop funds for the escrow account (if not now available), the loan being considered by the Lender may be increased by the amount needed to fund the escrow account. This loan is presumably collateralized within the overall loan collateral base. The escrow account will also earn interest for the Borrower. Generally, a cash-based escrow account, rather than a certificate of deposit, is preferable due to the need for rapid availability of funds to pay invoices of the remedial company.

Alternatively, the Lender could approve a separate loan against *additional* collateral and/or guarantees to generate the required escrow monies.

The Side Letter will contain provisions for periodic reports from the remediation firm and will authorize periodic inspections by both the Lender and the environmental inspection firm.

At the conclusion of the process, the Lender would not release any excess escrow funds until the proper certification(s) from the appropriate agency (ies) are received indicating all is now in conformity with existing regulations.

Consequences should be identified should the Borrower not satisfactorily complete remediation by the date required.

Sooner or later, the Borrower, as the owner of the property, may have to get the remedial work accomplished, if not for the current Lender, then for a new Lender—or later, at the sale of the property. There is usually no getting out of this; environmental issues, along with the associated costs of mitigation, *must be resolved.*

IMPORTANT: In considering the Side Letter strategy, the Borrower *must utilize* his legal counsel and take into account environmental requirements of local, municipal, state, and federal regulators. Preliminary discussions should occur between the Borrower's legal counsel, Lender's counsel, governmental agencies, and environmental and remediation companies.

REALITY CHECK

Before the Borrower commits to an environmental Side Letter, he should understand that this remediation commitment must be fulfilled. It could take considerable expense and a lot of time, including that spent replying to frequent Lender's inquiries as to progress made—taking away from the business of doing business. If the Borrower is totally pleased with the entire loan arrangement (terms and conditions), including the profile and personalities of the Lender, he may wish to proceed.

The Borrower does not have to proceed with the loan closing—another Lender may address a situation entirely differently—but "a bird in the hand" may be a prudent approach here. There may also be some Lender penalties for not proceeding with the loan closing.

It would be very difficult to get a replacement Lender when the Borrower is in the middle of an environmental remediation.

Remember—Always work with your legal counsel and consider running with two replacement Lenders when the opportunity arises (see Chapter 7).

CHAPTER 5

WHAT YOU DON'T KNOW ABOUT —BUT SHOULD!

"But I simply cannot provide a personal guarantee."

"The Bank took the insurance check—can they do that?"

"What—my supplier owns my inventory?"

"You're kidding—not another fee!"

"But he said the loan was going to be approved!"

Personal Guarantees and Their Options

Lender's approach: "You want us to stand behind your company, making you these loans, and you won't stand behind it by giving us your personal guarantee?"

Borrower's approach: "You already have fully collateralized this loan with all business assets, even those *now owned or hereafter acquired*–that's enough!"

Observation: Is a personal guarantee really "frosting on the Lender's cake"?

Or will the loan be in jeopardy without it? Be informed!

A Borrower may not wish to provide a personal guarantee based on:

- Lack of material personal assets or unencumbered assets
- Lack of *equity* in certain assets (real estate, business interests, and so on)
- Moral or religious grounds
- Refusal of a spouse or business associate to provide their supporting personal guarantees
- Personal guarantees that the Borrower has already provided to other creditors (other Lenders, suppliers, landlord, and so on)

If providing a guarantee is not absolutely necessary, don't hock your future—*but do negotiate with the Lender.*

First, consult with your legal counsel, accountant, and financial adviser.

Guarantees are not all created equal. Let's review some of the most common formats—the pluses and minuses.

There are two basic types of personal guarantees:

Unlimited Guarantee. "Unlimited" indicates that the guarantor is responsible for the entire loan, to include unpaid principal, accrued interest, and associated costs. Lenders feel the more *personally* committed the business owners are to the business, the more responsible they will be toward their debt obligations. The terms of, and any exceptions to, an unlimited guarantee, *should be negotiated.*

Limited Guarantees: These guarantees may be limited to an amount, a time duration, the Borrower achieving certain performance "benchmarks" (revenues, net profit, and so on), and may include collateral support, or none. Limited guarantees are generally more agreeable to a Borrower than are unlimited guarantees.

By authorizing a limited guarantee, the Lender may feel that there is an abundance of collateral to cover its position in case the business cannot repay its debt. A full guarantee may *not* then be necessary. In a collateral liquidation scenario, if the business collateral *does not* generate adequate proceeds to pay off the debt, the Lender may go after loan Guarantor(s) (either full or limited) for the loan balance deficit. In some arrangements the Lender may go after the Guarantor's assets first for repayment and then secondarily liquidate pledged collateral. The Borrower should, following his legal counsel's direction, seek to ensure that the Lender seeks a collateral liquidation first—*before* looking to the personal assets of Guarantors. If sufficient repayment cannot be obtained from the pledged collateral or the Guarantor(s), the Lender *may* take a net loss on the loan (see note that follows). Guarantors should remember that the Lender's *reimbursable* costs include all collection activity costs, to include the Lender's attorney fees and costs. Also, the continuing interest accrual due on the outstanding debt is part of the total amount due the Lender.

Note: In some instances, where there is a deficit loan remainder after all Lender recuperative actions have been taken, the Lender may suggest to the Borrower that he personally sign a new Note for the remainder due with specific repayment provisions. In this case, the Borrower should consult legal counsel.

Joint and Several Guarantees: Be careful here! This arrangement provides the Lender with choices when determining *which Guarantors* to approach when collecting on a loan; all Guarantors together or only one or a selection of Guarantors.

> In a "joint or several" situation, the Guarantors agreed to stand behind the total loan, either individually or as a group. While one or more individuals (or entities) may have guaranteed the loan, the Lender does *not* have to go after all on an equal basis. Rather, the single Guarantor that most probably has the necessary funds may be called upon for the *entire* debt due the Lender. *Consult legal counsel on "joint and several" issues.*

Prior to a loan closing, if joint and several guarantees are sought by the Lender, the Borrower may wish to oppose this. If an abundance of collateral is obvious and/or all Guarantors have substantial financial holdings, joint and several may not be really needed by a Lender. *Ensure that all Guarantors are aware of, and understand, guarantee specifics.* The Borrower should contact his attorney to confirm this information.

> **Time guarantees** are created to be effective only to a future point in time. This may be time-specific (a date) or based on certain benchmarks being achieved. These benchmarks are usually based upon the performance of the Guarantor's business or achievement of certain financial ratios. The Lender has agreed, within stated specifics, to "release" or adjust guarantee provisions once such a date, or benchmark, is achieved (which could be six months or years into the future). Such benchmark accomplishments by the business usually justify the releasing of the guarantee(s) by the Lender. Such satisfactory performance may further enhance the quantity and quality of the existing and/or added collateral. *The Borrower should make sure that agreed-to arrangements are satisfactorily documented at the loan closing.*

It is not uncommon for Lenders to require that all parties who own 20% or more of the business to guarantee the loan. This is not usually adaptable to a "public" company.

Updated personal financial statements (along with supporting schedules) and tax returns are usually sought at least annually by the Lender from all Guarantors. Lenders may then "track" assets and liabilities for addition or deletion activity. Some Lenders will also have Guarantors execute an updated guarantee agreement annually.

Options to the basic unlimited and limited guarantees:

Loan Deficiency Guarantee. An important guarantee feature for a Borrower's consideration is a loan deficiency guarantee. That means in a business closure or collateral liquidating situation, the Lender must first sell off all pledged collateral; applying the resulting proceeds against the loan balance. *Only then may the Lender proceed against the Guarantor(s)* for any deficiencies yet unpaid (this most likely will also include costs of liquidation). By utilizing the loan deficiency guarantee, the Guarantor's payment requirements could be considerably less—and the *Lender must do the work of collateral liquidation.*

It is most desirable that the Borrower always assist the Lender in a collateral liquidating situation, because the Borrower knows the products and the assets better than anyone. Doing this is to the Borrower's benefit because helping the Lender with the liquidation and sale of assets most likely will generate the maximum return—and ultimately fewer Guarantor responsibilities.

Validity of Collateral Guarantee: Another important option! If a Borrower is really opposed to providing a personal guarantee (family objections, moral grounds, feels the Lender is already too well collateralized, and so on), a Borrower may be able to convince the Lender to accept a "validity of collateral guarantee."

Primarily, a validity of collateral guarantee is a certification of honesty. There is no bogus collateral; just true reporting. The only claim a Lender may have to invalidate this type of guarantee could be the Borrower's misstatement or misrepresentation of collateral information or deficiencies in certain required reporting. Consult your legal counsel for what could result in invalidating this type of guarantee.

The validity guarantee may enable the Lender to "save face" by still obtaining a guarantee—possibly within the requirements of the terms and conditions of loan approval. If the Lender is not familiar with this type of guarantee, the LO should contact the Lender's counsel for clarification.

In this type of guarantee, the Borrower certifies that *all collateral is valid, genuine, and authentic.* All accounts receivable represent a bona fide existing obligation of a bona fide buyer in the ordinary course of business. All proceeds of accounts receivable are to be held by assignor (Borrower) in trust or as property of the Lender. A further certification indicates that all reports, statements, and schedules of assignor are true and accurate. Also, in the event of liquidation, the Borrower will assist the Lender in the collection and liquidation of the accounts and other collateral.

The type of personal guarantee that is used should be negotiated (whenever possible) to limit the amount of a Borrower's personal exposure. If a *limited guarantee* were to be called upon by a Lender, the limitation aspect might preserve (to an extent) the Borrower's assets. Prior to signing any guarantees, the Borrower *must* discuss ramifications with his attorney—*then negotiate!*

Real Experiences!

"In my opinion the bank already has an abundance of collateral and my personal *collateralized* guarantee is really not necessary" the potential real estate Borrower said to his Lender. The Borrower was involved in the financing of his first investment property, which housed a number of commercial spaces. The personal residence to secure the Full Guarantee was unencumbered and had significant equity. The pledging of his personal residence would effectively prohibit the Borrower from obtaining an equity loan elsewhere and possibly compromising the bank's overall collateral position. The Lender replied, "Inasmuch as the current commercial lease payments (positions currently occupied) do not cover the debt service (monthly loan payments), and irrespective of the other collateral we have, we see this collateralized guarantee as an inducement for you to do your best to rent out the remaining commercial spaces." The Borrower was not convinced, but wanted to do business with this Lender; the overall lending arrangement was favorable. Finally the Lender agreed that at the time all spaces were leased—as evidenced by a full rent roll and supporting signed leases—he would release the personal residence from the personal guarantee.

About eight months later, that benchmark was achieved the personal residence released. Inasmuch as the Borrower was a first-time lessor, the bank felt the full guarantee (uncollateralized) would remain in place until it could be determined that the entire venture was self-supporting. A short time later the Borrower obtained a home equity loan from the same Lender, using the proceeds as a down payment on his next property as well as additional improvements on the first. Most Borrowers understandably are reluctant to pledge their personal residence for any reason. However, a *limited* arrangement, with specific releasing benchmarks, can turn a difficult position into a positive result.

Note: Nontraditional Lenders may not be as demanding in the requirement for personal guarantees. Rather, they may seek a pledge of the business stock or other alternatives.

SUBORDINATED DEBT

Should officers, employees, or others (even other Lenders or suppliers) have made loans to the company, a Lender does not want to be "behind" these other creditors when it comes to loan repayment. The Lender wants, as is usually required by the *senior* Lender, *first place* (*or first position*) in the collateral *and* in loan repayment expectations.

Following the prospective Lender's analysis, the Lender may seek to improve its position by requiring, as part of the credit approval, that certain debt holders "step back." With such debt, whether in whole or in part, no longer requiring amortization, *cash flow and operating capital are also improved.*

Accordingly, the senior Lender may require, as part of the loan terms and conditions or later on during the lending relationship, that selected creditors "subordinate" their debt to the Lender. In other words, these creditors generally promise *not to accept principal debt repayment* from the Borrower *until the Lender's debt is first repaid.* Interest to holders of subordinated debt may be negotiated with Lender's approval.

Not all types of creditors to a company are candidates for subordination. Such creditors may be equipment term loans (finance companies), lessors, special services, and so on. Likewise, *some creditors may refuse to Subordinate* their debt to the Lender—*they want to be paid*! This is where the Borrower's negotiation skills come into play. The creditors must be convinced that it is to their long-term best interests to subordinate their debt.

Subordinated debt may result in:

- No further payments of principal or interest
- Payments of interest only (an inducement for a creditor to at least subordinate principal)
- Junior position in case of a business liquidation

Another plus with subordinated debt, insofar as the Lender is concerned, is that it is *no longer debt*. It does not have to be repaid—at least not on their watch. So, the Lender considers it "capital" and it is documented as such when the Lender analyzes the Borrower's balance sheet. The Borrower's net worth thus has just been improved.

Subordinated debt can substantially strengthen certain of the Borrower's ratios. The Borrower had debt, but it's no longer debt in the eyes of the Lender.

The only "losers," if you will, are the subordinated creditors; they may not receive principal payment for some time. Possibly, some interest may be authorized by the Lender. However, these creditors may also be friends of the company—friends who want the company to succeed. A loan from a Lender may materially contribute to further successes of the company. With improving Borrower performance the Lender may, upon Borrower's request, release the subordination agreement(s), allowing creditors to again commence their repayment process.

KEY MAN INSURANCE AND PROCEEDS

It is advisable, in most instances, for a business to consider "key man" insurance. This insurance coverage provides funds to the business in case of the death of a key owner, manager, or officer. Funds realized from insurance proceeds may then be used for loan repayment, settlements (or buyout provisions) with the owner's family, funds to attract a replacement officer to the business, working capital, or uses in accordance with other existing agreements.

It is the practice of many commercial Lenders to require that commercial Borrowers have key man insurance. The amount of the insurance coverage is usually at least equal to the total amount of the approved credit facility, *not necessarily* the amount of the loan at the closing or at a later time.

The potential insured party is usually required to pass a physical examination, which is part of the insurance company's underwriting process. It is not unusual for a business to already have key man insurance in place. In this case, the Lender may alternatively take an assignment of the *existing* policy; thus a new physical is avoided. If a Borrowing principal cannot qualify for coverage, the Lender sometimes may drop the requirement and go forward with the loan. It may happen that the periodic premium required is not realistic considering the Lender's potential exposure on the loan, availability of eligible collateral, or the health of the individual.

The Lender requires itself to be named as the loss payee on the policy, as well as within the insurance binder before a loan closing. Receipt of the actual policy may take some time; an insurance binder is acceptable proof of coverage at a loan closing.

Inasmuch as the policy is in the amount of the approved credit facility, the Lender has comfort that if the business owner should pass away, the loan will be paid off—no matter what happens to the business. *The designation of the loss payee clause results in the Lender, not the Borrower's company, receiving insurance proceeds.* Misunderstandings frequently occur during this process.

The point here is, what happens to the proceeds sent *to the Lender* by the insurance company. Here's one scenario of insurance proceeds expenditures:

1. The Lender receives the entire coverage amount—he is the loss payee.
2. The insurance company has fulfilled its obligation.
3. The Lender pays off the Borrower's *entire loan* with these proceeds.
4. Any remainder, following this loan payoff, is sent to the Borrower.

5. The Borrower's credit facility (credit line) is now at a zero balance.

6. The Lender's loan, once the source of the Borrower's working capital, now has no outstanding loan balance, but, most likely, the *credit facility still remains in place*. Credit line usage frequently remains available with the *same* terms and conditions as initially approved (however, see the following section).

Question: *Now that the credit facility is at a zero balance, can the business commence, once again, to use the line of credit?* The Borrower may need this source of funds *immediately*, especially if the Lender has retained the insurance check. The credit facility may have been used almost daily in the normal course of business, prior to the death or absence of the key person.

However, the Lender may now have some legitimate concerns:

The profile of the business may have changed to an extent (without the abilities of the deceased) that there is less confidence in the viability of the Borrower. Will the Borrower continue to be successful in business and able to repay future debt?

The Lender, if he wishes to continue doing business with the Borrower, *must be satisfied* with the selection of a replacement officer.

Will the Borrower, in fact, replace this person?

Will the Borrower need to borrow ("draw down") against this zero-balance credit facility in the same fashion as it has done in the past?

These concerns are usually satisfactorily resolved through discussions between the Borrower, his attorney, his accountant, and the Lender.

Lender considerations may include (but are not limited to):

- Providing a partial usage of the established credit facility until a satisfactory (to the Lender) replacement for the key person is employed.
- Expectation that a portion of these newly borrowed funds would be used to search out and attract desirable position candidates and address appropriate related costs.

- Requiring additional collateral and/or guarantees for credit facility usage until the replacement person has proven his or her abilities.
- Immediately authorizing complete credit facility usage in the same manner as in the past.
- Requiring the replacement officer to sign on to the loan agreements.
- Requiring the replacement officer to provide a personal financial statement and/or a personal guarantee.
- Requiring the Borrower to provide the Lender with key man insurance for the replacement officer.

The loss of a key person is an infrequent event, and *many Lenders don't know the process*. It can be a very confusing period while the Lender figures out what's going on.

Your business cash flow can easily suffer at this critical time.

Make sure your Lender is well informed as to key man insurance options and flexibilities!

Lenders work differently—yours may already have a satisfactory process in place.

REALITY CHECK

Check out, with your attorney, accountant, and insurance agent, the advisability of key man insurance for your company.

If such insurance is *already required* by the Lender, ask what the *exact process* is in the event of a death.

If procedures are fuzzy—clarify.

Get the negotiated results, as well as the process, *documented in a Lender's letter.*

PURCHASE-MONEY SECURITY INTERESTS

If the Borrower is financing his inventory (possibly on a formula basis), the Lender has filed a UCC-1 (see Chapter 1) indicating that these assets are pledged to him as collateral for a loan. Also, within the Loan & Security Agreement, a loan covenant usually states, in effect, that the Borrower will *not* borrow against or pledge identical collateral elsewhere.

Be careful in dealings with your suppliers because, in effect, they could put you in loan default.

This is especially true if the Borrower has been delinquent in his payments to a supplier. Sometimes the supplier will ask the business for a Note (rather than an open account) to more formally acknowledge his debt and establish a payment plan. By doing this, the account payable may then be removed from the Borrower's accounts payable aging (in whole or in part) and the debt amount is placed within the formal Note, which is reflected as a liability on the Borrower's balance sheet. The Note is signed by the Borrower. At this time *the supplier may file his own UCC-1 indicating his interest in your inventory*—in that portion of the inventory that represents goods provided by the supplier and is yet unpaid. The supplier can now establish his own collateral position.

So how is the supplier's position in Borrower's inventory relative to the Lender's?

- Superior to your Lender*
- Superior even if your Lender has a prior lien*
- Superior even if the inventory on the Lender's UCC-1 reflects "and all materials now owned or hereafter acquired"*

**Check with your legal counsel as to the laws in your state regarding purchase-money security interests and their priority filing status.*

The supplier simply has to send a letter to the Lender (the supplier can see your Lender's information at the office of the secretary of state) indicating that he has taken a security interest in a portion of the Borrower's inventory. The Lender usually does not have to acknowledge such a letter.

So, if the Lender does not have knowledgeable personnel reading the mail, this claim against a portion of the Borrower's inventory could go unnoticed, and the letter simply filed away. Remember, it is on the supplier's letterhead—not the Borrower's—so who knows where it gets filed?

Again, if the Borrower is financing his inventory, with values reported to the Lender on a periodic basis:

- The Lender may, in fact, be lending against portions of the inventory in which the Lender no longer has a perfected security interest.
- Also, the Borrower (unknowingly) *may be in violation of his loan agreement*, as this portion of collateral is now pledged elsewhere.

In a perfect world, the Lender would read the supplier's notification letter, reduce the appropriate amount of eligible inventory collateral by the amount of the Note (most likely equal to the cost value of the inventory portion), and the Lender goes on lending against only the eligible portion of the inventory.

In reality, things do not get read. When the supplier's filing is revealed through the Lender's routine UCC-1 search, the Lender will be surprised and concerned. Accusations may fly, and relationships may be damaged. *The Lender may feel that the Borrower knew of the Lender's eligible collateral being "compromised" and chose not to tell him.*

If the Borrower is considering converting a portion of an account payable to a Note Payable, and a supplier of inventory is involved, *check with the Lender first.* He may:

- Understand the situation and say OK to signing a Note to replace the account payable. Eligible collateral may then be reduced accordingly.
- Acknowledge the supplier's UCC-1 filing.
- But—and usually best of all—*the Lender may say there is no need for this.* He will *loan you* the amount to pay off the delinquent portion of the supplier's account—adding that amount to the current Lender debt owed (or even making a separate Borrower's Note). This has happened many times in my experience—keeps things simple!

That is the best scenario for every one—to *include* the supplier. The Borrower has just brought his supplier's account current—without the requirement of Notes—*and* the Lender has addressed a Borrower's need.

A Borrower may also collateralize *his* delinquent accounts receivable.

Switch places: The Borrower "files." The Borrower may wish to consider utilizing the reverse strategy to his benefit. The situation may be reversed when the Borrower is owed money by a customer who does not, or cannot, pay the Borrower's account on a timely basis. The Borrower may turn this "open" (and delinquent?) account receivable into a Note Receivable. This Note could also be collateralized. Legal counsel can advise the Borrower as to the benefits and mechanics of formalizing this Note, and the proper procedures for filing with the secretary of state. Note: Regarding collateral, don't forget to have the debtor name the Borrower as loss payee on his insurance, thus protecting the Borrower's interest in the collateral (if applicable).

INTEREST RATES AND LENDER FEES

It goes without saying that commercial lending is a business. This business involves risk and, considering these risks, the Lender seeks to make a profit. Lender's income, among other things, involves both interest rate and fee income. The Lender's cost of funds and administration expenses impact this income. Of course, there are other variables, but this will suffice for the current discussion.

The Interest Rate: This rate, expressed as a percentage, is applied to loans outstanding and represents the Lender's cost of funds and a profit margin. Interest rates (fixed or variable) are expressed on a per annum (per year) basis. For example, an interest rate of 7% on a $100,000 loan equals a $7,000 charge over a period of one year. This further could equate to $583.33 in monthly interest charges (if all months were of equal duration—they are not). So the Lenders actually charge interest on a *daily basis.* Even this has a variable—one Lender may calculate interest on a 365-day year, while another uses a 360-day year.

That is the *first* thing to look for—how many days in your Lender's year?

Using the same example above of a $100,000 loan @ 7%, a 365-day year represents interest at $19.178 per day (per diem).

But utilizing a 360-day year, the interest calculates out at $19.444 per day.

The Lender using the 365-day year will be the less expensive of the two considerations. Inasmuch as many Borrowers borrow much more than $100,000, the difference can be material. Many loans are structured for 30, 60, 90, or 180 days, and thus daily calculations become important.

In reality, most of the lending institutions are locked in to their policy on the stated interest rate "year." However, I have seen some Lenders "give away" (lower) the daily rate (days in a year) in order to avoid other concessions. *It never hurts to ask.*

Fixed and Variable Rates

Fixed rates are not usually subject to change for the term of the Note or Loan Agreement. The rate is negotiated up front—before the loan closing—and is entered into the loan documentation. The Lending organization is subject to a rate that reflects its cost of funds. From that point, prescribed margins above this base rate, and regarding particular loan types, are established by Lender's policy. Above these base margins, the Lending Officers are free to establish a rate for specific loans, considering each loan's risk potential. The higher the risk, the higher the rate. Sometimes the credit committee, during the loan approval process, will adjust the loan officer's rate considering *its* estimate of creditworthiness.

Generally, it is advantageous to *strive for a fixed interest rate* so as to benefit the Borrower's interest expense when variable rates begin to climb. Fixed rates also complement the Borrower's financial forecasting, considering the constant interest expense each month.

Variable rates fluctuate. These fluctuations are based upon a supporting index or multiple indices utilized by a Lender that reflect its cost of funds. The Federal Reserve Board meets monthly to determine whether the cost of funds from the federal government will rise, be lowered, or stay at the same level as the previous month. The purpose of the board's review and pronouncements is to guard the country's economy from inflation or deflation. Changes in Federal Reserve rates are often reported on nightly news broadcasts.

The most common rate category (or index) offered by a Lender is referred to as the *prime interest rate*. The prime rate is quoted daily in *The Wall Street Journal*. Also, the prime rate is frequently touted as the rate offered by commercial banks to their "best" customers. In practice, the best customers may very well experience a rate *below* prime. This can be accomplished because the Lender has a "margin" between its cost of funds and its announced prime rate—in other words, its profit. This profit margin must of course deliver income sufficient to cover expenses and provide a net profit for the Lender. However, there is still some flexibility, as evidenced by rates "below prime."

Just a note on LIBOR (London Interbank Offered Rate). This interest rate is based upon an average of those rates offered by selected provider London banks. This *rate index* is utilized for many adjustable-rate business loans, mortgages, and in global market transactions. The LIBOR rate is quoted in *The Wall Street Journal* and is referenced within a number of Internet sites (search "LIBOR"). This rate travels *roughly about 3%* (300 basis points) below the prime rate. One advantage of utilizing this rate index is that it may not change as frequently as the prime rate. There are one-, three-, and six-month quoted LIBOR rates, as well as a one-year LIBOR rate. It should be noted that Lenders usually do not provide Borrowers with the LIBOR option unless their loans are significant.

A variety of indices and/or combinations are available for loan structuring purposes. The Borrower's accountant should be a help in analyzing such rate variables.

Considering a Borrower's cash flow situation, the *repayment amortization* (the amount paid against principal periodically) may be just as important, or more so, than the interest rate to the Borrower.

In a real cash bind? It is not out of order to ask for an "interest only" loan for six months or a year.

This arrangement is surprisingly available, because there can be a good reason for such a request. One of the most effective reasons is that loan closing costs will eat up much of the anticipated initial loan proceeds, which means that cash flow could be strapped for a short period. The Borrower simply will receive less at the loan closing than he had anticipated.

And, as all Borrowers make commitments for utilizing specific amounts of loan proceeds following a loan closing, an unanticipated cash shortage could be damaging.

This is, of course, a good deal for the Lender. The loan principal is not reduced whatsoever during this interest only period. At the end of the interest only period, the Lender continues to receive interest income; the principal loan balance is still at its original amount, and principal payments now commence. Obviously, this should only be done in a reasonably strong credit relationship in which immediate principal reduction should not be seen as an important item by the Lender.

First negotiate the basic loan you seek. Get all terms and conditions as complete and agreeable as you can make them. *Then* ask for the "interest only" provision. This should be negotiated and resolved *before* the loan is finally approved. *You may wish to discuss such actions with your accountant and financial adviser before the fact.*

An option to the request for an "interest only" accommodation would be to have the Lender include loan closing costs within the basic loan. The net amount to be received at loan closing would be much more predictable.

"Caps" and "Collars"

You may also discuss with your accountant the possibility of obtaining loan caps and collars from the Lender. These accommodations are usually addressed within the larger loan relationships (over $1,000,000) and prior to loan approval.

- An *interest rate cap*, on a loan with a variable rate, restricts the Borrower's interest rate from increasing over a specific rate. A cap is functional regardless of increases in the supporting interest rate index. *The Borrower is essentially including a fixed-rate feature: a cap on his variable-rate loan.* For example, suppose the Borrower has a variable rate loan priced at the prime interest rate of 7.75% + 2%, or 9.75%. A cap structure of 11% is negotiated and incorporated within the loan agreement. In no event will the Borrower be charged more than 11% for the loan—even should the prime rate go to 18%! This accommodation (or risk) on the part of the Lender is fee based—*it will cost you*. But the cost *may be justified* when a Borrower strategically forecasts future interest expenses anticipating an environment of increasing interest rates.

- *A collar* functions as an opposite to a cap, and is of benefit to a Lender. A collar agreement is an additional inducement (other than fees) for the Lender to approve a loan cap. The collar reflects the Borrower's agreement not to pay less than a stated rate. If the Borrower's variable rate loan index decreases, and would normally justify a reduction in rate, the interest rate will not be reduced lower than the collar rate agreed upon. Again, the reason the Borrower would agree to this collar arrangement is to induce the Lender to provide an interest rate cap. Usually *both* elements (a cap and a collar), when negotiated, are placed within the loan terms and conditions.
- Also, an *interest rate swap*, sometimes available within the larger lending institutions, effectively changes a variable rate loan into a fixed rate loan. Two (unrelated) borrowing parties agree to exchange or swap the interest payments on a specified amount, for a stated period of time. Typically, this involves one Borrower who wishes to pay a fixed rate and another Borrower who wants to pay the variable rate. These borrowers may be identified by the commercial loan department of the Lender. Following a Borrower's discussion with his accountant, these types of "hedges" should be addressed first to the LO and then to the treasury department of the Lender. The Lender makes the necessary connections with the *other Borrower* to gauge his interest and then operationally structures the arrangement. Most smaller banks do not offer interest rate swap accommodations.

More on Cumulative Lender Fees

There are a number of other Lender fees that can accumulate and amount to thousands of dollars unless the Borrower, and his advisers, recognize the purpose, validity, and reasonableness of these "required" fees. A good number of these fees are not truly "required." In many cases, they are applied considering what the market (or the Borrower) will bear.

Remember: If the Lender cannot get his desired yield within the assigned interest rate, he *must* get it in fees.

Lender fees can be assessed at many points during the relationship:

- The commencement the loan application review
- Upon a loan approval
- Upon issuance of a commitment letter by a Lender
- At the point loan closing
- During the normal lending relationship
- When loan problems develop
- Upon termination of the credit facility

Let's review the *most common fees* at various points within the loan relationship.

Loan Application Fee: As the name implies, this is an amount of money (usually between $100 and $500) required to be sent in with a Loan Application. This fee ostensibly pays the Lender for the review time spent on a preliminary application. This amount of money never would come close to covering the actual time spent in a comprehensive Lender review, but for a brief review, it's more than enough. So, either the Borrower is really not paying enough money to cover Lender costs or he may be paying way too much for a quick "look-see."

Initially, of course, it is really a quick (but educated) Lender's look-see. Usually, in less than an hour, a seasoned LO can evaluate the key pluses and minuses of a loan request. The LO quickly determines whether or not this could be an acceptable loan.

So if the application fee is really almost irrelevant, why impose it? Primarily to see *whether the Borrower is serious* in applying to this specific Lender or just "shopping the loan." The Borrower may be spreading his loan request all over town—and not all Lenders charge application fees. In the aggregate, the potential Borrower is consuming many hours of these Lenders' time, but who cares, as long as there is no cost to the Borrower? The Lender thus is attempting to ferret out those less-than-serious Borrowers by imposing an application fee. The serious ones usually will pay and wait for the Lender's initial consideration. In some cases, if the loan is approved and funded (loan closed) the fee *may* be credited against closing costs.

If you, as a Borrower, *seriously want to be considered* by two or three competitive Lenders, *do not make an issue* of the loan application fees involved. Otherwise, a Lender may make the judgment that, if the Borrower is excited about this small fee, what will happen when the necessary (and higher) fees are required? *If the Borrower is serious with a particular Lender (or more than one), he should pay the fee(s) without a challenge.* Even if the Borrower is turned down, the reasons given for his turndown, and the understanding gained, may in itself be worth the expense. Read Chapter 7 regarding the option of courting *two* prospective Lenders and paying *two* application fees.

Audit Fees: These fees are *not to be confused with a Borrower's periodic CPA engagements.* Rather, these audit fees are for professionals engaged by the Lender (or sometimes *employed* by the Lender) to examine the books and records of Borrowers involved in specialized loans. One example would be asset-based lending (ABL). Borrowers utilizing ABL may provide customer invoices or sales journals *daily* to a Lender to support *daily* loan advances on these sales. Likewise, customer payments are sent to the Lender (usually directly) to reduce the ABL loan balance. Due to the propensity for fraud (bogus invoices, overstated inventory values, and so on), these specialized auditors visit Borrowers one to four times a year, providing specialized audit reports to the Lender.

In Asset-Based Lending there is also an initial (pre-approval) audit fee, sometimes referred to as a "survey," which assists the Lender's credit group in initially determining the adequacy of the Borrower's books and records. Audit fees (passed on to the Borrower) may be upwards of $750.00 per diem for *each* auditor *plus* expenses.

The Borrower won't win if he debates the per diem price. The Lenders pretty much accept the going rate among these specialized outside contractors. *All* costs and expenses are passed on to the Borrower. Lenders are billed by these audit firms following the audit and report. The prospective Borrower may be required to put up a "deposit" to cover these initial audit costs on a loan yet to be approved. This deposit is not usually refundable, especially should the Lender's audit be completed. If not yet completed, it's possible a refund may be considered.

The Borrower *can* win in addressing the *frequency* of these audits. Most Lenders want to conduct audits three or four times annually (which can be very expensive to a Borrower). A single audit may last between two and four days and may additionally include the travel time of auditors. These audit costs mount rapidly. Ask the Lender to commence with two audits a year. If problems develop, the Lender can then accelerate the frequency of the audits. If the books and records are "squeaky clean" at the initial survey, ask the Lender to schedule these audits only once annually—preferably *following* completion and delivery of the Borrower's annual financial statements. *Do not debate price—debate frequency*! Infrequently, a Lender may agree to a cap on such audit fees.

> **Credit Report / Dun & Bradstreet Report (D&B):** These two reports cover both personal financial information (from a major credit bureau) and information on the business (borrowing) entity (from D&B) as well. Costs of all such reports will be passed on to the Borrower—usually at loan closing. These fees are not something that is reasonably negotiable. The Lender contracts out for many reports annually from various agencies, and costs are passed on to the Borrower.

Individual credit reports are drawn on the key business owners, possibly select officers, and on individual loan guarantors. The business D&B report covers the basic business entity; identifying certain officers/owners as well as related divisions and affiliates. Reports may also be drawn separately on affiliates. Other common ownership situations may become apparent when reports are drawn.

Considering other costs of borrowing, report costs are negligible and are not normally negotiated. Lenders, by vendor contract, usually are not permitted to share, copy, or give reports to their Borrowers.

Good Faith Deposits: Following acceptance of a loan proposal, the Borrower may be required to have appraisals or environmental inspections completed. The Lender realizes that the Borrower may, at this point, not yet be committed to concluding the loan. A loan approval or commitment letter may not as yet have been issued nor a commitment fee paid. Before final loan approval, appraisals and environmental inspections usually must be completed to the satisfaction of the Lender. A deposit in the amount of these estimated costs is frequently required by the Lender. Should the Borrower decide to go with another Lender, the original Lender has funds to liquidate these remaining (and incurred) costs. It does happen that commercial loans may be approved subject to satisfactory appraisals and environmental inspections, all of which are completed before the loan closing.

Also see the information about collection days and prepayment fees later in this chapter.

Commitment Fee: This fee is usually a percentage (½% to 3%) of the approved credit facility for a new relationship. The fee is determined based upon the Lender's perceived lending risk and what is generally customary in the marketplace. The fee may be payable upon acceptance of the Lender's commitment letter or at the loan closing. Upon loan *renewal* (one to three years down the line) this fee may again be the same, may be less than initially quoted, or could be eliminated altogether.

The execution by the Borrower of a commitment letter, which is returned to the Lender along with the commitment fee, indicates that the Borrower is serious about dealing with this Lender—demonstrated buy putting *his* money up front.

Note: The Borrower can still "walk away" from this deal, although any commitment fee or deposits provided earlier may be lost.

Your Best Option: Whatever the commitment fee quoted, *always attempt to reduce it.* The "norm," if there is one, is 1%. In other words, a

$100,000 loan would require a $1,000 commitment fee. Extrapolating this into the larger loans, one can see that this fee can be a significant loan expense. If this fee can be negotiated below 1%, the Borrower usually has done a good job. Zero would be better– you don't know if you don't ask. Frankly, a zero commitment fee is very rare unless the new lending relationship is of a *very special* nature. The accountant may assist the Borrower during these periods of fee negotiations.

> **Loan Origination Fee (Processing Fee or Loan Closing Fee):** Among other fees and Lender expenses to be reimbursed at the loan closing, there may be a loan origination or loan closing fee. This fee is designed to generate reimbursement to the Lender for the time and expense expended in successfully bringing in the loan application, processing credit and loan approval, and reaching the point of loan closing. Depending upon other fees assessed by the Lender, these fees could be relatively small. However, if there was *not* a commitment fee, either paid along with the signed commitment letter or scheduled to be paid at the loan closing, this loan origination or loan closing fee could be significant. It is *somewhat unusual for a Borrower to pay both a loan origination and a closing fee.* Of course, the Lender may try to acquire as much in fee income as is reasonable (and customary within the market area).

Your Best Option: In order to reduce, as much as possible, conflicting or ambiguous fees at the loan closing, the Borrower should *ask the Lender for a schedule of all fees to be paid.* This is frequently presented within the commitment letter format from the Lender. However, between the receipt of the commitment letter and the actual loan closing, weeks or even months could pass, with additional Lender expenses developing. Once the final loan closing date is set, ask the Lender for an updated schedule of all expenses. Compare the list with the commitment letter and with the verbal statements made by the Lender relative to fee requirements. The Borrower should indicate his displeasure with the loan origination or closing fees if a commitment fee was already required. A commitment fee usually sticks, while some other fees may be waived when reasonable Borrower pressure is applied.

Broker Fees: Borrowers frequently use the services of loan brokers to find appropriate lenders for their current situation. Brokers, for the successful placement of the loan on behalf of their Borrower, will receive a fee from the Borrower. This fee may range from ½% to 5% of the approved loan facility—normally around 1%. A separate broker agreement is signed between the Borrower and broker long before a Lender gets into the process. A broker agreement usually is limited in time. See Chapter 8 for more about loan brokers.

Your Best Option: Inasmuch as the broker arrangement has already been set, the only "after the fact" event is actual payment to the broker. The Borrower usually requests that the broker's check be distributed from the loan proceeds at the loan closing. Usually the broker attends the loan closing and waits for his check—or funds are wired to his account from the loan closing.

Infrequently the Borrower will *not* want the Lender to pay the broker's fee—the Borrower will take care of it later. This could be an opportunity for the Borrower to renege on the broker's fee. The comment may be made, "This is too much money—he didn't do that much work." The Lender could suggest that the broker be paid as agreed, with disputes settled later. The Borrower should seriously consider ramifications of a broker dispute—especially because the broker, who now knows the Borrower thoroughly, could be useful in the placement of future financing requirements.

Legal Fees: The Borrower is usually responsible for the *Lender's* legal fees, associated fees, and costs. Services that incur fees involve research and advising the Lender, preparing appropriate legal documentation, administering the loan closing, and possibly certain post-closing considerations. The total amount of such fees is not usually determined until just before the loan closing. They may be estimated earlier, but it is only that—an estimate. Fees may be substantial and may bear some relationship to the part of the country in which the business is located. Lender's legal fees and post-closing fees may be added to the loan balance, paid at loan closing, or billed separately to the Borrower. The net loan proceeds realized at the loan closing will determine the Borrower's strategy and requests to the Lender.

Your Best Option: Remember two things:

1. These legal fees *do not cover* the Borrower's own legal fees. The Borrower's legal services are provided by his attorney and are usually billed separately from any loan closing activities.

2. It is not wise to assume that a Borrower does not need an attorney inasmuch as the Lender already has one. The *Lender's attorney has only the best interests of the Lender at heart*—he is not responsible for the Borrower. It is advisable for Borrowers to always be represented by legal counsel.

It is not unusual for a Borrower to ask the Lender for a *cap* on legal fees, especially in the case of a loan that has:

- A complex loan structure
- Many collateral components and/or site locations
- Many loan participants (more than one Lender is involved). The possibility of drawn-out loan negotiations and delays exist before a loan closing is accomplished (environmental holdups, and so on)

One does expect that, as an attorney for the Lender develops his cap on legal fees, he will overestimate his probable expended time, as is expected and reasonable, to cover contingencies within the final billing. However, more than not, even these potentially inflated estimates can be smaller than what is actually and finally incurred.

However, the Borrower should remember that such a cap will not involve associated costs such a filing fees, recording requirements, copy work, mailings and special deliveries, and so on. *A cap is usually the best way to go—and most Lenders and their legal counsel may consider such requests.*

Collection Days: Collection days (business days) represent the amount of time a payment against the loan is held by the

Lender before posting it against the outstanding loan balance. In other words, the *loan balance is not immediately reduced when the Borrower's payment is received.* It is obvious that the Lender earning more interest by retaining a higher loan balance. The Lender may indicate that customer checks that are from "out of the area" may not clear for a time. However, collection days are usually applied against *all* types of loan payments—local payments and even *daily* payments made on asset-based lending relationships. The exception is payments wired into the Lender from an outside source; these are termed "collected funds" and usually applied upon the day of receipt.

Frequently, the Borrower is not aware of the collection days feature until the loan closing. *Collection days are infrequently discussed prior to the loan closing, but they are presented within the final loan documents.* Unfortunately, the issue of collection days seldom surfaces until the Borrower's bookkeeper is reconciling the Lender's interest statement after the fact. Generally three or more collection days are quoted by the Lender, and sometimes as many as five. It can be that loan reduction payments don't get posted for up to a week after the Lender's receipt! Your accountant can calculate the impact of payments being applied at such later times. Collection days are usually common, but the number of collection days are all over the board. *Fight for the fewest days possible.*

Your Best Option: Find out what the number of collection days will be. This is usually determined by the Lender and appears on the Lender's terms and conditions sheet. Strive to reduce these collection days using logic provided by your accountant. For example, the Borrower may state, "XX% of checks received from my customers are *within* the Lender's region." "The loan interest rate is high enough already—this only makes it higher." "Four collection days is unconscionable."

Non-Usage Fees (aka Facility Fees): Essentially, the Borrower is *paying interest on money he is not borrowing.* It would seem a Borrower *should* be striving to borrow less, but with this annual fee he is penalized for such frugality. For example: A Borrower has a credit line of $1,000,000. He uses an annual average of only $890,000 over the year. The non-usage fee agreed upon is

1%. In this case, 1% of the unborrowed $110,000 results in a fee of $1,100. This fee, if involved in the loan approval, will be within the terms and conditions of the loan agreement. Non-usage fees are rather infrequent, as Lenders are often challenged on these fees.

Your Best Option: The Borrower argues that, what with all of the other fees, the *Lender is more than well compensated* should the Borrower not utilize all funds available to him. The Borrower may wish to indicate that fees such as this make the Lender seem less competitive in the marketplace. In my opinion, this fee, if required, should not exceed ½%. Even at that level, try to get to ¼%.

Lockbox Fees: Within certain types of lending relationships (primarily ABL and factoring), the Borrower's daily receipts (check payments from customers) are not mailed to the Borrower's business but rather *sent directly to the Lender's bank by the Borrower's customers.* The Lender thus exercises dominion over the proceeds of collateral (customer payments). The Lender accumulates the data and reports to the Borrower the amount of daily collections and which customers paid their bills. The Lender also returns to the Borrower any remittance advices or other communications that may have come in with the payments.

Your Best Option: The lockbox fee is partially a base fee that can be impacted by the number of items flowing through the lockbox *daily.* While the basic provisions of an asset-based lending relationship require lockboxes, Borrowers frequently experience operational problems. The Lender knows, usually a day or two earlier, that certain customers have *already* paid their bills—*but this is not yet known by the Borrower.* If the Borrower is following payment promises from certain delinquent customers, timely tracking of payments by the Borrower's bookkeeper is difficult. Embarrassing situations could occur. Also, the Borrower's customers have previously been notified (or there is an imprint on the invoice) to send payments directly to the Lender—not to the business. *The Borrower's customers now know that the Borrower is financing his receivables and is "in hock" to a Lender.*

If the survey (initial) audit showed the borrower's books and records very clean and the delinquency rate on the accounts receivable low, the Borrower may request that *customer checks be sent directly to the business—not to the Lender*. The business will then deposit the checks into its normal operating account. Customers are no wiser as to the Borrower's method of financing, and collection information is all recorded by the Borrower on a *timely basis*. Should the Lender seek daily reductions to the loan balance based upon Borrower collections, the Borrower informs the bank of the amount deposited and the funds are then wired (or "swept") daily to the Lender for loan reduction. **It's all about control!**

Forbearance Fees: Substantially a fee for a Lender to *not* proceed with a specific action, which usually revolves around a Lender's concerns of a potential loan default. There is more about this subject in detail in Chapter 3.

> **Loan Prepayment (Penalty) Fee:** Should you elect to *pay the Lender off before the maturity date* of the loan, there may be a prepayment or penalty fee. This is stipulated within the terms and conditions of the loan. The Borrower should clarify this before the loan closing. This is one of the *few* times the Borrower will have any leverage in this situation.

The fee *may* be 3% (of the then average unpaid loan balance) during the first year of the loan, 2% during the second year, and 1% during the third year. On a five-year loan, the formula may be 5% during the first year, and then 4%, 3%, 2%, and 1% on the final year. Penalty fees are not necessarily evenly incremental and may fluxuate by multiple percentages, but this is somewhat infrequent. There are a number of ways to calculate prepayment penalties, but the method chosen will be quite specific within the loan agreement. The Lender will especially attempt to enforce this if the Borrower is going to a competitor.

A high prepayment fee frequently has the affect of leaving the Borrower *unable to switch Lenders—it simply costs too much*. The Borrower will then wait to switch lenders until the end of the lending contract, when there is little or no prepayment penalty remaining.

Note: Once in a while, if the *new* Lender is anxious to obtain your business, it will pay the prepayment fee for the Borrower, enabling the

Borrower to move to the new Lender. This works most often when the Borrower is moving into nontraditional lending (see Alternative Lenders in Chapter 9).

Real Experiences!

In many instances, especially in the occurrence of real estate mortgages and term loans, there may be a requirement for loan prepayment penalties. These are usually part of the original loan agreements. These should have been, if possible, aggressively negotiated between the Lender and the Borrower before the loan closing. A larger relationship with a manufacturing company involved their two plants, which were mortgaged in the total amount of $6,000,000 to a commercial bank. The Borrower was approached by a potential replacement Lender, who offered a *much* improved mortgage relationship. In validating the prepayment penalty amount it was learned that the amount would be approximately $350,000. The current bank would neither negotiate nor lower the penalty. The bank did not relent, and the Borrower remained with his initial bank for the next three years. Needless to say, the Borrower no longer addressed any of his future needs with the current bank. At the end of the period their new Lender, still interested in the relationship, closed the mortgage loans.

Then there was the case of a large door manufacturer who wanted out of a line of credit relationship. A prepayment penalty was to be imposed based upon his average outstanding loan balance during the entire term of the relationship. The potential new alternative Lender earnestly wanted this pristine credit. The alternative Lender paid (and absorbed) the entire prepayment in order to facilitate gaining this new business. Occasionally the prospective Lender will provide a *separate* term loan (at a *preferred* rate) to a potential Borrower, thus providing the Borrower with the cash to pay the prepayment penalty. The Borrower would, of course, be obligated for the new debt with his new Lender. Should timing be important, and prepayment penalties are involved, the latter is one way to get from one Lender to another. And, from time to time, a current Lender may waive *any* requirement for a prepayment penalty, even if such a requirement is currently within the lending agreements, due to a special relationship or circumstance.

Your Best Option: Prior to loan approval, have the Lender commit to no prepayment penalty. At this point in time, the Lender wants to obtain the Borrower's business. Sometimes this fee is a "giveaway"—a Lender will try to get it, but it may not be a deal killer if he does not. After the Borrower argues (unsuccessfully) for *no* prepayment penalty, the Lender may be ready to opt for a *very low* prepayment penalty.

Fees Peculiar to Real Estate Closings: Real estate mortgage loan closings may have a variety of fees peculiar to such transactions:

- Processing or application fee
- Environmental testing fees
- Appraisal fees
- Flood searches
- Land surveys
- Local, state, and federal government searches
- Notary fees
- Recording fees
- Points (or commitment fee)
- Prepaid interest (usually if loan is not closing at month-end; this can be a significant expense at closing if the closing date is not planned correctly)
- Prepaid taxes
- Funding of escrow accounts
- Periodic tax searches by the Lender
- Insurance tracking fees

The Borrower should discuss all of these fees with an attorney who specializes in real estate transactions.

REALITY CHECK

Most Lenders can structure the loan so that many of the fees discussed in this chapter are *added into the loan balance*. The aggregate of fees then may not dilute the *net* loan proceeds (or loan availability) that the Borrower anticipates at the loan closing.

WHAT (REALLY) HAPPENS AT CREDIT COMMITTEE?

I have attended hundreds of credit committee meetings, in many types of lending institutions, as an observer, as a loan officer seeking credit approvals, as a sitting member of the committee, and as a Lender's consultant. I've seen the gamut of scenarios. Sure, most are of a routine nature, but a few will always stand out. Considering confidentiality, of course, I must keep silent on the more unusual ones. Let's go over some of the structures and lesser-known aspects of this decision-making group.

First of all, almost always, *the Borrower is excluded from this process*. The committee members believe that the presenting lending officer has (or should have) all the pertinent facts concerning this credit application. If the Borrower were invited to attend, he might immediately challenge comments or judgments of committee members. This is not a forum for confrontations. If the information is not now on the table, it is usually too late—*not always*, but usually.

Note: Although a Borrower and his LO may be expecting a timely review by the credit committee, it is not unusual for loan requests seeking credit committee approval to be put off from one week to another as other accounts, of a more immediate nature, are brought before the committee. It is best for the Borrower to give a reason why his loan must be on this day's agenda—he is catching a plane and will not be available to answer LO questions, a competing Lender is pressing the Borrower to go with its institution, and so on.

There are usually three or more members of a credit committee. These may be:

- Active lending and/or credit officers (one is the presenting LO)
- A senior officer solely acting in an approval mode without account responsibilities
- Loan workout officer
- Head of the credit department
- Selected division, department, or group heads (involve on a routine or exception basis)

- Consultants who specialize in the industry under discussion, who in certain instances may be invited to participate

Not infrequently, the credit committee members may be aware of certain internal and confidential facts or happenings that could impact the current credit approval. These facts are not usually known by the Borrower's potential LO (or presenter). In such a case, the presenting officer is at distinct disadvantage, and chances of obtaining an approval may be slim. These situations may arise because of:

- A recent unfavorable occurrence with an industry—a Lender has been "burned" in similar loans. The industry is no longer attractive to the credit committee.
- Lender policy changes may be in process which could, if the credit is approved, adversely affect the terms and conditions of credit approval.
- The type of financing the Borrower is seeking may no longer be a part of the Lender's long-term product offerings. Possibly, the department that would handle the lending relationship has not been historically profitable or has suffered a number of losses.
- Regulators have criticized the Lender's handling of specific types of high risk credits—such as the one currently under consideration.

The LO generally makes a verbal presentation while the credit committee scans the formal credit report (narrative and numbers). The credit report may be only a few pages long, or as thick as a book. The presenter will usually emphasize the strong points of the Borrower; *the committee attempts to identify risks.* The presenter is then expected to suggest changes to the terms and conditions that may mitigate identified risks. Loan pricing, risk rating assignments, management capabilities, adequacy of guarantors, and the like also may be discussed.

It is not unusual that the credit committee may have already discussed the credit and is predisposed in rendering its judgment—*prior* to the lending officer's presentation. The level of experience of the presenting LO will dictate whether or not he will be able to sway the credit committee back into an approval mode. Of course, in some cases, continuing to argue a Borrower's case could hurt the LO's future and be fruitless. Much can be lost with an inexperienced LO—*so it is in the Borrower best interests* to ensure, early on, that his presenting LO is mature and seasoned in the lending business.

Note: The LO's compensation *may* be tied into the new loan business he is able to fund, so *he has a real vested interest in getting the Borrower's loan approved—and funded.* However, it does not necessarily follow that the LO will wind up being the "officer of account" (running the loan on a day-to-day basis after closing). Some LOs perform only new-business duties and do not have loan portfolio responsibilities. In this instance, and following credit approval, the Borrower and his loan will be turned over to a LO who performs portfolio management.

Key credit considerations of the credit committee, in a general order, are:

1. Quality of management
2. Quality and quantity of collateral
3. Financial strength of the borrowing company
4. Strength of guarantors
5. The Borrower's ability to service debt (make the monthly payments)
6. Overall cash flow
7. Satisfactory mitigation of risks
8. Realistic loan covenants

In real life, there is generally a *key officer* on the credit committee, and his direction influences other members. *His judgment may be influenced by the creditability and respect he has for the presenting LO.* A seasoned LO is the absolute best to have on the Borrower's side. Of course, the lending institution usually has a desire to book new business, and that in itself may be marginally in the Borrower's favor.

The Borrower may have been assured by the LO that "everything will proceed fine." *It is very dangerous for the Borrower to take such a remark "to the bank."* Should a Borrower commence to make financial commitments based on such a comment—and the loan is ultimately turned down—disaster can only be a short distance away. Such early assurances by an LO should hold little weight with a Borrower. The credit committee can, at the eleventh hour, insist on stricter loan covenants, higher interest rates, and collateralization of a personal guarantee before approving the loan.

In some cases, with such dramatic last-minute changes, the wisest avenue for the Borrower is to forget the approval. *The Borrower simply may not wish to do business with this Lender!*

Never make post-loan "commitments" to others until the loan proceeds are in your bank account! It's tempting—but don't.

Remember—things can happen:

- Outside of the Borrower's control
- Outside of the Lending Officer's control
- Even outside of the Lender's control

Thus surfaces the case for maintaining dual "potential" lending options: The Borrower's immediate financial future then will not be placed in jeopardy with a single disapproval or failed loan closing. See Chapter 7.

CHAPTER 6

YOUR WORST CASE SCENARIO

"They can't do that—can they?"

"Hey, I really need more time."

"The Lender took our customer checks?"

"*Great*—our cash flow is now zero!"

Emergency Procedures - Now!

A commercial Borrower received a form of the following letter ("30-day letter") from his Lender. Some detail and specific phraseology is omitted for the purposes of brevity, but the message is unmistakable:

> March 17, 2008
>
> Dear Borrower:
>
> After due considerations, and within the terms of our Loan Agreement executed 11/15/04, you are herewith notified that the bank will no longer extend to you our secured lending credit facility. Your Line of Credit, in the amount of $2,000,000, is herewith terminated as of the date of this letter.
>
> Accordingly, you have thirty (30) days from the date of this letter to repay your obligations in full to this bank. Should you not repay all obligations within the time provided, the bank may then exercise its rights and remedies as provided for within our Agreements and the Uniform Commercial Code.
>
> Very truly yours,
>
> Senior Credit Officer

The Lender is trying to get the Borrower's attention—and it just worked!

A letter like this really shouldn't come as a shock to a Borrower. Chapter 2 detailed many of the danger signals that would be apparent prior to such an action being undertaken by a Lender.

If the danger signals were observed, and *recognized* as such by the Borrower, he may already be a long way into resolving the situation or considering his next two Lenders.

If you receive a 30-day letter, these are your initial responsibilities—to yourself and to others:

1. **Don't panic!**
2. Inform and copy your legal counsel, your accountant, and business consultant as to the receipt of the letter.
3. Do not hide the facts from your business partners or appropriate shareholders. Full disclosure to owners, officers, and guarantors is important. Of course, such notice to the principals should be followed up by the Borrower's *immediate* (and later long-term) plans to address and remedy the situation.
4. At this time it is *usually* not essential to inform employees, business customers, or suppliers about these business concerns.

Work with your legal counsel on item #4. *There is a correct and necessary time for such an internal notice, but it probably has not as yet been reached.* Of course, there are exceptions. There is more information about proper timing for such notice later in the chapter.

Premature notice could needlessly upset employees and cause management distractions at a time when management should be planning and implementing strategic solutions. Also, promoting what would become public knowledge of internal company problems could prejudice potential replacement lenders. If the Borrower is one of the major employers in a small town, undue and possibly unnecessary community unrest could also develop.

I have seen situations in which employees, customers, and suppliers *were never aware* of any such financial concerns. The Borrowers resolved the problems—replacement Lenders were attracted and the new loans were closed with acceptable (and often *improved*) loan terms and conditions—without internal notice.

The reality: In these days of considerable Lender due diligence and unpredictable economic times, the current Lender knows it is *highly improbable* that the Borrower could conclude a new financing transaction within 30 days. Of course, it is recognized that the Borrower may also be experiencing business difficulties. It may take an innovative and aggressive Lender to satisfactorily address key issues.

Realistically, *even in the best scenario*, it will take about 90—120 days to finally close on a new (replacement) lending relationship.

So why has the Lender issued the *30-day* letter?

The Lender has simply given the Borrower incentive to actively seek a Lender replacement. In any event, the Borrower should not let the Lender know that he recognizes that there is, in reality, an extended avenue of valuable time in which to act to resolve issues.

The 30-day letter is not to be ignored. It is a serious action by the lender, and should not be taken lightly.

I do not—nor should a Borrower—minimize the intent of the letter, but cool heads can prevail if the Borrower keeps his.

The decision to send this letter has been arrived at by Lender's management. Their considerations may have involved:

- Credit policies of the Lender (either currently existing or new)
- Loan covenant violations
- Supporting collateral
- Strength and liquidity of Guarantors
- A deteriorating risk rating
- Borrower's past history with the Lender
- Condition of the Borrower's business
- Borrower's past history with the Lender
- A review of the Borrower's credit and legal files
- Possible discussions with Lender's legal counsel

Real Experiences!

Lender pressure to perform finally became too much for this Middle Atlantic Borrower. Performance in this case meant that the Borrower's business had to recover from unprofitable trends and deliver additional collateral to the Lender. This road paving company's job bonding requirements, customer base of municipalities and the state, and poor cash flow made compliance with the bank's loan covenants difficult. The Borrower seemed to be contending against insurmountable odds. A particularly critical meeting was held at the bank—a bank with many years of experience with the Borrower. The

> Borrower also had operating and payroll accounts with this bank. The Borrower was unaccompanied and was surprised when confronted by a phalanx of bankers from loan workout, the credit department, and the local branch. After an especially heated discussion, the Borrower lost it. He said, "You guys want more collateral—here it is!" as he flung the keys to his business across the conference table. "Congratulations, you're in the paving business!" He stormed out of the bank. The Lender was not prepared for this response, nor should the Borrower have been subjected to such an organized assault. The tenor of the meeting was completely unexpected. Hindsight, of course, suggests the Borrower should have first determined the purpose of the meeting, who was attending and, once the purpose was clear, he should have been accompanied by legal counsel. The Borrower finally obtained another Lender, who successfully restructured all loan obligations. He never again did any business with the first bank. The bottom line: Prepare meticulously for all such meetings!

As in situations described in previous chapters, the strategy now is to buy time!

Tactics—Three Action Meetings

First Action Meeting: The first thing for the Borrower to do is request a one-on-one meeting with the LO. Do not permit the Lender to "load" the meeting with other Lenders or bank counsel. There will be a time for this—not now, but later on—and then *on the Borrower's terms.* The Borrower must emphasize that this initial one-on-one meeting is necessary for "personal clarification purposes." The Borrower is *not* there to negotiate—just to gather the facts.

Note: If, once you're at the Lender's place of business, you find that the meeting involves additional Lender representatives—no matter who they are—indicate that you respectfully requested an initial one-on-one meeting with your Lending Officer. *Your wishes were not respected and you must leave. The one-on-one meeting was personally important to you and* *you will be happy to reschedule.* It could develop that all other persons will come to a consensus to leave the room and permit the "one-on-one" to commence.

> IMPORTANT: Both the *first and second action meetings* should occur within the *30-day window* of the first letter.

At the commencement of the one-on-one meeting, ask permission to take notes (seldom refused). Do not agree to the Lender taking all of the notes—take your own—and do not agree to the meeting being recorded. At this meeting:

- Clarify the reason(s) behind the issuance of the "30-day letter."
- Push for specifics. Obtain copies of the Lender's supporting documentation (if any); if reasonable, make copies on the spot.
- Obtain the name, address, phone, and fax numbers, and the e-mail address, of the Lender's legal counsel in this matter. Your reason? "I need to keep my legal counsel informed."
- *Do not sign* anything, "on advice of counsel"; *do not agree to anything.* State that you must *always* talk to your attorney first.
- Do not establish the next meeting time, agenda, or who will participate—*you* will get back to *them.* You must check your calendar and the calendars of your attorney and accountant.
- Leave graciously.

Upon returning to the business, the Borrower should prepare a written memorandum of the meeting detail for his records. Don't forget to include the date, time, and duration, and the person (with title) who was in attendance at the meeting. Copies of this Borrower's memorandum will immediately be sent to the Borrower's lawyer, accountant, and business adviser. It may also be provided to *selected* members of management, *selected* guarantors, or other business owners (on a *need-to-know basis*).

The Borrower can rest assured that the LO is doing exactly the same thing and is providing copies of his memorandum to his senior management—who may, in fact, have authorized the 30-day letter to be issued in the first place.

Now, as soon as possible, a roundtable meeting with the Borrower's business participants should be held. Participants do not include any of the Lender's personnel or representatives. The meeting will most likely include the Borrower's lawyer, accountant, business adviser(s), and senior business management. Whether "outside" loan guarantors should be present would be a decision of the management team and legal counsel. This "insiders" meeting will determine strategies and prepare rebuttals to those issues emphasized by the Lender—those that can realistically be rebutted. Finally, prepare Borrower's supporting documentation for the next meeting with the Lender.

Second Action Meeting: Following the Borrower's roundtable meeting, arrange a second appointment with the Loan Officer, at the Lender's place of business. The Borrower will be accompanied by his lawyer at this meeting, and, if the situation dictates, also by his accountant and/or business adviser(s). In addition, the Borrower should take any supporting documentation developed by management.

The difference between this and the prior meeting is that the Borrower *will require his lawyer, among possible others, to attend with him.* The Borrower's counsel in attendance may add creditability to the Borrower's position. Do not announce to the Lender that your attorney is attending, unless you are specifically asked. This two-on-one scenario could place the Lender somewhat at a disadvantage, with any flexibility to the Borrower's favor!

Again, the Borrower is to take detailed meeting notes. The purposes of this second meeting are to:

- Discuss clarifications needed as to the Lender's position.
- Discuss the Borrower's *preliminary* plan(s) of action. Detailed and explicit plans will be addressed in the following section. *Don't tip your hand now.*
- Clarify the Lender's expectations (may be obvious—but you never know).

- *Ask for an extension* of the 30-day letter to a 60- or 90-day letter. The longer time period will "allow the Borrower to discuss requirements and opportunities with those who were not able to be present at the meeting."
- Get a *new* Lender's letter. Do *not* agree to initialed pen changes to the current 30-day letter. You can say, "It's OK—you can mail the new letter to me." Again, all of this is to create time to develop and execute strategies. *Do not sign any new documents at this time.* Wait for the new letter.

The point of the Borrower's efforts at this point is to *continue to seek extensions of time* regarding the expiration dates on the letters. *Gaining time is frequently the only flexible factor of this entire scenario—but it is very important.*

At the end of the second action meeting, Borrower and his legal counsel will provide their closing comments. These should be along the lines of, "We must take back the understandings gained here today to the (other) owner(s), shareholders, and loan guarantors. We appreciate the alternatives you have provided, and these must be thoroughly discussed. We'll get back to you shortly."

Note: During this second meeting, the Borrower's rebuttals, documented support, and appropriate comments from the Borrower's attorney *may create some doubt with the Lender as to the validity of the Lender's position.* This is a plus!

Two meetings have been concluded. The Borrower may now be waiting for a new extension letter or a written synopsis of the past meeting from the Lender. During the next few days the Borrower, his accountant, his lawyer, and his advisers must meet again to formulate a detailed plan of action. They may need to address these key concerns:

- Seek to be reinstated with the current Lender —even if for a short term. After this "notice" action by the Lender, the Borrower most likely wants out of the relationship anyway. For any kind of reinstatement (remember—create time to attract a new Lender), benchmarks may have to be instituted by the current Lender to assure himself of the

Borrower's progress.

- Obtain certain guarantee(s), individual or governmental, providing the current Lender with satisfactory and *additional* margins of comfort.
- Following the previous step, the Lender could possibly obtain a participant in the loan, thus reducing the primary Lender's exposure. Much of this would depend upon the current status of the Borrower's business performance and available collateral.
- Seek replacement Lenders (consider alternative lenders, as discussed in Chapter 9).
- Seek additional contributed capital.
- Consider an "ESOP"—Employee Stock Ownership Plan.
- Sell, or otherwise liquidate, portions the business.
- *Combinations* of all of the above.
- Bankruptcy may also be an appropriate consideration—consult legal counsel.

You should discuss *all* considered options with legal counsel and professional advisers.

Then read Chapters 7 and 8.

Of course—it is possible that an absolute decision has already been made by the Lender to terminate this borrowing relationship. If this is self-evident, obtaining a replacement Lender is imperative. Chapter 7 provides suggested courses of action.

Third Action Meeting: Now plan the final (strategic) action meeting—*with a full cast.* The Lender is invited to the *Borrower's place of business* to hear about "action proposals and accommodations by business management."

If the selected strategy is to convince the current Lender to stay in the loan (even for a short time) it is *imperative* to have the third meeting at the business site. This process must be accomplished *even if* the Borrower may be considering a replacement Lender(s). At this point in time, dual scenarios may have to be conducted simultaneously to "cover all bases." Dual scenarios include delaying negotiations with the current Lender while attracting a replacement lender(s).

The Borrower should invite the current Lending Officer, the loan department head, key credit department representatives, and other relevant individuals. The Lender is not to be restricted in his level of attendance. I would not invite the Lender's attorney, but if he does attend there should be no problem. In fact, the Borrower will also have a large contingent: his attorney, accountant, special consultants, selected company officers and owners, possibly *selected* guarantors, and key company department heads.

The *upbeat agenda* (which may be printed and handed out to participants) will be especially choreographed with company department heads, highlighting to Lenders the pluses (or recent business successes) of the business. Exchange business cards with all participants you have not met prior to this meeting. The chief financial officer of the business will present (and provide copies of) financial forecasts and assumptions—*supported by the primary assumption that the Lender will remain in the loan relationship*. Marketing will indicate the business's unique competitive position and the department's plans to grow the business. The Borrower's president or CEO will finalize the presentation, providing closing comments and hosting a tour of the facilities. Some of the Lender's personnel, although frequently analyzing the credit, probably have never been on the premises. Refreshments should be available during the presentation.

If the Lender provides a proposal for the Borrower to remain in the relationship, it should be confidentially evaluated, after the meeting, in concert with any other new Lender loan proposals (see Chapter 7). Such loan proposals may already be in-house or on the way. *Even an extension of the 30-day letter to a 90-day letter is a win!*

Mission accomplished: The Borrower is gaining valuable time.

REALITY CHECK

If it is apparent, following the first or second meeting, that there is *little redemption probability* with the current Lender—*now is the time to commence the search for two replacement Lenders!* That is, if you haven't begun already. See Chapter 7 for specifics.

Should the current Lender accept an extension of the date of the final payment, the Lender should send (another) *new letter* to the Borrower's attorney. Any problems with this letter should be rebutted until a "clean and acceptable" letter is in evidence. This letter will be signed and acknowledged by the Borrower. *Do not accept initialed changes—ask for a "clean" letter.* This takes up more time, which the Borrower needs as he sources replacement Lenders.

Working with the Borrower's accountant, attorney, business consultant, or loan broker, the Borrower begins to identify an acceptable replacement Lender. Actually, the Borrower should consider selecting at least two acceptable proposal letters from Lenders. Both of these "candidate" Lenders will commence their due diligence to approve the loan. By doing this, the Borrower will rule out any eleventh-hour problems with one lender, which would jeopardize all of the previous plans and forecasts. *The second Lender will then be ready and waiting "in the wings" to close the loan.* Again, read Chapter 7.

Note: Most *prospective* Lenders will initially provide the Borrower with either a "term sheet" or a proposal letter. These documents are developed by the Lender prior to the issuance of a commitment letter. A commitment letter is not issued until a *formal* loan approval has been achieved. The Borrower should prepare *his own* preliminary terms and conditions (Chapter 7), both as a worksheet and as an inducement for a Lender to address the Borrower's precise needs. *The completed format may then be presented to a potential Lender as a well-formatted description of the Borrower's requirements.*

The *term sheet,* which some Lenders are able to issue in one day, is a presentation of the basic elements of a suggested loan structure before the Lender has done much in the way of *formal* due diligence. In essence, the Lender is saying, "Here's what we might do, but no guarantees." If the first is unacceptable to the Borrower, a series of alternative, and improved, term sheets may be provided. In any case, it is the Borrower's decision to go forward with the Lender—or not. If a term sheet is acceptable to the Borrower, the Lender will commence to work toward a credit approval. Always remember that the final approved loan structure could be *completely different* from the initial term sheet.

The *proposal letter* contains more detail than a term sheet, usually giving the Borrower a more inclusive representation of potential terms and conditions. The detail involved in a proposal letter reveals that the potential Lender has probably put more effort into identifying and attempting to respond to the Borrower's goals. As is the case with term sheets, unacceptable proposal letters can be rewritten by a Lender—again, trying to achieve Borrower satisfaction, at least to a point. However, if a proposal letter is acceptable, it is usually then signed by the Lender, the Borrower, and possibly the loan guarantor(s). The proposal may further require a good faith deposit or deposit(s) specifically addressed to cover the *estimated* costs of appraisals, environmental inspections(s) and/or legal costs (see Chapter 5). The Lender wants to make sure that if the Borrower decided to quit the loan process *after* the Lender had incurred certain expenses, these would be paid by the potential Borrower in the form of his early deposits. The Borrower's deposit check is attached to the signed and accepted proposal letter. A proposal letter may take one day to a week or more to be issued by a Lender.

The signing of a term sheet or a proposal letter by both the Lender and Borrower *is not an indication* of a Lender's loan approval. It is only the Lender's approval to go forward with its normal credit underwriting (credit approval process). *Only* the commitment letter, following a loan approval, represents the actual loan approval. Due to the comprehensiveness of a proposal letter over a term sheet, a Borrower may feel more comfortable with a proposal letter.

The commitment letter, issued to the Borrower by his new Lender, is like "money in the bank" to the *former* Lender—he's going to be paid off. More than not, at this point the former Lender will back off, allowing the remaining elements of the new Lender's approval and closing process to move forward at a normal pace.

Note: Not infrequently, a commitment letter may contain some "*subject to's*." In other words, the Borrower does have a commitment, but there are other agreed-upon loan elements that must be satisfactorily completed or reconciled by the Borrower before the Lender will close the loan. These may be appraisals, environmental inspections, obtaining key man life insurance, legal opinions, certain compliance certifications, and the like. Many times these items remain open right up to the loan closing date. Fortunately, in real life, the new Lender may give further time or considerations as to these tardy items (post-closing items) in order that the loan can close as scheduled. Not doing so could play havoc with the Borrower's cash flow.

To a new potential Lender, an important aspect of issuing a term sheet or proposal letter, is to "get the deal off the street." Once either of these documents are signed by the Borrower, the potential Lender, to some extent, has a "lock" on the loan deal. The potential new Lender feels he no longer has to worry about a competitor taking the deal away from him—*preliminary* documents are signed. Deposits or early fees may even be given to the prospective Lender. The Lender can now address deal specifics on his own time and not feel pressured that he may be working against a competitor. Within any of the documents mentioned in this section, the Borrower *is not required to reveal* that he may actually be working similar arrangements with another potential Lender at the same time. More important, the Borrower *should* not reveal any such information. *These are confidential Borrower strategies.* See Chapter 7.

The next step is to comparatively review all proposal letters and term sheets with your accountant and business consultant. The loan broker, if any, will also become involved in attempting to find the best deal for the Borrower. Then review, with legal counsel, what is thought to be the final version. (Chapter 7 demonstrates some comparative loan proposal techniques and worksheets.)

If a loan broker is engaged by the Borrower, he should be the primary intermediary between the Borrower and all prospective Lenders. After all, the Borrower is paying him to find desirable Lenders and handle communications. The broker plays a very important liaison role in sourcing Lenders, determining which Lenders will be most receptive, advising the Borrower on what the broker sees as a good deal, addressing potential Lender questions, and coordinating and transmitting supporting documentation. The use of a qualified commercial loan broker may save a lot of shoe leather and critical time. There is more about loan brokers in Chapter 9.

The point of the action meetings and emergency procedures is that the 30-day letter, or an extended 60- or 90-day letter, *must not be allowed to expire*. Rather, it must be *reborn*—a number of times, if necessary—until the Borrower achieves his objective:

A new Borrowing relationship, or the reinstatement of his existing relationship.

THE 30-DAY LETTER (OR EXTENDED ONE) HAS EXPIRED

Once this happens, a whole new level of negotiations could commence. However, the Lender *may* proceed with the following scenario. Be forearmed and forewarned!

Worst Case: A few days following letter expiration, the Lender may arrive at the Borrower's business, *unannounced and possibly with a sheriff*, to take possession of the Lender's collateral (the Borrower's pledged assets).

The Lender may say he is not putting the Borrower out of business (he cannot do that); he is only recovering the collateral pledged to him. This could include:

- Accounts receivable
- Invoices and shipping documents
- Accounts payable (to determine any offsets against receivables)
- Sales journals, cash receipts journals
- Inventory: Either raw materials or finished goods; inventory may be identified, segregated, or moved out of a Borrower's plant for security purposes.
- Work-in-process (to the extent salable)
- Supporting inventory records
- The file cabinets in which records are stored

The Lender can even go so far as offsetting (emptying) the business checking (and sometimes payroll) account(s), and immediately applying funds against the loan(s).

I have been involved in a number of these disturbing situations. Just reviewing such happenings can help a Borrower recognize the seriousness of the situation. Sometimes the Lender's collateral is left at the business site, protected by the Lender's employees (or by personnel from an outside firm hired by the Lender). These people protect the premises and the collateral and look out for the best interests of the Lender. Tractor-trailers may back up to the shipping bays to load the inventory and transfer it to a more secure location until a sale or auction can occur. The paper records may be taken to the Lender's offices. Accounts receivable debtors may be notified that any money owed to the Borrower should be sent directly to the Lender (a receiving lockbox may be established by the Lender).

The Borrower should consider keeping a backup set of business records off premises, to include the detail of the accounts receivable and accounts payable. (Maintaining backup business records is good business practice for any company these days.) Business records may be seized by a Lender within certain of his rights and remedies. As mentioned, in such a scenario, it is most likely the Lender's intention to *notify* the Borrower's customers to send receivable payments directly to the Lender's lockbox. Back up records now!

Note: The Lender may not have the immediate internal capacity to generate periodic billings or post activity to the Borrower's business accounts on a timely basis. Such things tend to slow down the continuance and accuracy of the Borrower's record keeping. *A real mess can occur if the Lender does not have dedicated personnel and systems for this type of daily monitoring and posting.* Certain accounts receivable debtors may seek to take advantage of the situation and not pay.

An important discipline within the banking and commercial finance industry is liquidating collateral to the benefit of a Lender and doing so in what is called "a commercially reasonable manner." This side of the business comes with its own set of experts.

The Lender's "possession team" has now entered the premises.

Borrower's action:

1. Upon arrival, the Borrower ensures that *all* individuals, including Lender(s), Lender's attorney, and law enforcement, are

shown to a secluded common private office or conference room. Once they are in the room, *the door is closed.* These people are then left in the room alone.

2. Next, the Borrower *contacts his attorney* (in private). This should be regarded as an *emergency* call! Call on a cell phone so others cannot pick up and listen in.

3. *Insist that the Borrower's attorney be present before any further conversations or actions take place.* Offer to send out for coffee or sandwiches while waiting for attorney. They wait alone. You are gaining valuable time. They are getting nervous.

4. While all are waiting for the Borrower's attorney to arrive, the bookkeeper should prepare a copy of the accounts receivable and accounts payable agings. While the Lender will ask for a "master" list of all customers, including name, address, and phone numbers, the Borrower should ensure that he has a duplicate copy. The Lender *requires* the receivable aging records in order to notify the business's customers (and the Lender will do that quickly) that remittances should now be sent to the Lender—not to the Borrower. The Lender will also seek a copy of the most recent inventory report for his retention. The Borrower, if possible, will hold on to the larger, detailed inventory report, with a summary report going to the Lender.

5. Bookkeeper should *quickly verify cash balances* in all operating and payroll accounts.

6. Once the Borrower's legal counsel arrives, the Borrower should *only converse with his counsel—not the Lender* or his various representatives. Let Borrower's counsel resolve immediate concerns, requirements, and/or compromises.

Note: The Lender's collateral consists of accounts receivable and "proceeds." Proceeds of accounts receivable are payments from customers. It is likely that most of the cash sitting in the operating account (A/R payments) belongs to the Lender. Consult with your attorney and *try to retain cash.* You may be able to dissuade the Lender from offsetting the accounts—but then again, it may be too late.

7. Borrower's counsel may work without delay with the Lender to ensure that the accounts receivables (and their proceeds) that

were created *after* the Lender's termination of the credit facility *belong unencumbered to the Borrower and not to the Lender.* This can be the beginning of restoring the Borrower's cash flow.

8. The Lender may permit the continuation of payroll (to include associated taxes and health-care plans) through special loans to address the payroll of employees involved in completing work in process, the bookkeeper, plant manager, and other key employees, and the salaries of officers.

9. Employees: The information will get out to the employees, but it must be done *in an orderly manner*. Remember, the payroll account may already have been "set off," and payroll checks may not be honored. Find out if adequate payroll funds are available in the payroll account to *meet the current payroll.* If not, the Borrower's counsel should prevail upon the Lender to deposit (a loan advance) enough funds for payroll purposes, to include taxes and health insurance—an important symbol of "good faith" on the part of the Lender.

10. Meeting of Employees: Upon the advice of Borrower's counsel and once the Lender's group has left the premises, or activities have settled down somewhat, it *may* be time to call a meeting of employees—*out of earshot of the Lender's representatives.* Management may also make the decision that it is *not* the time to notify employees until the continuing situation has been clarified. The Borrower (president or senior management) will disclose happenings *to the extent advised by counsel.* Employees will have many questions: What were the Lender's actions, and why? Do they still have jobs? Will they get paid? Are the last paychecks OK?—and so on. Lender's counsel should also remain available in the background to answer legal questions. This may be a difficult time for all, but it does not mean business operations will be shut down. Possible concessions may be arranged with the current Lender, and possibly alternative lenders could loan emergency funds until a new and permanent and replacement Lender is selected. See Factoring in Chapter 8.

11. Daily Monitoring Functions: The Lender may wish to have a Lender's employee, or other third party, conduct certain daily monitoring functions on the Borrower's premises. Do not agree to this without counsel approval. If such a scenario does develop, the Borrower and his employees *should not become friendly with these representatives.* Unguarded comments could come back to haunt the Borrower. It's best *not* to leave the Lender's employees or other Lender representatives alone in, or on, the business site.

12. Take Notes: The Borrower should, as soon as possible, commence taking notes regarding all activities as observed. It is also advisable to *have the bookkeeper prepare similar notes* as to all actions accomplished during this period.

13. Notification to Customers and Suppliers: This letter notice from the Borrower will provide pertinent information to (perhaps selected) customers and suppliers. The extent and tone of information provided will be dependent upon determinations of the Borrower, his legal counsel, and associated professionals. Information provided must be clear, accurate, timely, and *not overly pessimistic.* If reasonable, being upbeat always helps. The *continued good faith* of these business supporters may be paramount.

14. *In many cases, daily business operations actually continue,* almost at a normal pace. Employees may not be aware of any unusual activities as the business works its way out of difficulty. Also, new Lenders may provide interim business financing. Borrower's counsel will explain to the Borrower various *legal* scenarios through which positive opportunities or solutions may exist.

REALITY CHECK

The key to a Borrower's success in these most critical of scenarios can be *cooperation with the current Lender.* Such cooperation could change a difficult problem into a manageable one!

Caution: *Cooperate only to the extent approved by the Borrower's legal counsel.*

LENDER'S RIGHTS AND REMEDIES UNDER THE UNIFORM COMMERCIAL CODE

The Lender has certain legal rights and remedies as provided by law under the Uniform Commercial Code ("UCC"). The "UCC" has been adopted in most states and there are attorneys who specialize in such commercial law.

Continuing our discussion regarding the deteriorating borrowing situation, it is important to note that the Borrower acknowledged many of the Lender's rights and remedies upon initially executing the loan documents, to include the Loan and Security Agreement. Unfortunately, these loan documents are filed away and not read until one crisis or another arises. When a Borrower has a spare moment, he should review these loan agreements, in some detail, and clarify questions with his attorney.

The following points of information are only the author's general comments and opinions as to certain aspects of the UCC and its practical application. The Borrower should contact his legal counsel for a complete understanding, applicable provisions, and updates concerning these laws. As highlighted throughout this book, the Borrower is strongly advised to have the benefit of legal counsel when dealing with all aspects of business financing.

Among the Lender's rights may be the right to:

- Declare all obligations due and payable.
- Enter the Borrower's premises and take possession of and /or remove collateral—even to the extent of the cabinets in which records are kept.
- Within the provisions of the UCC, or other applicable laws, operate specific portions of the Borrower's business. Such efforts may include completing work in process through the utilization of Lender or third-party personnel and, upon completion, subsequent customer billing.
- Requiring the Borrower to marshal selected assets, bringing these to a single common location (at the borrower's cost).
- Prepare for the public or private sale of selected assets. Lenders usually use outside professionals for such services.
- Set off, *without notice*, bank accounts (to include payroll), applying funds obtained against the loan(s) outstanding, interest due, and expenses (not necessarily in that order).
- Open Borrower's mail and endorse checks due to the Borrower.

- Pay taxes, rent, insurance premiums, and other authorized expenses on behalf of the Borrower. Such expenditures may be added to the existing loan.
- Following Lender's account notification, Lender collects balances due on existing accounts receivable. Proceeds pay down amounts due to Lender.
- Should court actions result, a Borrower may be tried in court by a judge rather than a jury. Clarifications should be obtained from the Borrower's legal counsel.

Generally, it is a requirement of a lending agreement that a Borrower maintain his business operating account within the Lender's institution. This is where loan advances are usually credited and, as learned, where "offsets" can occur. The exception to this may be a Borrower who is geographically distant from the Lender. In that case, the Lender usually allows the Borrower to pick (or remain with) a locally convenient bank.

The Borrower may consider, as a practical matter, to have his payroll account at a bank other than the Lender's bank. This should be done at the beginning of the relationship and with the Lender's permission. To move accounts at a later date may be a violation of the lending agreement. An appropriate reason is that a local bank may be more convenient to the employees so that they may cash paychecks.

Discuss actions taken, or contemplated, with your legal counsel.

Some Additional Operating Account Concerns

Inasmuch as word of the Borrower's situation will shortly find its way to suppliers, vendors, and customers, and considering the actual situation, the Borrower may consider the following:

- Have a new endorsement stamp prepared for accounts receivable check deposits. This is done so it is not easy for a third part to identify the Borrower's main operating account. Make it something like, "For Deposit Only to the Account of the Within Named Payee." Certain customers may try to renege on recent payments and try to get their money back. Don't make it easy for them. And yes—this has really happened!

- The Borrower should consider paying certain nervous suppliers or trade accounts by money order or bank check. These vendors will not then know the number of the Borrower's operating checking account. It will not be so easy for them to seek to attach account funds. It is possible that selected accounts payable had agreed, at a prior time, to extend special payment terms. These terms generally fall apart at times like these, and suppliers want their money. It is important to protect all funds from such intrusion.
- Your Lender may have already set up a special address (lock box) to receive proceeds of those *accounts receivable that existed up to the time of the Lender's termination of the lending arrangement.* If the Borrower still receives checks pertinent to the Lender's accounts receivable, these are usually required to be forwarded "in kind" (the actual check) to the Lender.
- The Lender is now receiving and processing accounts receivable checks on behalf of the Borrower. The Borrower should insist on *timely reporting* to his bookkeeper so business records may be kept current.
- Upon advice of counsel, the Borrower should not let third parties, including sheriffs, IRS officers, leasing companies, vending machine companies, or other creditors, into the premises. All such parties should talk only to the Borrower's legal counsel. *Keep doors locked at all times* (even during working hours) with a competent and informed employee responding to inquiries through the glass. Another way to handle this is to post signs at all entrances (on the *interior* of the glass) indicating that all inquires should be made to "[Attorney's name] [attorney's phone number]." Do not respond to doorbells or knocks. Other creditors of the Borrower may arrive at the business and attempt to remove property or indicate, by the placement of stickers or tags, that selected property, certain pieces of equipment, desks, and computers are *their* collateral for *their* debt satisfaction. Only with the Borrower's counsel's

permission (keep notes) will anyone be let in to perform such actions.

- A similar profile for answering the phone is also appropriate—all inquiries should be directed to the Borrower's attorney. A private cell phone may be used for other calls.
- As before, maintain a detailed daily log of *all* events and telephone calls. Such documentation could later be invaluable.

PRESERVATION: YOUR LIFE BLOOD—CASH FLOW

Sources of cash flow during a *routine* lending restructuring process were discussed earlier in Emergency Procedures—Now! Some of these sources could take one to four months to conclude.

However, once a Lender has taken possession of its collateral (especially accounts receivable and inventory) the Borrower's short-term cash flow is seriously jeopardized.

Some short-term sources to consider are:

- Accounts receivable (post–Lender possession)
- Extended amortization of existing term loans
- Grace periods on debt payments
- Sale of items "excess" to needs
- Salary cuts (across the board, and hopefully temporary)
- Selective layoffs
- Special accounts payable accommodations (discussion follows)
- Personal funds
- Supplier or customer loans and/or equity involvements
- Reduction of business space requirements

Work with *legal counsel and accountant* in addressing these short-term cash-flow enhancements, including the following considerations.

Accounts Receivable (Post–Lender Possession): The Lender would now be collecting on those accounts receivable that are *his* collateral—*up to the date the credit facility was terminated.* Accounts receivable generated by the Borrower *after* this date are generally free and clear, with all such collections belonging to the Borrower.

To speed up customer receivables:

- Fax invoices to customers—do not mail. Call in advance.
- Consider offering discounts: Customers who pay within seven days will receive a 10%–15% discount (Borrower's choice). Such discounts would apply *only* to the basic product billing, *not* including shipping costs.
- Offer a 20% discount (or less) if a payment is received by overnight mail. This may be a bit aggressive, but right now the Borrower is concerned about making payroll and keeping the lights on.

Note: The percentages suggested in the preceding list are shown only as samples. The Borrower and his professional associates would determine the actual percentages, their reasonableness, and potential effectiveness.

Extended Amortization of Existing Term Loans: Borrower asks for a 30-, 60-, or 90-day deferment of loan payments from each term Lender (or lessor). Monthly term loan payments (principal and/or interest) can total a meaningful amount, especially if deferred for a few periods. The reason you may give is that the Borrower is in the process of obtaining a replacement Lender—and the old one is seeking an accelerated repayment. Borrower may be without a "line" Lender for 90 days, considering the time it takes for the regular credit and approval process. The Borrower is just seeking some short-term slack. Is the Borrower worried about the business credit rating? Don't be—the fact that the Lender has "called" the loan may have already damaged the rating. Working with the accountant can clarify some of these issues.

Grace periods on Debt Payments: Most term loan agreements (equipment, auto, computer, and so on) provide for grace periods, which enable more time in which to make the required monthly payment. Find out what these are, and take advantage of them.

Sale of Items "Excess" to Needs: The Lender is "filed" against certain assets of the Borrower—which constitute the Lender's collateral—and possibly all assets are encumbered. Sometimes "hereafter acquired assets" are also the Lender's collateral per the loan agreement. These assets, *as they existed at the time of termination of the credit facility*, are the Lender's collateral and cannot be disturbed until the Lender's loan is paid off. *Exception*: With Lender's permission, in writing, certain agreed-upon assets may be liquidated by the Borrower. It is likely that all, or only a portion of such proceeds, must go to the Lender. If the Lender is "filed" only against accounts receivable, excess inventory may be sold by the Borrower with proceeds going to the Borrower. Of course, if the Lender is "filed" against inventory, this excess inventory sale, without Lender's permission, may not be possible. A similar rationale may apply to machinery and equipment or other assets. Again, the *Borrower should check with legal counsel* to ensure that certain assets are available for such sale considerations.

Personal Funds: This may be the time to mortgage that unencumbered piece of vacation or investment property or take a residential second mortgage for short-term cash. The Borrower's accountant may advise that these funds be placed into the company as short-term loans so that, once the new Lender is "on board," the Borrower can retrieve these personal funds (with the new Lender's permission). Be careful here. If the Lender had previously collateralized the Borrower's personal guarantee with the personal residence, or other personal assets, funds through an equity mortgage may not be available at this time. Will the Lender release this equity mortgage? If the Borrower can convince the Lender that such a release will not jeopardize the Lender's position (and will assist the Borrower) it may be a consideration.

Special Accounts Payable Accommodations: In the most difficult of situations, trade suppliers still expect to get paid. It is probable that a handful of loyal and important suppliers have worked with the Borrower over a number of years. *These suppliers do not want to lose their long-term customer.* They want to continue to ship their goods as their customer recovers. Calls to the most needed (and faithful) suppliers *usually* will bring desirable results.

The Borrower may request that *new shipments* (new vendor payables) will be paid 33.3% in 30 days, 33.3% in 90 days, and 33.4% in 120 days. Any *current balances due* will be paid 50% within 60 days and the remainder in 120 days. The presented percentages are *examples only*—the Borrower and his accountant must determine what is reasonable and what will best improve the Borrower's cash flow. Suppliers may then get their money, customers may be retained through continued production or services, and the Borrower will have accounts payable relief with supplies delivered. Any variation of the above may be considered—each situation is different. Remember, the Borrower, *at the same time he is doing all of this*, is working toward a replacement Lender, which can bring relief to all.

Supplier or Customer Loans and/or Equity Involvements: Sometimes suppliers and/or customers value the Borrower's company and the mutually important business benefits of the relationship so much they will offer to put some needed cash into the company on a short-term loan (Note) basis, *or even as equity*—but the Borrower has to ask! The Borrower's attorney can help with the legal aspects.

Reduction of Business Space Requirements: Generally, business space concerns represent long-term cash flow considerations (rent, lease, or buy). That said, businesses have successfully moved a good portion of their machinery and equipment to half or three-quarters of the prior usage area, and leased out the newly available space to smaller businesses. What with first and last month rent payments, and then continuing monthly rental payments, a new source of income has been developed. Security deposits may also be required, but these are usually restricted in their use (see your accountant).

There are entire books written on the subject of improving and accelerating cash flow—get one!

TRANSFERRED TO LOAN WORKOUT? MANAGE IT!

The Borrower has now left the realm of Loan Officers and credit departments. The loan workout group or special assets department (among other names) is usually the last stop for loans destined to leave the Lender.

The decision for the Borrower's loan relationship to be placed in the workout group may have been based on:

- Loan agreement violations
- Failure to live up to subsequent agreements
- Providing unreliable information to the Lender
- Inability to get along with the Lending Officer or other Lender personnel
- Important "trends" that are down and, in the opinion of the Lender, have little hope for recovery
- Lender authorities deciding this is not a relationship the Lender wishes to continue
- Risk rating analysis that reveals there is a potential for a loss to the Lender
- The Lender deeming itself insecure

NOTE: Businesses assigned to the loan workout group may be operating companies or non-operating companies. Simply because a Borrower has been assigned to a workout group doesn't mean business operations cease. Continuing operations is not a decision of the Lender; it is the Borrower's decision. This decision is best made in conjunction with counsel from his attorney and other professionals. It is, however, time for the Borrower to effect *aggressive repairs* to the financial health of the business. See Chapter 7.

In the realm of loan workouts, the Borrower is very small and the loan workout department is an elephant. There are only two kinds of people who dance with elephants—the quick and the dead. *So let's be quick!*

Once transferred to loan workout, and depending upon the size of the Lender, the Borrower may be one of hundreds of loans in this department. Loan types can range from small investment property loan defaults and small-business credit line defaults to multimillion-dollar secured credit lines. Supporting collateral for these loans are all over the board, from real estate, accounts receivable, and inventory to equipment, vehicles, and even intangible properties. Many loans may be further guaranteed by Individuals or municipal, state, and/or federal agencies.

The mission of loan workout is to maximize loan recovery, to include the outstanding loan principal, accrued interest, and associated expenses.

In order to accomplish this mission, and because some of these Borrowing relationships are the most difficult, this department is usually staffed with only the Lender's most seasoned lending / workout officers.

The Borrower's current Lending Officer is usually replaced by a loan workout specialist. From time to time the loan workout officer may contact the former officer, but typically only in an advisory capacity.

The fact that this is a most unique situation for the individual Borrower should not inordinately disturb the affected Borrower. However, and to the Borrower's advantage, the situation is not unique to the workout officer. These are the only types of accounts he handles—and he has probably been doing this for years. It can be a great benefit to the Borrower to have such an experienced officer to handle the workout arrangements and provide guidance.

One interesting note: The loan workout officer's compensation may be affected by the amount he is able to recover. In many instances, the loan may already be "charged off" the books of the Lender at the time it *enters* the workout department. When this has happened, Borrowers usually don't know. Any recouping (total or partial) of the loan can be a plus to the loan workout officer—and *may* result in a bonus situation.

While a total loan write-off is not a desirable outcome for the Lender, *a meaningful "limited" recovery may be acceptable.* In other words, after all that can be reasonably obtained from the pledged collateral (also considering the workout department's time involved), the Lender may write off the remainder of the loan due. The Borrower may be released from the obligation, and a portion of it may not have to be repaid. Of course personal guarantees, as well as other guarantors, may play a part of the Lender's overall recovery potential.

During the Borrower's time assigned to the Lender's loan workout group, he should stay in close touch with his legal counsel. As all situations are different, the following comments and suggestions again must be tempered by legal counsel and other professional advisers.

Some major Borrower considerations during this period of time:

1. Work cooperatively with the current lender

2. Seek continuing advice of legal counsel
3. Aggressively seek a replacement Lender
4. Run your business

More directly, during each of these processes:

1. Once assigned to loan workout, request an *immediate meeting* with the workout officer assigned. Your attorney and accountant (or business adviser) should also attend.

The meeting must be an immediate go! *It may only be a matter of time* before the Lender exercises certain rights and remedies to which he may be entitled, such as taking possession of his collateral, including the Borrower's premises; conducting an accounts receivable notification and commencing a collection program; offsetting bank accounts; or planning for appraisals and or an auction. The Borrower must be aware of the Lender's *immediate intentions*. It is possible that a "grace period" may be provided by the Lender, enabling the Borrower to get his strategies in order—or the Lender may be planning some immediate and unfavorable action.

This meeting should be face-to-face and most likely will be held at the office of the Lender. That's OK—get to know the lay of the land. You may also be introduced to the head of the loan workout department, and that never hurts.

Note: It is *possible*, through business performance and collateral improvements, to work one's way out of the loan workout area and back into a normal lending relationship with the same Lender, *but usually not probable or feasible*. Too much history—and a new Lender is really the best route. The Borrower's internal credit file with his existing Lender may already have permanent and derogatory information—not a good foundation for attempting to rekindle the relationship.

What is the Lender's posture; hostile, benevolent, middle-of-the-road? This seasoned workout officer may have some beneficial up-front suggestions. Also, options may be put forward to shorten the Borrower's time within the loan workout group. Certainly successful refinancing, capital infusion, mezzanine lending or additional guarantees may be all or part of the answer to closing out this lending relationship. But remember, most any of these can take from *two to four months* before concluding a successful closing with a replacement Lender.

The Borrower should expect, and ask for, the time necessary to obtain a new Lender. The workout officer already knows how long this may take.

Accordingly, this workout officer could indicate that everything is "on hold" while the Borrower commences to attract a replacement Lender. The Borrower should keep close to his legal advisers during this period.

These are the most likely initial scenarios within a loan workout group:

- In good faith, and *only if possible,* the Borrower agrees to pay *interest only* on the loan(s). The Borrower is going to pay this anyway, now or later. Alternatively, a moratorium on interest and principal payments could be put in place. Then the Lender will usually expect the total debt to be paid off at the replacement loan closing.
- Borrower agrees to commence looking for a new lender. He will keep the loan workout officer updated with *weekly* memorandums regarding this developing search. Keep these memorandums going—even if not asked. It is a good sign to the workout officer that he has a cooperative Borrower. The loan workout officer also has to write up-dated periodic reports. The Borrower's report will help the officer write his own report, and the report will be accurate. For the first few weeks, or months, the Lender need not know with which Lenders the Borrower is negotiating. If a loan broker is utilized to assist in the search, it is usually OK to inform the Lender which loan broker has been engaged. There is no need to detail the terms of your agreement with the broker. Only the day or so before the replacement loan closing would the Borrower's new Lender contact the prior Lender. This is only for the "payoff amount" of the relationship. The new Lender may then close the new loan the next day.
- This is also the time to ensure the workout officer recognizes that *newly created receivables and inventory purchases* belong to the Borrower and *not* to the Lender. Likewise, all such collateral belonging to, and existing *prior* to the time of credit facility termination, is a part of the former

Lender's collateral package.
- Following the meeting with loan workout, ask the Lender to write a letter to the Borrower confirming agreements reached. *Keep it in writing.*
- After a month or so, it may again be necessary to have a face-to-face with the loan workout officer. Thirty days may have passed without any loan repayment, but through the Borrower's memorandums, the Lender knows progress is being made. Again, take your attorney, as well as the others who attended the prior meeting. This type of support gives everyone a chance to think, and the Borrower's commitment will be impressive. Should any new agreements, or time concessions be reached, have the Lender *again* confirm these in writing.

When meeting flow is conducted in this manner, the Borrower may be creating favorable concessions with the Lender as well as generating a significant amount of time to source a replacement Lender.

REALITY CHECK

The loan workout group really does not want to have to take possession of a Borrower's collateral. Too much work—too costly—and the loan officers assigned to "watch the store" cannot perform their regular duties. The Lender wants out "clean"—and the best way is being paid off *completely* is by the Borrower's *new* Lender.

IMPORTANT: It could be imperative that the Lender hold off from selling any part of the Borrower's collateral. The Borrower needs to continue to reflect a whole and solid collateral base (even an *attractive* package) to potential lenders, suppliers, customers, or even a business buyer.

Should there be no "takers" in the search for a replacement Lender—and that does happen—the Lender may have no choice but to work out a continuing arrangement with the Borrower. The Lender may consider a term loan with a payout over a number of years, including interest only for the first year (providing time for the Borrower to get back on his feet). Another structure may consider a reduced periodic payment but include a long-term loan amortization until an agreed upon "balloon" payment (final remainder loan balance) is achieved. It must be realistically anticipated that the Borrower would be stronger at that point in the future. A replacement Lender may then *again* be sought, with the replacement Lender paying off the outstanding "balloon" loan balance.

Assignment to a loan workout group is not necessarily the "swan song" of a Borrower. *A positive outcome is realistic to anticipate.*

The Borrower's aggressive actions (in concert with legal counsel's advice) can result not only in a new Lender, but a new Lender with a more flexible loan structure.

Legal Counsel and the Borrower—Time for Strategic Planning

While I have mentioned a number of times that you should consult with legal counsel as various situations occur, a bit more explanation may be necessary to clarify this important legal association.

There are many advantages to engaging legal counsel as the Borrower addresses various aspects, or situations, within his commercial lending relationship. The Borrower's attorney performs many vital functions:

- Acts as an informed advocate for and representative of the Borrower, as necessary
- Advises the Borrower as to possible or probable outcomes of a situation
- Attends Borrower meetings to protect Borrower from making impromptu or inappropriate agreements
- Forms rebuttals to Lender's requests and requirements
- Proposes appropriate and/or alternative countertactics
- Coordinates correspondence responses
- Reviews all Loan Agreements
- Is present at agreement and loan signings to protect Borrower's interests

The attorney selected for these important functions is *not the family friend or the family affairs lawyer*. Counsel selected should be:

- Well versed in commercial lending
- Experienced in loan workout situations
- In practice within the business financing field for at least five years

- A member of a firm with multiple partners, should the engaged attorney become unavailable
- Able to provide client references
- Able to ensure that there are no conflicts of interest (the firm will most likely represent Lenders as well as Borrowers)

Counsel's experience in the commercial lending area is paramount—he must be used to dealing (day in and day out) with Lenders and Borrowers. Such an attorney will be aware of the latitude a Lender possesses in the area of loan workouts.

In my opinion, the competence of the selected attorney can determine the effectiveness of the Borrower's delaying strategies and tactics.

If the Borrower is unaware as to where to find such an attorney, try these two avenues of information:

1. Local bar association
2. A "friendly banker" in another institution (one that will *maintain confidence*), who will know which firms have lawyers specializing in *commercial lending*

Commercial law firms frequently represent Lenders *against* Borrowers. The Borrower must find a qualified attorney whose firm does *not* represent the Borrower's current lender, or a conflict of interest may occur. A prospective law firm will make this determination promptly. *If a conflict exists, ask for a referral to another firm.*

Most communications will be between the Borrower's selected counsel and the Lender's attorney. The Borrower's counsel will not appreciate it if the Borrower talks directly to the Lender's attorney or the Loan Officer (without his permission and/or presence). A verbal or impromptu agreement may be made, or alleged, without Borrower's counsel's knowledge.

Competent commercial loan counsel can be the best friend the Borrower has in these difficult commercial lending and business recovery situations.

The Borrower will not make any agreements with the Lender until the Borrower's attorney is able to review. The Lender understands this approach, and it will gain you time.

It cannot be repeated enough that it is prudent to maintain a call log, posting calls from the Lender, all legal counsel involved, and all other third parties. Indicate the date, time, person involved, telephone number, and subject discussed. Such a log may be valuable in future legal proceedings, documenting timing or event resolutions.

DO NOT PROVIDE MORE AMMUNITION

Even in a deteriorating situation, the Borrower is *still* subject to all agreements and covenants executed for the benefit of the existing Lender. Exceptions, due to circumstances, *should be acknowledged* by both the Borrower and Lender in writing.

Likewise, the Lender is still bound by covenants made by the Lender to the Borrower. One of the most important is the *Lender's requirement to advance funds* to the Borrower under certain circumstances.

The Borrower may feel that the *Lender is not performing as agreed.* The Lender may not be making loan advances as agreed. This action (restriction of funds) could seriously damage the Borrower's ability to pay suppliers and subsequently harm customer relationships. The Borrower should notify his legal counsel. Some Lenders may capriciously stop loan advances when, in fact, loan agreements *do not* provide for such arbitrary actions. The Borrower should always document in detail what has, or could happen, if the Lender exhibits what is believed to be Lender nonperformance.

The Borrower must continue to demonstrate to the Lender that the Borrower is complying with loan covenants:

- Payment of the Lender's loans on a timely basis, if possible
- Deposit of payroll withholding taxes on a timely basis
- Maintaining open communications with the Lender (or counsel to counsel)

Continue to report accurately and timely all aspects of collateral. To get caught in a falsehood could undermine all of the Borrower's work, as well as his attorney's efforts.

The Borrower should not "badmouth" the Lender in outside circles or idly threaten the Lender with liability lawsuits outside of counsel chambers. If a proposed replacement Lender heard of these things, he could be less inclined to consider this Borrower for a loan. Who needs the grief?

The Borrower should hold his temper with lending personnel (as well as suppliers and customers). When practical, and approved by legal counsel, the Borrower should be accompanied by a witness to collaborate the Borrower's version of what transpired.

Remember—the Borrower must *maintain open communications.* Silence on the Borrower's part may leave the Lender with little choice but to take severe action.

Effecting a Loan Officer Change

There may be a time when a change of loan officers is justified in the Borrower's mind:

- Absolute inexperience
- Lack of confidence in the Loan Officer
- Lack of confidentiality
- No interest in the business or its problems
- Personality conflict (domineering, no patience)

The Borrower, or his Lending relationship, should not have to suffer because of such obvious shortcomings. Do consider that such incapability may also be apparent to the Loan Officer. Maybe both the Borrower and the Loan Officer really want out!

The Borrower will, in the normal course of events, be aware of the Lending Officer's immediate superior. The Borrower should bring to the attention of this superior, in writing, the specifics of the problem relationship. This letter is to be prepared without recriminations—only the facts as perceived by the Borrower. It is a good idea for the Borrower to have his attorney preview this letter, indicating at the bottom that the attorney received a copy.

The Borrower could also admit some shortcomings of his own. By such action the Borrower is not necessarily putting the entire burden on the incompatible Lending Officer. The Borrower then respectfully requests that his relationship be assigned to another Lender without prejudice.

It is always possible that the Lending Officer's superior would accept responsibility for the Borrower's account—this does happen frequently. Be careful what you wish for! However, it usually works out, as the superior officer will most likely be at a higher level of experience and maturity than is his junior. This superior would also usually have higher approval authorities and more clout with the credit committee.

Should the transition to a new Lending Officer be effected, the Borrower can be sure the departing Lending Officer will voice his biases to the new officer. The Borrower should not badmouth the former officer, but rather go forward doing business as pleasantly as possible. Good luck in your new relationship!

CHAPTER 7

TAKE CHARGE OF YOUR BANKING DESTINY

"Create my own loan terms and conditions?"

"I'm supposed to find **two** new Lenders?"

"Not to worry—our Bank doesn't know we're seeking a new Lender."

"*Terrific*—it was all worth it!"

Fully Maintain Your Current Relationship

It may be in a Borrower's best interest to continue to work with his current Lender's commercial loan department or its loan workout group, for some weeks (or months) even while contemplating a move. A Borrower's strategy may include:

- Attracting a new Lender
- Attracting a non-traditional Lender
- Achieving a reconciliation with the current Lender
- Seeking a buyer, equity funds, or a merger partner for the business

It is imperative that the Borrower continues to maintain the confidence of the current Lender to the fullest extent practical, considering the current situation, the advice of the Borrower's legal counsel, and professional advisers.

The obvious reason for maintaining a good relationship with a Lender is that there must not be any reduction in the current Lender's financing commitments while the Borrower seeks a change or amendment(s) to the existing relationship. In fact, it is possible that throughout the Borrower's search for a new Lender (possibly lasting one to four months), the Lender will be unaware of such activities.

This scenario is preferable, since the Lender will continue, as always, to provide necessary periodic loan advances and be receptive to developing financial needs. Frequently, the first time the current Lender knows the Borrower is leaving is when the new Lender calls up, the day before the loan closing, for a payoff number. It really can go that smoothly.

However, if the Borrower is in a workout scenario, it is important that the Borrower continues on good terms with his Lender. In this case, the Lender mandates that the Borrower seek a replacement Lender. The Borrower is usually required to report the status of this search, on a continuing basis, to the Lender. It is possible that during the Borrower's search process, even in a workout situation, the Lender will actually grow more comfortable with the departing Borrower. The Lender will see light at the end of the tunnel through the upcoming loan payoff. As directed, the Borrower is making progress toward an ultimate payout of the relationship. The Borrower continues all required reporting to the Lender—no matter what the numbers look like. The Borrower also responds to the Lender's questions and requirements on a timely basis. All of these actions could be the basis for additional loans (advances) by the existing Lender to help the Borrower over the "hump" as a new Lender is in the middle of his credit analysis and approval process.

Keep in mind that the existing Lender does not want to jeopardize the chance of a replacement Lender paying it out, so it may continue, to an extent, to assist the Borrower whenever possible—to include additional and periodic loan advances.

The Borrower should continue to demonstrate to the existing Lender that this relationship is vital to the company's well-being. It may very well be.

Some less obvious reasons for continuing to maintain this relationship, even though the loan may be paid off by another Lender in a short time, are:

- Financial product realignments—New financial products announced by the existing Lender may now be able to address the company's needs, whereas before, these capabilities just were not there.
- Departmental changes—Management or personnel changes within the commercial loan department could favorably impact a loan relationship that was on the way out; it may now be retained under a new management philosophy.
- Risk rating classification changes—It is possible, due to regulatory inspections or improved credit analyses, that the Borrower's risk rating may be improved, changing the loan relationship to an acceptable status.
- Lender mergers or acquisitions—As a result of, or in contemplation of, a financial institution's merger or acquisition, most internal activities are addressed as to how they will mesh within the new institution. On the flip side, use caution—the new owner of a financial institution

(bank) frequently "cleans house" in the commercial loan portfolio within two to three months. *If the Borrower is thinking of leaving this Lender, he should get a head start and commence the search for a new Lender immediately, before he is compelled to leave.*

What also happens some times is that a Borrower's current Lending Officer quits and invites the Borrower to apply at his new institution. Some of the more seasoned Lending Officers do have a following of such loyal Borrowers, who will travel from one institution to another with the same Lending Officer. The LO understands the Borrower's needs and the Borrower is very comfortable with the LO's integrity and experience level. Generally, there is little trouble getting these relationships approved at the new institution.

TAILORING YOUR FINANCIAL COVENANTS

As the Borrower approaches the preparation of a Borrower's terms and conditions sheet (T&C; see later in this chapter), certain elements deserve special planning. The Borrower should address his potential and desired financial covenants (Chapters 1 and 2) with his accountant. Professional advice will enable the Borrower to better focus on his specific situation and goals. The Borrower's T&C will ultimately be provided to potential (and possibly multiple) Lenders. This document will present a potential and comprehensive loan structure agreeable to the Borrower. Of course, it is hoped that Lenders will then respond by providing their formal proposal letters, but they will now know the Borrower's *primary* requirements.

Regarding non-financial covenants: Most of these relate to what the Borrower must or must not do (*without* the Lender's permission). These covenants may include, but are not limited to, types of financial statements, periodic reporting, business changes, other borrowings, environmental and real estate issues, loan defaults, lender visits, insurance requirements, ownership changes, and so on. Many are usually non-negotiable and may resemble boilerplate text from loan agreement to loan agreement.

REALITY CHECK

The Borrower often may not get to see these covenants until a commitment letter is issued. Even then, some may not show up until the Borrower's review of the loan closing documents. The Borrower and his attorney should review these loan closing documents and covenants *well in advance* of the loan closing. It does happen that Borrowers get "locked" into covenants they have never seen, nor had time to negotiate, at the loan closing. Borrowers usually do not want to postpone the closing, so unplanned covenants are accepted. *Don't let this happen!*

Regarding Financial Covenants: The Borrower and his accountant should actually calculate these key ratios as they now exist within the company, in advance of completing the Borrower's T&C. Eight basic covenants are:

1. Gross profit margin
2. Cost of goods sold
3. Current ratio
4. Minimum net worth
5. Debt-to-worth (or tangible net worth)
6. Accounts receivable turns
7. Accounts payable turns
8. Inventory turns

Some of these ratio calculations were reflected in Chapter 1. The Borrower's accountant or financial adviser, or any good accounting book, can provide the Borrower with the necessary ratio formulas. An excellent ratio development and analytical publication is published by the RMA (Risk Management Association). It is called RMA's *Annual Statement Studies*. Not only are formulas provided for a variety of ratios, but ratios peculiar to most industries are provided. For further information, contact the association's Web site at *www.rmahq.org/RMA*.

The base information utilized by the Borrower to determine financial ratios for input into the Borrower's T&C is initially derived from the Borrower's own historical financial statements. From these financial statements, business financial *forecasts* are developed (either extrapolated or new information) from which the *future ratios* may be constructed. Finally, the average ratios within the Borrower's industry, related to the Borrower's size, are located within his industry association's database or in publications such as those mentioned in the previous paragraph. Thus, the past and forecasted ratios and the industry comparables establish base ratios to be considered for insertion within the Borrower's T&C.

If the Borrower's historical financial statement ratios are way off industry comparables, the Borrower must determine why. However, if the Borrower knows the forecast to be accurate, the Borrower's ratios may be appropriate regardless of national averages.

The Borrower should cut himself some slack before placing his final suggested financial ratios within the Borrower's T&C. He mustn't lose sight of the fact that as a Borrower he is presenting financial ratios to a prospective Lender. He is suggesting that the Lender live with his suggested ratios rather than accept those developed by the Lender's credit department.

Deviations to the established financial ratios will happen. If actual profit projections are missed, the net worth may be reduced more than was forecast. Accounts receivable may not be as high as expected, so the current ratio may not be as strong. A couple of key customers may stretch their payments and the accounts receivable turn slows. Inventory has increased, due to a good buy of materials, so the inventory turn may be slower. Anything can, and usually does, happen. The Borrower should then be conservative and, depending upon the probabilities, *consider adjusting preliminary ratio forecasts by*:

- Increasing the accounts receivable turn
- Reducing the inventory turn
- Increasing the debt-to-worth ratio
- Reducing the gross profit margin
- Reducing the current ratio

All of these actions speak for conservatism. If the Borrower's operational results vary from ratio projections, these early ratio adjustments (by the Borrower) may provide the cushion needed so as *not* to be in violation of the Lender's financial loan covenants. Of course, there is the chance that the credit department, and the Borrower, could be very close to each other's numbers. That's good—the Lender will be more likely to accept the Borrower's recommendations as to financial ratios.

These "adjusted" financial ratios, as finally determined, will find their way into the Borrower's T&C. Prospective lenders are usually pleased to see such effort and will consider the Borrower's recommendations.

Let's just cover some additional covenants that could impact financial constraints of the business:

Capital Equipment Purchases (Limitations): The borrower may have to justify requirements for projected capital expenditures. The Lender may have such a restrictive covenant and will usually request from the Borrower a schedule of intended equipment purchases for the year. If the Borrower initially states that he will need $300,000 for new equipment during the year and then buys $500,000 worth, that constitutes a covenant violation. Simply forecast for the year (or even two years), by month, the cost of equipment required (including "soft costs," such as shipping, setup, and so on). Then plug in another few percent for unforeseen items as a cushion in the forecast of equipment requirements. The Borrower *may* wish to further indicate that equipment purchases do not include equipment, or tools, under a certain value. Such purchases are made from operating capital. Again, the Borrower is striving for flexibility. These requirements *must* be made known within the Borrower's T&C.

Officers' Salary May Be a Restrictive Covenant: Lenders like to know what the officers (owners) are paying themselves before and after the loan closing. Be careful here: Lenders look for what they believe to be exorbitant compensation. It is generally reasonable to indicate within the assumptions to the financial forecasts that officers will receive a 10% to 15 % (or whatever) annual gross salary increase. While gross officers' salaries can be determined from forecasts, individual officers' salaries cannot. Lenders may ask for a separate schedule of individual officers' salaries. Excellent business performance may later justify increased salaries or bonuses—with permission from the Lender. Likewise, with developing losses, the Lender may seek to restrict increases in officers' salaries.

Officer Loans: Are they on the company books now, or will you need them in the future? Does the Borrower, or the Borrower's officers, currently have loan(s) outstanding due to the company? The prospective Lender may look to see if there is an executed Note to the company with a stated plan of repayment. Are officers abiding by their individual loan terms? If the Borrower anticipates that such a loan(s) will be necessary in the future for college costs, new residence, and so on, *this should also be noted within the Borrower's T&C.* The Lender will then be (or should be) prepared for such future officer loans. More important, two or three years down the line, the Lender will not be able to say that it was unaware of these needs. Plan ahead and reflect this within the Borrower's T&C.

ENHANCING COLLATERAL VALUES

Yes, collateral is collateral—and it is worth what it is worth. It doesn't get much plainer than that—or does it? Collateral does, however, lend itself to purging, classifying, protecting, and evaluating. We will define "collateral value" more explicitly, and by doing so, values *may* actually be amplified.

While Lenders "file" against selected pledged assets (see Chapter 1), they are taking an interest against *all* of these assets—good, bad, or indifferent. While the Lenders may now "own" all of these assets, they do *not* necessarily loan against 100% of asset values.

The Lender, through his own internal operations, determines what portion of pledged assets are "eligible" collateral, i.e., what percentage is eligible to lend against. These eligible assets should be unquestionably valid, accurate in stated value, quantity, and quality. Eligible assets should be insured, housed in a protected area, and available for Lender's review and validation at reasonable times. The Lender expects timely, accurate, and periodic collateral reporting. This is important because elements of certain pledged assets may be volatile over time. Frequent (and in some cases daily) collateral reporting may be required, as is the case, for example, within asset-based lending.

Especially volatile collateral elements are accounts receivable and inventory. Determining such eligible collateral within a revolving loan structure described as asset-based lending requires specially trained Lender personnel. While initially confusing to the Borrower, actual daily usage clarifies eligibility determination. (Asset-based lending is presented in detail in Chapter 8. The eligible and ineligible collateral flow, along with loan potentials, are clarified there.)

The loan percentage, known as an "advance rate," is applied against the determined eligible collateral, as computed by the Lender, usually prior to loan closing. Advance rates may also be presented within term sheets, proposal letters, and commitment letters. Such advance rates are usually a topic of continuing negotiations between the Lender and the Borrower during the entire relationship. That percentage is then applied toward the specific asset's eligibility value so the actual loan amount can be determined.

The Borrower should consider, with the assistance of his accountant or financial advisers, the appropriate elements of collateral enhancements discussed in the following list. These enhancements may result in the assessment of the total asset, or the eligible portion, to be of more value to the Lender. Value increases loan eligibility. Eligibility increases the amount that the Borrower may borrow.

- **Accounts receivable insurance:** A/R insurance protects the Borrower and Lender against delinquency losses. This insurance may be obtained for both domestic and foreign accounts. With such insurance, ineligible accounts may turn into eligible accounts for borrowing purposes. If accounts are of large value (large borrowing potential), premiums for such insurance can be worthwhile. Your accountant or financial adviser can inform you of companies providing such insurance coverage.

The aging of A/R's may reveal a large number of accounts over 90 days in age, termed "aged receivables." This large delinquency position will detract from the value of the overall accounts and the advance rate against A/R's. Consider, with the cooperation of the account debtor, converting the largest over-90-day account to an amortizing Note format. The debtor will sign a Note for the entire account (or delinquency portion). The Note should also contain a repayment plan. In appropriate cases the customer may also provide collateral support to the Note (see Index—accounts receivable conversion to Note). Then the delinquent account may be removed from the accounts receivable aging. Selectively cleaning up the aging by this method results in an aging reflecting a lesser percentage over 90 days. This by no means indicates that the Borrower cannot continue to sell to this Debtor. In fact, if the entire balance were converted to a Note, three months may pass before the account would again be close to a delinquency situation. Ensure that the Lender concurs with the process of formalizing selected accounts receivable to a Note Receivable. Legal counsel should assist in Note preparation.

The Borrower may consider offering a discount for prompt payment within the billing format. The purpose is to speed up accounts receivable collections, keeping accounts current within the A/R aging. For example, the Borrower may offer terms of "3% 10 days, net 30 days." This means if the debtor pays his bill within 10 days, he may take 3% off of the total amount due. If the debtor does not pay within the discount terms, the entire bill must be paid in 30 days according to the seller's terms. An additional comment on the bill head may indicate that this discount percentage does not apply to shipping charges, only product charges. Of course, the amount of the discount, and other terms of payment, are tailored to the Borrower's calculations to generate the most favorable results. The Borrower's accountant can be of assistance in determining the most practical discount provisions.

The nature of the Borrower's business, seasonal or otherwise, may dictate that account delinquency does not really occur until a period of 120 days (or more) from the billing date. Sometimes lenders are not familiar with an industry and they default all delinquent accounts into the traditional 90-day-and-over grouping. An extension from 90 days to 120 days in *eligibility determination* may add much to a Borrower's available cash flow. Lenders must be schooled in the uniqueness of specified industries in order to provide Borrowers with realistic account eligibility limits. The construction and fabrication industries lend themselves to "progress billings" with overall receivables due in portions (following certain benchmarks of job completion) rather than a single amount. Some Lenders are reluctant to lend against such receivables as it is difficult for a Lender to substantiate that a certain percentage of a job has actually been completed. Specialized or on-site collateral inspections are usually required the Lender.

- **Inventory:** Inventory values (raw materials and finished goods) may be affected by inclusion of excess, obsolete, or unsalable inventory. When a Lender determines that inventory values are impacted by such ineligible inventory, a lower advance rate will be implemented. When an inventory is absent of such items, the overall value of a Lender's advance may be increased. The Borrower should consider eliminating this burden on the eligible inventory. Consider a sale to customers, or even employees, or a take-back to suppliers (may be a restocking charge), make a donation (see accountant for tax advantages) or simply write it off. The message is this: *clean up the inventory to enhance Lender advance rates.*

- Another approach to enhancing inventory values is to contract for an *independent inventory appraisal.* Like real estate and equipment, inventory appraisers are in the marketplace. Most likely your current Lender may be aware of these. Also, you may contact the Commercial Finance Association at (212) 594-3490 in New York City. This association (with regional chapters) is an excellent location to source commercial lenders and associated services (further described in Chapter 9). While inventory appraisers may not be as plentiful as with real estate and equipment appraisers, their operations and valuations are somewhat similar. They may separately value raw materials, work in process, and finished goods. Generally Lenders will lend against eligible aspects of raw materials and finished goods but *not* work in process. Such an appraisal may provide clarifications as to the market value or lesser valuations of an existing inventory. At least, the Lender and the Borrower will be on the same page as far as determining an eligible inventory figure is concerned. Appraisers are usually ordered by the Lender (especially a new Lender). Lenders usually use an internally approved appraiser, so it is best, rather than the Borrower engaging an appraiser, to let the Lender arrange for the appraisal. The Borrower may, of course, obtain his own inventory appraisal absent a Lender's request. Either way, the Borrower will pay for it. The appraiser may recommend certain inventory exclusions, such as printed shipping cartons and catalogs. As a matter of interest, it should be noted that certain elements of raw materials, in certain industries, may actually *increase* in value should these be on an allocation basis.

Machinery and Equipment (M&E): In maximizing advance rates on machinery and equipment, new equipment purchases since the last appraisal should be added to former list of appraised values. Of course, it follows that disposal of equipment should also be deducted from prior values. In unique circumstances, certain pieces of equipment may have actually increased in value since the last appraisal. Examples may be certain types of printing presses and extruding equipment. Generally customers' tooling is not recognized as eligible equipment. An accurate re-appraisal is usually needed by a *new* Lender. Again, it is the Lender who ordinarily arranges for these updates or new appraisals. There will be little room for disputes as the Lender and Borrower review results. Here the decision will be whether the Lender will accept the appraiser's higher orderly liquidation value or the lower "auction value" as the eligible number—the number against which advance rates are applied. The fair market value may also be presented, but it will not be a valuation that a Lender would lend against; they usually seek the lower discounted values. (A fair market value is usually more appropriate to business valuation considerations.) Lenders seek a realistic comfort margin when determining eligible collateral.

Infrequently there is a process whereby an appraiser may "guarantee" to the Lender that a specific amount will be obtained at an auction. This is referred to as a "put." These types of offerings by an appraiser are not routinely promoted, but it's worth asking. It is expected that such an appraisal would be more expensive to the Borrower than the more common formats. Of course, if an M&E appraised value is *guaranteed to the Lender*, such a valuation may result in a preferred advance rate of benefit to a Borrower. Weighing the cost (price of the appraisal) over the benefits (amount of loan proceeds that could be generated by the higher advance rate) is up to the Borrower.

- **Real Estate:** Much like M&E above, the Lender seeks a reasonably current appraisal—usually within the past year or two. As property values do, to an extent, continually rise, it could be to the Borrower's advantage to arrange with a new Lender for an updated appraisal. Most likely this would be a Lender's routine requirement.

Real Experiences!

Don't waste valuable time when you are in the middle of a Lender's credit approval process if you already know there may be potential appraisal complications. These issues can jeopardize your loan approval or significantly delay your loan closing. For example, the owner of a manufacturing plant sought to have his current real estate mortgage Lender taken out by a new Lender for a much better deal. The owner had owned the property for over 20 years. The former Lender had never ordered a flood search. Considerably into the credit approval process the new Lender, according to policy, ordered a flood search and discovered that the Borrower was in a sizable flood plain. Flood insurance of a considerable cost would now be required. The Borrower contested this finding for over two months. Through a re-examination, the authorities finally revised their survey and the property was judged to be outside of the flood plain. The Borrower's real estate deal closed *much later* than was planned and at additional cost to the Borrower.

In another instance, a rural loan applicant felt an eighty-year-old commercial property he acquired at limited cost would be excellent for a commercial storage facility. Certain walls and other structural elements were already in place. The Borrower thought that because of the property's perceived business potential it would appraise well. He really had no basis to support his optimistic commercial property value. The Lender, upon touring the property, quickly determined this was not a deal to follow until the Borrower learned more about his own property. The Borrower then ordered his own appraisal, which came nowhere near the amount to support his loan request. The Borrower definitely lost credibility in this case. Inasmuch as a potential Borrower (or Buyer or Seller) will have to accomplish inspections or appraisals for some

> Lender, at some time, the Borrower should consider doing these up front so he will not be surprised, or lose valuable time. Most Lenders will insist that the Borrower pay for *all* inspections or appraisals as part of the closing costs. As a Borrower, you should arm yourself with relevant and current information before you seek a Lender. Waiting until after the fact will not add to your credibility.

When real estate must be a part of the overall lending package, consider suggesting to a working capital Lender that the Borrower will place the real estate portion of the loan elsewhere (with another Lender). This has the effect of reducing a working capital Lender's overall exposure. This action may also result in an improved risk rating and a larger working capital line or improved advance rates with a working capital Lender. The real estate portion of the loan could then possibly be refinanced through a local thrift or credit union—and most likely at better terms than through a larger commercial bank. For large real estate loans, there are national Lenders that could address such portions. Consider also that the Borrower could be removing a large piece of the working capital Lender's (additional) collateral. In reality, most working capital Lenders really would rather not have real estate as collateral.

Other General Collateral or Loan Structuring Enhancements

- Offer Lender "A" (new Lender) a second position on collateral for which Lender "B" already has a first position (such as real estate). This gives Lender A a second position in that portion of unencumbered equity. This second equity position also increases as Lender B's loan is gradually paid down. Such additional collateral may provide an inducement for Lender A to provide the Borrower with improved advance rates or other concessions elsewhere within the loan structure. This can work with real estate or M&E collateral. *Caution*: Make sure it is not a violation of the Borrower's loan covenants to offer a second position in Lenders B's collateral to the other party.

- While addressing what most likely is a remote future event, the Borrower may offer to increase the amount of assigned life insurance, with the Lender being the beneficiary (see Chapter 5). While not directly affecting the operating terms and conditions of the loan, this demonstrates good faith on the part of the Borrower. This tactic has, in fact, resulted in loan structuring concessions by Lenders.

- Utilizing what is termed as a "step-up agreement," the owner(s) or officer(s) of a business agree to put in additional personal funds, of a specified amount, into the company (equity or subordinated debt due to officers could be negotiable) at a specific point in time. This could be an inducement for the Lender to back off from an unrealistic financial covenant position. Such a covenant may be one of maintaining a minimum net worth. Usually there is a required benchmark that triggers the step-up requirement. An example is the company's financial results falling below certain (negotiated) levels. The contributed personal funds may then be used to reduce Lender debt, pay down accounts payable, or whatever else is negotiated. Identification of the probable sources of such potential additional funds may add reality to the proposal. Sources may include liquidation of personal investments (property or securities), obtaining new mortgages (first, second, or more) on other properties owned, or even involving additional Guarantors.

- While working to enhance the collateral, the Borrower may consider enhancing the *entire* loan structure by attracting additional loan Guarantors. These do not necessarily have to be relatives and friends but may, in fact, be good customers or important suppliers to the Borrower. These outside entities may have a vested interest in the continuing success of the company. They do care and may "step up to the plate" if asked.

- Overall collateral may be enhanced by offering to the Lender the pledge of "intangible collateral." This may involve patents, copyrights, and other intellectual properties (Borrower should check with his attorney and accountant). These types of intangible properties, while having worth, *generally* are not regarded by a Lender as base or eligible collateral (no advance rates). However, they may be assigned to the Lender as simply "other collateral," with no value assigned. Again, a Borrower's commitment is demonstrated and there may be flexibilities from a Lender as a result of such an assignment. The Borrower should be extremely careful in assigning these assets and work closely with his professional advisers when considering this tactic.

Note: There are some unique Lenders that *may* lend directly against selected intangible assets.

Discounting Payments Due at or after a Loan Closing

Depending upon relationships with certain trade creditors, or other Lenders, who are seeking a *full* payoff or a material payment from your loan closing, one collateral enhancement may be interpreted as not having to spend as much of the loan proceeds as was initially expected. In other words, preserve your loan proceeds. Such payments may include debt to a large supplier, the delinquency debt portion to an important supplier, smaller term debt in a current condition, or debt to a former business owner or business associate. After consulting with your accountant, attorney, and business advisers, consider negotiating to pay less than 100% of the debt. *Do not initially offer* to pay 100% of principal and interest. Instead, you might say, "I'll pay you off in cash *immediately* after the loan closing for a 15% (or whatever can be negotiated) discount." Or, "I'll pay you off (a certain number of months or years) early, in cash, for a 15% discount." Again, such a tactic is *not* intended to jeopardize a favorable relationship but may be used selectively on those other "special" relationships.

PUTTING IT TOGETHER—A NEEDS WORKSHEET

The following format is a worksheet that may be tailored to a specific Borrower's requirements. This format assists the Borrower in the development of the size of loans or credit lines to request, determining the supporting collateral, manipulating different advance rates, and calculating the loan proceeds potentially generated. (See following pages for narrative analysis of worksheet.)

CREDIT LINE, COLLATERAL, LOAN & "AVAILABILITY"
9/10/XX DEVELOPMENT WORKSHEET

Johnson Wire, Inc.

Credit Lines **Current Lender / New Lender** **(000's) Collateral, Ineligibles, Eligibility, Availability, Usage**	**Funds Availability**	**Loan Payoffs**
Accounts Receivable: @ 9/1/06	$1,362	
Less: Ineligibles: Over 90 days	$109	
Other: Foreign Accounts	14	
Affiliated Companies	50	
Total Ineligibles	$173	
Net Eligible A/R's	$1,189	
$1,000/$1,500 A/R Availability (x 80%)	$ 951	
Inventory: @ 6/30/06 total $913M		
RM $643 (Inel. $13M) x 55%	$347	
WIP $ 47 (Inel. $47M) x 0%	0	
FG $223 (Inel. $ 0M) x 50%	112	
Other $___ x __% (Inel. $ _ M)	0	
$500 / $600 Inventory Availability	$ 459	
Aggregate A/R + Inventory Availability	$1,410	
Less: Letter of Credit "carve out"	25	Prior Lender
Net Revolving Credit Availability	+ $1,385	$1,219
$2,118 / $2,269 **M&E**, Orderly Liq. Value		
$3,025 x 75%	+ $2,269	1,913
$ 800/ $800 **Real Estate**, FMV		
$1,230 x 65%	+ 800	648
$____/$____ **Other:** $____ x __%	$____	$____

New Cr. Line	**Total Borrowing**			
	Base Availability:		$4,454	$3,780
	Less: Former Lender Payoffs:	—	$3,780	
$4,418 / **$5,169**	**Loan Availability**			
	after **Lender's Payoff:**		$674	

Estimated Closing Costs:	
New Lender Fees: 1% Overall Credit Line	$52
Loan Broker Fee: 1% Overall Credit Line	52
Appraisals (2) + Environmental Asses.	6
Less: Good Faith Deposit Paid	- 2
Legal Fees + Costs: Lender + Borrower	15
Other Closing Costs: (Real Estate, etc.)	6
Total *additional* Funding Usages:	$129
Excess Loan Availability:	$545

This internal form, once initially drafted by the Borrower, should be reviewed by the Borrower's accountant and business advisers. This is a Borrower's internal *working document* and should *not* be presented to a potential Lender. However, the Lender will receive a good portion of this information within the Borrower's T&C, to be discussed later. The format is only a *suggested* worksheet and may be tailored to better meet a Borrower's specific needs.

Narrative Analysis of Worksheet

Revolving Credit Line—new and former: The left margin column indicates first the existing credit line the Borrower has with his *current* Lender. Following the slash (/) is the new credit line sought by the Borrower. The sample indicates that the Borrower currently has a $1M revolving line of credit against accounts receivable and seeks to increase it to $1.5M.

The Borrower came up with the new amount as he calculated his current A/R availability of $951M. Assuming eligible receivables will increase as the company grows, the Borrower wants further room for loan growth (increased borrowings within the credit line). This new credit line total amount ($1.5M) is the amount that would also be placed within the Borrower's T&C (loan request). Of course the Lender, following his own calculations, may either agree with the Borrower or choose to make changes, which would be reflected within the Lender's proposal letter. These changes could be further negotiated should the Lender not fully comprehend the Borrower's collateral or his rational.

The *inventory credit line* is determined in the same way. It is noted on the sample that the inventory value is of a prior date. Numbers are frequently only available periodically; the most recent numbers available were for the six months ended 6/30/06. The inventory value is reduced by the ineligibles *before* applying the advance percentages. These ineligibles could be imprinted packaging materials, obsolete or slow-moving inventory, and/or supplies. In this case there is no cap on inventory borrowing. A cap may be established by the Lender. It means that no matter what the inventory borrowing formulas determine, the Lender will loan *no more* than the cap amount expressed in dollars. This cap may unfavorably impact the Borrower's cash flow, should his forecasts reflect *full* usage of the inventory loan availability.

Credit Line determination on other collateral: Reflected are current borrowings on machinery and equipment and on real estate. The appraisals have been updated with current values as shown. The prior Lender's M&E loan has been paid down to $2,118. Considering the loan availability after the 75% advance rate against the new appraisal of $3,025, the loan value is $2,269. In the cases of M&E and real estate, the new credit line usually matches the actual loan. It is noted that there is no change to the real estate credit line between Lenders. However, the prior Lender's balance of $648M will, against the $800M line, generate some $152M in new money.

At the conclusion of the left-hand column is reflected the total of the old Lender's credit lines ($4,418M)—as well as the total credit lines ($5,169M) now sought from the new Lender.

The far right-hand column reflects the estimated payoffs to the prior lender within the three loans that are now outstanding ($3,780M). These amounts are only estimates because, at the loan closing, there may be additional interest due and possibly even prepayment penalties (see Chapter 5).

The Funds Availability column reflects a running balance as to how the loan availabilities are developing. This concludes at the Total Borrowing

Base Availability (all credit lines), totaling $4,454M. It then reflects (and this is usually the largest expenditure item) the estimated loan payoffs ($3,780M) due to prior Lender(s). Not all Lenders are necessarily paid off at the loan closing; only those with a security position in the *new* Lender's collateral. After all availabilities are calculated, minus the former Lender's payoff, we are left with unencumbered funds (Loan Availability—$674M)—*before* closing costs.

A number of uses are detailed with the last section, Estimated Closing Costs. This section should include loan closing costs as are known or estimated. This area also can include credits for prior deposits, payoffs to other creditors, payment to a Loan broker, debt due to company officers, litigation settlements—for wherever funds are required. It is desirable to achieve, in the final analysis, an "excess" loan availability. This means that, after all is said and done (and paid), the Borrower has funds remaining to be later borrowed (or "drawn down") for working capital or general purposes. Remember, as collateral values change and loan balances are paid down, or increased, the loan availability constantly changes.

STRUCTURING YOUR OWN LOAN TERMS AND CONDITIONS

Now that the Borrower is satisfactorily maintaining his current Lending relationship, has determined where he is within the stages of financing, has developed a working schedule for credit line development and loans required, he is ready to develop his own terms and conditions.

Generally, within the *Lender's* internal credit analyses and pre-loan processing, a document is formulated summarizing the basics of the transaction—at least as is currently envisioned by the Lender. This document is known as a terms and conditions sheet (T&C). In these few pages the basic loan structure is capsulated. By viewing this document, a quick grasp of the key loan details and important offerings are achieved. Further, inasmuch as the format is somewhat generalized nationally, it is relatively easy to make comparative analyses between many Lenders' proposals.

The Borrower, utilizing this recognized format, will now convey to prospective Lenders his most desirable loan structure. As the Borrower investigates potential Lenders, it is to the Borrower's benefit that these Lenders recognize the Borrower's essential requirements. The Borrower's T&C performs this function.

The following is a fictitious financing request from a Connecticut company involved in the wire extrusion business. This company is probably in the third stage of financing (see later in this chapter). The request is to an unidentified Lender. This Borrower's T&C sheet may be sent to a number of potential lenders, either by the Borrower or by his loan broker. It is best to leave the potential Lender's name off of the document in case things get mixed up. In real life, the loan broker often prepares this type of T&C document, with the assistance of the Borrower and his professional associates.

SAMPLE ONLY **SAMPLE ONLY**

JOHNSON WIRE, INC.
FINANCING REQUEST

Proforma Terms and Conditions

CONFIDENTIAL

1. **Borrower:** **Johnson Wire, Inc.**
1246 Liverpool Park West
Manchester, CT 06403

Contacts: Mr. Robert Johnson, President
Mr. Robert Sail, Senior Vice president
Ms. Mary Foley, Chief Financial Officer

2. Secured Credit: $5,169,000
Purpose: Support expanding working capital needs.
Pay off current lender.

3. Type: A. Revolving Line of Credit (
A/R + Inventory)—$2,100,000
(Initial RLC draw estimated at $1,410,000)

B. Equipment Term Loan: $2,269,000

C. Real Estate (First) Mortgage: $800,000

Line of Credit availability up to $200,000 may be carved out of Revolving Line of Credit. Ability required to wire funds to foreign suppliers.
All senior secured debt may be cross-collateralized and cross-defaulted.

4. Expiration/Maturity: Revolving Line of Credit Three (3) Years.
Equipment Term Loan Five (5) Years.
Real Estate Mortgage Ten (10) Years.

5. Repayment Schedule: A. Revolving Loan (Evergreen —Annual Renewals)
B. Seven (7) year amortization schedule, $17,553.44 monthly to include interest. Matures XX/XX/XX. Interest only first three (3) months.
C. Twenty (20) year amortization. $10,301.06 monthly to include interest. Matures XX/XX/XX. Interest only first three (3) months.

6. Pricing: A. Prime Interest Rate + 1%, "0" Float Days (Current bank depository provides Lender with Collected Funds.)

B. Fixed Rate @ 9.5 %

C. Fixed Rate @ 8.5%

7. Prepayment: No prepayment penalties.
No fees for the unused portion of the credit line.

8. Guarantors: All Loans: Robert Johnson and Robert Vail in the aggregate: Limited to $1,000,000 or deficiency; whichever is less.
Fifty Percent (50%) limited guarantee on Real Estate loan through State Loan Development Fund (application pending).

9. Collateral: Accounts Receivable, Inventory and Proceeds
Machinery & Equipment
Real Estate (Main manufacturing plant in Manchester, CT). Garage on adjacent parcel.
Assignment of Life Insurance on Mr. Johnson and Mr. Vail in the amount of $500,000 each.

10: Appraisals: Machinery & Equipment Appraisal conducted XX/XX/XX by Robert Vaughn & Associates of Meriden, CT.
Orderly Liquidation Value $3,025,000.
Real Estate Appraisal conducted XX/XX/XX by C&J Appraisers, Inc. of Danbury, CT.
Fair Market Value $1,230,000.

11. Subordinations: Not applicable.

12. Covenants/Default
Provisions: Annual officers' salary increases not to exceed 15% each annually.
Fixed Asset purchases not to exceed $250M annually without Lender's written authorization. Detailed purchases forecast available.
Minimum Tangible Net Worth of not less than $1,400,000 will be maintained.
Debt-to-Worth not to exceed 6.5 to 1

13. Formulas & Advance Rates:
A. Revolving
Credit Line: Accounts Receivable. 80% of eligible (not over 90 days in age). U.S. Government A/R's to be eligible within the provisions of the Assignment of Claims Act. Employee receivables ineligible.

Inventory: 55% of raw materials, 50% of finished goods inventory. "0"% of work-in-process. Supplies, catalogs, packing and shipping materials ineligible.
An inventory cap is not applicable.

B. Machinery & Equipment:	75% of Orderly Liquidation Value.
C. Real Estate:	65% of Fair Market Value
14. Special Conditions:	An update of the XX/XX/XX Phase 1 Environmental Site Assessment was conducted on XX/XX/XX by Hanover Environmental Services, Inc. of Hartford, CT. The update resulted in non-material findings. Borrower may seek equipment financing credit facilities through the Lender. Borrower will have the flexibility to place such financing (to include equipment leasing) elsewhere.
15. Expenses:	Johnson Wire will be responsible for reasonable, typical out-of-pocket expenses incurred in connection with this refinancing, associated fees, and closing costs. Expenses are not to be incurred until Lender issues, and Johnson Wire accepts, a Commitment Letter.
16. Management Reporting:	Per Requirements of new Lender.
17. Depository Account:	Currently Johnson Wire's area bank wires collected funds to the secured lender. Payroll bank account is maintained locally.
18: Accountant:	(Name, address, phone, fax, and cell.)
19: Attorney:	(Name, address, phone, fax, and cell.)
20: Financial Adviser:	(Name, address, phone, fax, and cell.)
21. Loan Broker:	(Name, address, phone, fax, and cell.)

The preceding represents a *general* terms and conditions sheet, prepared by a Borrower, to inform and induce a potential Lender to meet the Borrower's proposed terms and conditions. The specifics indicated are what the Borrower is trying to achieve—not necessarily what the responding Lender will meet.

At least the potential Lender has a benchmark as to where to start—and the plus is that the Borrower has set the benchmark! In actual practice a Lender will generally try to follow the targets of the Borrower—and if it is a competitive Lender, may even improve on some items. However, the Lender may be precluded from granting certain concessions due to current policies. But it is a very good start for both the Borrower and the proposed Lender.

Let's just review the this Borrower's T&C. We'll cover most items but not necessarily every one. Paragraph explanation numbers that follow match the preceding terms and conditions numbers.

You will note that, under the name of the Borrower, it is indicated that this is a "Financing Request." This Borrower's T&C may ultimately be under cover of the Borrower's (or the Loan Broker's) cover letter. The Borrower's T&C letter may also be an attachment to a Lender's Loan Application.

1. The Borrower and the Borrower's contacts are identified. Reflected are only the key officers (or owners). The personal Guarantors will be listed under #8.

2. The Secured Credit amount represents the *total amount of all loans and credit lines sought*. The word "secured" indicates that qualified collateral will be provided supporting all loan categories. This amount may be expanded upon by adding "plus the costs of loan closing expenses." That is appropriate if a Borrower wishes to finance these expenses rather than having them deducted from loan proceeds. Most Lenders can accommodate this request.

Purpose: It is customary to provide a simple "purpose" statement. This, of course, can be more explicit than indicated in the sample. It may include paying off officer loans or subordinated debt. If the Borrower is paying off another Lender, this should be stated. At this point the specific Lender need not yet be identified. The statement may additionally include: "For loan closing expenses and working capital purposes."

3. The various types of loans sought are identified along with the amount of each loan. These amounts were determined in

concert with discussions with the accountant, the CFO, and other appropriate management and professionals. The total of all items should total the amount reflected under #2. Also, in this section, it is advisable to add other financial services required. The statement, "All senior secured debt . . ." indicates to the proposed Lender that the Borrower does not have a problem for *all* collateral to support *all* debt. Also, if one loan goes into default, it triggers a default on all loans. Such a provision indicates that the Lender's collateral is cross-collateralized and cross-defaulted. Whether the Borrower puts this into his proforma T&C or not, the Lender will usually include it in his T&C. If the Borrower does not have a problem with it, putting this statement in reflects the Borrower's recognition that he must meet the needs of the Lender as well. "Overall initial draw" indicates that while the *Revolving* Line of Credit totals $2,100,000, only about $1,410,000, less any special "carve outs," will actually be "drawn down" from the revolving credit facility by the Borrower at loan closing (approximations are OK). The remainder is available to the Borrower for later usage. The Revolving Line of Credit draw maximum is based upon the loan advance reflected within #13. A Borrower almost never receives 100% of the collateral's value. A lesser amount is calculated to give the Lender a margin of safety. If a Borrower will need funds for future purchases of equipment, he should ask the Lender for a "CapEx" line of credit (capital expenditure). This separate credit line may be approved and the new equipment being purchased will collateralize the loan. Usually advances are up to 75% of "hard" costs. Hard costs exclude shipping, insurance, and installation costs. The credit line is gradually used as new or used pieces of equipment are purchased.

4. The expiration/maturity date of each loan is listed. Revolving Line of Credit will expire in three (3) years. It may, however, be reviewed annually by the Lender to make sure everything is working satisfactorily. Adjustments to the Revolving Line of Credit loan can be made by the Lender and/or requested by the Borrower at any time. In a loan default, loans may be "called"

(immediate repayment required), regardless of the maturity date. While the Equipment and Real Estate loans indicate a five- and ten-year maturity, the actual payment duration (called "amortization") can be (and usually is) considerably longer. A longer amortization is usually of benefit to the Borrower as considerably less cash is paid out monthly for repayment purposes. In that case, the total of payments produced in a longer amortization (longer than the maturity date) results in a "balloon" payment—a larger one-time payment becoming due upon loan maturity.

5. The most favorable Repayment Schedules have been requested by the Borrower. He has, along with this accountant, calculated the payments and determined that the company's cash flow is adequate to service this debt. Interest rates have been determined based upon current marketplace rates and "shaved" a bit to get a better rate from a Lender. The "interest only" comments are a "try for." The rationale is that closing expenses may have reduced the aggregate loan proceeds to be received at the loan closing. Thus, the Borrower does not have the cash he thought he would have to meet planned payoffs and other post-closing expenses. So, for a few months, the entire amount, or a portion, of the new loan principal payments are put on hold by the Lender to ease cash flow. This interest-only period may be from 30 days to one year. This depends upon the size of the deal and the Borrower's other financial obligations. I have seen a year's worth of loan payments put on hold because of serious and unidentified environmental remediation expenses, and everything worked out well. There are many reasons for this arrangement. You can't be faulted for trying, and you could improve your cash flow!

6. As mentioned previously, interest rates ("Pricing") reflected with the Borrower's T&C are based upon the current marketplace rates. The Lenders also relate their rates to the cost of funds and their required margins. Rates are then adjusted (by Lenders) to reflect the perceived risk involved in the loan, the size of the

loan, and possibly the amount of additional bank business that may develop from this particular Borrower. Rates may be fixed or variable (see Chapter 5). The Borrower may check with his accountant, or other associated professionals, about the "going rate" for his type of loan. The Borrower should *reduce* the rate that he determines to be most reasonable by ½ to 1 percentage point. Competitive Lenders may attempt to address the lower requested rate or ultimately the Lender may actually come up to what the Borrower sought in the first place. Then again, the Lender *may grant* the lower rate! It's one of those things. You don't know if you don't ask.

7. Prepayment penalties have been around forever and most any type of loan could be subject to these. See the discussion and possible calculations of this fee in Chapter 5. Some lending institutions promote themselves as having no prepayment fees on any loan. This is, of course, a marketing device, and the Lender may make up this income through a higher interest rate or other fee. If a prepayment penalty is a part of an agreement, and is significant, the Borrower may wish to wait until loan maturity to relieve any such burden. At that time no prepayment fee will be due. It is always advisable to indicate within the Borrower's T&C that "No prepayment penalties" are desired. At least, the Lender may, while still wanting a prepayment penalty, choose a lower-cost penalty due to the Borrower's T&C indication. This is also a good place to enter other restrictions the Borrower wishes to employ.

8. Guarantors: Rather than have the Lender determine who will guarantee the loan and for how much, it is best if the Borrower indicates *up front* what he is *willing* to do. Again, see Chapters 3 and 5 for more information about guarantees. It is noted that, in the sample, CFO Mary Foley is *not* a Guarantor. This may be because she is simply a paid employee without any ownership interest in the company. She may also be a relative of the owners, without material assets, making her guarantee of little value. The Borrower knows the reason and is indicating, by the absence of

her name, that she is not available as a Guarantor. The Lender may question this and try to loosen the Borrower's stance. Frequently an owner's spouse will refuse to provide her personal guarantee. Again, this is an instance where information provided up front may result in the desired outcome. If it is contemplated that the federal government (Small Business Administration), state, or local development agencies will guarantee all, or a portion, of the loan(s), the Borrower should so indicate in this area.

9. Collateral that the Borrower is willing to pledge is listed here. Should the Borrower feel that the Lender will most likely want as additional collateral an Assignment of Life Insurance, for example, that should be so indicated in the collateral section. Be sure to reflect the limits of this life insurance. Without the up-front information from a Borrower, the Lender could seek much more insurance than the Borrower is prepared to provide. See more on the assignment of insurance in Chapter 5.

10. Should the Borrower or other Lenders have conducted previous appraisals, these results should be briefly listed. If these appraisals are older than one to three years, the new Lender may seek updates or even want an entirely new appraisal and a new appraiser. It is to the Borrower's advantage to seek an "update" rather than a new appraisal (see Chapter 3). The update means that the prior appraiser, who is already familiar with the collateral, has only to update his records rather than conduct an extensive new appraisal. The "update" approach could save the Borrower significant expenses.

11. Subordinated debt is debt that the company officers or creditors have agreed not to require repayment on until the senior Lender is paid off. Such debt usually includes debt due to officers. The Lender does not want the Borrower's officers pulling funds out of the company that should be used for working capital. Suppliers and other creditors may be required to also subordinate their debt to this Lender. If certain debt is now subordinated to the Borrower's current Lender, this is the time to indicate to the *prospective* Lender that the Borrower no longer wishes to subordinate this specific debt. Indicate this information under number 11 as follows: "Currently Subordinated Debt in the amount of $250,000 exists. This debt represents two separate loans made by the officers to the company in 2004. These officers request, as a result of this new financing, the developing strength of the company, and its supporting collateral, that this debt be paid off at loan closing." See more on subordinated debt in Chapter 5.

12. Covenants/Default Provisions: The covenants the Borrower elects to include within the Borrower's T&C may include both financial and non-financial covenants. The actual commitment letter from the final Lender will have all of the Lender's boilerplate (standard legal language) covenants as well as those peculiar to the specific Borrower. The Borrower should, by entries placed in this section, highlight what will be important to him: ability to increase salaries, make new equipment purchases as needed, and the like. Also, as regards special financial ratios, the Borrower may wish, *working with his accountant*, to propose certain parameters on these ratios. Of course, following the proposed Lender's analysis, he will also have his own ratios in mind. However, because the Borrower has proposed specifics, the Lender may tend to lean toward the Borrower's request.

Note: When a financial ratio is violated by a Borrower, it sends up a red flag to the Lender that something is happening out of the norm—something that was not planned for at the commencement of the relationship. That is why financial ratios are established (see Chapters 1 and 2). The Borrower usually is required to send in periodic financial statements to the Lender. These statements are analyzed by credit personnel to see if the Borrower is abiding by these ratios.

13. Formulas & Advance Rates: Items B and C under number #13 within the Borrower's T&C, are somewhat standard advance rates. While machinery and equipment *may* be appraised at a fair market value (FMV), the Lender is interested in more

conservative valuations, orderly liquidation values (OLV), or an auction value, sometimes referred to as a "knockdown value." Market value is usually the highest of values. OLV is reduced from FMV, sometimes by as much as 50%. The lowest value is an auction value, which may again be reduced from the OLV. Lenders seek to lend against a *percentage* (formula or policy) of one of these more conservative values. So it is very unusual to lend 100% against the FMV; there would be no safety margin for a Lender. Usually, if a Lender wound up selling the machinery and equipment collateral to recoup his loan, proceeds from such a sale would most likely not reach 100% of FMV. The normal advance consideration is generally 50% to 75% of the equipment value. Likewise, on commercial real estate, 65% to 85% may be considered normal. The reader must recognize that each situation is different and negotiations frequently determine the *final* advance rate. The Borrower should enter an aggressive advance rate on the T&C that will generate maximum loan proceeds. It's all about the marketplace, the Lender minimizing his risk, and the Borrower maximizing his loan proceeds. Likewise, regarding the accounts receivable and inventory, advance rates are developed and approved by the Lender, addressing a number of considerations. See asset-based lending, Chapter 8.

14. Special Conditions refers to additional information points or other requests by the Borrower. If the Borrower feels, through the analyses or other investigations routinely conducted by a prospective Lender, that other important business or collateral concerns will be revealed (positive or negative), he should address these briefly in this section. Revealing the Borrower's position (and his requests) on these points will provide advance guidance to the Lender.

15. Expenses: It is appropriate to reflect the Borrower's perceptions as to what are "acceptable" expenses. *Should the Borrower wish that loan closing costs be added to the loan balance (maximizing loan proceeds at the loan closing) this request should be entered here.* Also, if it is the Borrower's intention that his Loan

Broker be paid directly from loan proceeds, with the check cut by the Lender, this information may also

be provided. Of course, the Loan Broker may be paid later by a regular check from the Borrower. (See About Loan Brokers in Chapter 9.)

16. Management Reporting is where the Lender will *later* indicate the Borrower's periodic reporting requirements. However, within the Borrower's T&C, he may place any relative comments. If no comment is necessary as yet, fine. He may put in a statement similar to the sample. But if the Borrower has no clue what potential lenders may seek, a discussion with his accountant would be valuable. The accountant may deal with many different size companies that utilize various types of Lenders. A small company may not be able to afford an annual reviewed financial statement—only a compilation. Then again, a complete audited financial statement (or "certified") may be too expensive for a medium-size company. In that case, a reviewed financial statement may be considered (see Chapter 1). In many situations, the Lender considers not only the size of the lending relationship but also the loan's risk in order to determine the type and frequency of reporting. Generally it is okay to stay with the current format of the Borrower's financial statement until at least the conclusion of the first year with the new Lender. Then a change may be required by the Lender or requested by the Borrower. There may also be quarterly or monthly requirements for internally prepared income statements and/or balance sheets. If this is a hardship, especially for a company with only an inexperienced bookkeeper, remedies should be addressed. Read Chapter 11.

17. Depository Account: Comments similar to the sample are appropriate. Should a bank, in close proximity to the business, be used for payroll purposes, mention this here. Also, if the company currently uses a payroll service, indicate the name of the service and of the bank where the payroll account(s) will be maintained.

Items 18–21 are self-explanatory fill-ins.

Within a Lender's proposed terms and conditions, *additional specifics* may be addressed. But remember, we are only addressing at this time a *Borrower's* T&C, assisting the prospective Lender to focus on what the Borrower is specifically seeking. This type of Borrower's T&C will go a long way to achieve the Borrower's goals, and will indicate to the prospective Lender that he has a well-informed Borrower.

PROACTIVE SELECTION OF YOUR NEXT TWO LENDERS

Let's say that, for whatever reason, the Borrower wants (or needs) to leave his current Lender, or that the Lender wants *him* out. The process for selecting a new and suitable Lender must now begin.

If the Borrower recognized the danger signals of a deteriorating relationship (Chapter 2) the search for a new Lender may have begun in the previous month or two. Or, if unexpectedly placed in loan workout, the Borrower is now scrambling to "make a deal" with a new Lender within a limited amount of time. Or, finally, it may have become apparent to the Borrower that his company is actually doing quite well. He had received an unsatisfying loan structure in the beginning and now he simply wants to "get a better deal."

The process is somewhat similar under all these circumstances, but there are many subtleties and nuances that can make the difference between an adequate deal and an outstanding deal.

There are a number of sources from which replacement loans, of many types, may be obtained. There are two basic types of commercial Lenders: traditional lenders and alternative lenders. These are identified in some detail, with additional sources provided, within Chapter 9. Suffice it to say, for current purposes, that traditional lenders are commercial and saving banks and certain credit unions, and alternative lenders are all others. Don't be misled—within "all others" there are major players.

First, it is highly recommended that you select at least two prospective Lenders. I don't mean review only two lenders, but rather review many and come up with the *final two* with whom you would like to do business.

Why come up with two final candidates? This way the Borrower will avoid the "eleventh-hour snafu." The Borrower *thinks* he has a loan approval—loan documents may be in process, a loan closing has been scheduled, the Borrower may even be at the closing—and then Murphy's Law kicks in. The new relationship suddenly changes:

- The new Lender decides that he cannot proceed unless the Borrower's personal guarantee is collateralized by his personal residence. The spouse never did want this. The Borrower did tell the Lender up front that a pledge of the residence was not doable.
- The appraisal finally comes in and it's far short of the expected value. Because of the Lender's loan-to-value ratio, there is a significant shortfall of collateral and thus reduced loan proceeds.
- The "risk" has been "re-evaluated" and the interest rate will be increased by 2%.
- A $7,500 loan closing fee is now due—in addition to $10,000 in points already agreed upon. The Lender said the bank put in more time on this request than expected.

Or, the Lender informs the Borrower by phone, *the day before* the loan closing, "I'm really sorry—but my boss said we really cannot do this loan."

Deal killers, all of them, and the preceding are only a sampling. Many Borrowers are forced into a deal that they would have earlier, during their preliminary review process, immediately declined.

But *this* Borrower has been "traveling" with two Lenders (one not knowing of the other), and the second one, which also has approved the loan and is preparing to close, has no material changes within its terms and conditions sheet. A *second* loan closing settlement sheet has *already* been provided by the second Lender. This is a "go"! The Borrower is saved. Those commitments made to certain suppliers and other creditors can now be honored without any problems. Otherwise, it could have been a disastrous outcome. It just makes sense to travel to two approvals, because you never know.

Real Experiences!

For two months this middle-America plastic extruding company was leveraging two prospective lenders, one against the other, attempting to achieve the very best interest rate. One Lender was a national commercial finance company (alternative Lender) and the other was a large regional bank with a local office. The bank had its local Lender visit the business. The bank indicated it would do the best it could—subject, of course, to policy and approved terms and conditions. The commercial finance company had also been making a number of visits to the company from their East Coast offices. Its travel expenses and the time devoted were impressive to the Borrower. The regional bank had the marketing advantage of proximity.

Over time, the Borrower developed an excellent rapport with the commercial finance company's Lending Officer. This Loan Officer was accompanied from time to time by a senior lender, a loan approval authority from the finance company. That was a good sign. It was interested in his business, receptive to ideas, and appeared flexible and especially seasoned in the business of lending.

Final loan proposals were as close as you could get, except the bank was 1/2% cheaper on rate. Based on rate alone, the Borrower accepted the bank's proposal. The Borrower then called the commercial finance company, apologizing and thanking his contact for all of the company's patience, expense, and structuring ideas (which the Borrower had further supplied to the bank to assist in its loan structuring).

At the bank's loan closing, certain loan covenants and structuring elements were unilaterally amended. The Borrower was becoming disillusioned with his selection. Following the loan closing, the bank's attitude had immediately cooled and the lack of loan flexibilities was apparent. There were no prepayment penalties involved.

Considering the timing, what could he do? He had already closed the loan with the bank. He described the situation to the commercial finance company Loan Officer, asking if the company could possibly reinstate its last proposal, even though he had already closed with the bank. Within six weeks the commercial finance company closed the deal. Needless to say, the bank was surprised to receive a complete payoff within six weeks of its closing.

If your gut feeling says your comfort level with one Lender is significantly better than with another Lender, pay attention to it! An interest rate reduction of 1% or less is *not* a reason to ignore these feelings. **Note:** The Borrower thereafter remained with this commercial finance Lender for years, enjoying a friendly and productive relationship.

An initial consideration: The Borrower, together with his professional advisers and attorney, should decide whether a loan broker or the Borrower will do all the legwork:

1. Sourcing and qualifying the preliminary lenders to be reviewed
2. Preparing the financing packages for each reviewing lender
3. Material back-and-forth time with each potential lender answering questions and faxing supporting materials
4. Reviewing all incoming term sheets and proposal letters; analyzing the pros and cons of each proposal
5. Accomplishing all of this within a mutually agreed-upon time frame

Also, there may be a need to prepare a formal business plan. Again, the Borrower may be able to do this with his accountant and company staff. But do they really have the time? Then again, there are professionals who make their living preparing business plans. Read more about this in Chapter 12. Loan brokers generally serve their clients competently and have a good track record with Borrowers and Lenders alike. A Broker can be an indispensable tool in many transactions. Brokers provide fee estimates and are generally hired to perform within specific time frames. Please read Chapter 9 should you seek to engage a loan broker.

In selecting preliminary Lenders through which to place commercial loan applications, the Borrower should consider the following basic concerns:

Financial Stability of the Lender: If considering commercial banks, thrifts, or credit unions, the Borrower could obtain financial statements (annual reports and/or quarterly reports) by directly contacting the financial institutions. The Borrower's accountant may review these reports and provide any cautionary advice to the Borrower. Also regarding commercial banks, thrifts, and credit unions, the Borrower may wish to contact the following rating companies: Veribanc at *www.veribank.com* and Bauer Financial, Inc. at *www.bauerfinancial.com*.

While the FDIC operates a toll-free hot line at (877) 275-3342, it does not "rate" financial institutions. It can only indicate whether an institution is FDIC insured and active.

Note: FDIC also suggested contacting the aforementioned two firms for rating information.

If the Borrower, or the Borrower's professional advisers, have heard of any regulatory difficulties with regard to a potential lender, it is best to reconcile these to reality. The Borrower does not want to be in the middle of the loan approval process when the Lender is taken over or the doors are shut.

Note: For the Borrower's future reference, at the end of the financial institutions' annual reports is a list of directors and senior officers. Usually the senior lender and/or senior credit officer is identified. This person's identity could come in handy in the future should one have to go to the executive committee to resolve an issue.

Size of Institution: Is this Lender large enough to provide adequate credit facilities? If it is a small city bank or state bank, a credit requirement of $2,000,000 to $5,000,000 may be too much for it to handle. The Borrower doesn't necessarily want to be the largest loan in the portfolio (too high of a profile should there be difficulties). For a loan from $100,000 to $500,000, or possibly to $1,000,000, the small local bank may be just fine—if it makes commercial loans at all. For larger credit lines, over $4,000,000 or so, the larger regional or national lenders are ones that could effectively address a Borrower's needs. There are a few select lenders in the country that routinely address mega-million-dollar loans. In some cases, a number of these lenders will together "subscribe" for only a *portion* of the larger loan (forming a syndication), thus spreading risk among the many participants.

Relationship or Transaction Oriented: A relationship-oriented lender not only seeks to fulfill the Borrower's primary need but also cross-sells most of its other services, emphasizing to the Borrower that he is part of the family. The transaction lender, however, seeks to provide a line of credit, term loan, or a mortgage, whatever is *specifically* sought, and that's the end of it. This type of Lender selection is determined by what the business owner feels his needs will be in the near and medium term—does he want a relationship or just the transaction?

Specific Lender Specialties/Capabilities: Does the potential Lender fulfill requirements by having an asset-based lending group, offer lines of credit, or have a leasing and/or factoring division? Do loan accommodations require an annual "cleanup"? Smaller Lenders are frequently able to handle only moderate credit lines, term loans, and mortgages, and offer few commercial services.

Wide Range of Support Products: Does the Borrower require a wire transfer department (to receive funds in or transfer funds out, even overseas)? Will letters of credit be required for local or worldwide credit arrangements? How about business credit cards for selected members of the Borrower's business? Will the Lender provide personal services for principals of the Borrower? If minimal support products are required, a smaller lender may be fine. But considering future growth, and the financial requirements of such growth, the Borrower may want to rethink the Lender's size.

Loan Guarantee Programs: Is the Lender a Preferred or Certified SBA Lender? Does it have knowledge pertaining to state, county, or community development grants, loans, and loan guarantees? Such programs can make the difference between a loan approval or a turndown. (See more on such guarantees in Chapter 8.)

Industry Specialists: Some larger regional banks are prominent as specialists in selected industries. They do very well concentrating on these special Borrowers. The Borrowers are usually very comfortable in these relationships in that the Lender is completely knowledgeable as to the needs and peculiarities of an industry. For example, there are lenders on the Atlantic and Pacific coasts, and the Gulf Coast, who specialize in the fishing industry. Likewise, in the Midwest, lenders specialize in agriculture, meat packing, and poultry processing. The timber industry is well represented in the Northwest and northern New England. The entertainment industry also has specialized Lender representation.

Lender Well Regarded: Ask the potential Lenders for commercial customer and professional references. These lists are usually available. Also, the larger accounting firms within the area are usually knowledgeable as to the Lenders and their offerings—call a few.

Note: Do not ask the *current* Lender, the one the Borrower is leaving, for potential new lender referrals. *The Borrower should keep his specific prospecting details confidential.* Likewise, at this time, a prospective Lender does *not* have permission to call the Borrower's current Lender. Let the prospective new Lender do its own due diligence.

Lender Credit Inquiries: Banks are required to respond to general credit inquiries, providing a minimum of information: "Yes, ABC Company, Inc., does maintain accounts with us. Balances are in the low five figures, a secured loan relationship exists in the middle six figures, and accounts are handled as agreed." The inquiring party is then usually asked the reason for the inquiry, and guidelines may require a response: "Our bank is considering a credit facility for this company." Words are chosen very carefully, and this established protocol is usually observed nationally.

A problem with this process, from the Borrower's viewpoint, is that the current Lender is quick to identify that a Borrower is seeking to move the relationship. If the current Lender is not aware of these Borrower actions, such an inquiry may be transmitted immediately to the local Loan Officer. Questions will be raised. "Why is he leaving, should we curtail the credit line, and what did we do wrong?" The current Lender could then make life even more complicated for the Borrower. It is best not to authorize the new reviewing Lender to call the current bank. At this time the new Lender should be able to get enough preliminary information from the reports of national credit agencies and state records. Most Lenders subscribe to these credit information services.

Convenience Doesn't Count: In the Borrower's selection of a Lender for a business lending relationship, proximity of the Lender should be of minor concern. (Where a payroll account is to be housed is a different story. A bank in the immediate area is perfectly all right for the convenience of employees.) The Borrower may ultimately determine that the optimum new Lender is located out of state or across the country. With online banking, computers, and videoconferencing, a distant Lender can seem almost next door. *Pick the Lender—not the geography!*

PS: Make sure you like the people, too!

Stages of Business Financing

Where is the Borrower positioned in the hierarchy of business financing maturity?

Seed Financing: Small amounts of funding to substantiate concept or qualify for startup capital.

R & D Financing: Tax-advantaged partnership set up to finance product research and development.

Startup Financing: Provided to companies completing product development and initial marketing.

First Stage Financing: Company has expended its initial

capital. Now requires funds for full-scale operations and sales.

Second Stage Financing: Working capital for initial expansion of a company that is producing and shipping. Company may not yet be profitable.

Third Stage or Mezzanine Financing: Major expansion of company whose sales volume is increasing. May be at break-even point or profitable.

Bridge Financing: When a company plans to go public (within six months to a year). Funds may be used for restructuring of stockholder positions or other interim concerns.

Lenders recognize the preceding segmentations within the financing ladder and use such terms in the financial arena. Over the years, a niche has been established by a variety of Lenders for almost every situation.

> This is not the time to provide detail—only an overview. As Lenders become seriously interested, they will (during their due diligence credit phase) ask for more details in most all areas. Each party, the Borrower and Lender, are developing first impressions.

Put Prospective Lenders to the Test

If the Borrower has followed the progress of suggestions as presented within this chapter, this is the status of the Borrower:

- Still with his current Lender
- Tailored financial covenants have been calculated to his best interests
- Collateral values have been enhanced and improved where appropriate
- A Needs Worksheet has been developed
- The Borrower has structured his own terms and conditions
- Borrower has selected a number of *potential* Lenders (Chapter 9) and is ready for the interview process

Following the completion of the preceding items, to the extent the Borrower and his accountant deem necessary, the Borrower may now prepare for meetings with a series of what *appear* to be qualified Lenders.

The purpose of these meetings is to determine the extent of their legitimate interest. Before inviting potential Lenders to the business site, the Borrower should prepare a "lender's overview" package for each Lender's representative attending the meeting.

This lender's overview package (no slides or transparencies—only hard copies) is really no more than a mini business plan, and is similar to a press kit. Keep each of the following items to *one or two* pages (consider "bullet" formats)—do not staple. *Each* business segment sheet(s) will be handed out separately during the meeting. By meeting's end, each guest will have received a *complete* package.

- **Management Team:** Brief key management profiles (one paragraph each), organizational chart, general employee information, and union involvements, if any.
- **Company Summary:** Nature of business, short history, stages of development, and prognosis for the future.
- **Product Lines (or Services):** Show-and-tell is OK here. Display products or hand out promotional materials. An *overview of operations/production* may be given by the plant manager with a local plant tour following. Do not commit to visit distant, off-site facilities, as the agenda could be compromised. Distant locations may be viewed later in the review process. Discuss private label and proprietary products, patent features, applicable licenses, and pertinent regulations.
- **The Market:** Nature of industry. Borrower's size, share, and growth potential. Key competitors and the Borrower's competitive edge.

Note: Such brief summaries of the basic business functions will assist the Lender in its credit write-up function. The Borrower has done much of the work for the Lender. In fact, much may be extracted verbatim by the Lender into the request for loan approval. This is to the Borrower's benefit—the Borrower is selling himself.

Additional items and information to provide for the lender overview:

- A sheet of company *business cards* may be attached within each package.
- *From your accountant:* If possible, the Borrower's accountant should be available for the financials presentations. If not, a knowledgeable member of the staff (or financial consultant) should be the presenter and answer questions. Cash-flow and profitability forecasts, covering the period of the proposed loan, and a brief historical financial summary will be presented at this time. Upon advice of the accountant, it is usually appropriate to include the most recent Balance Sheet. These items *will not be included in the package* but will be provided *later* during the meeting. Otherwise, Lender participants will be reading the financials and not paying attention to the presented information. **Note:** Financial forecasts should be prepared on the basis that the loan request *was approved* and loan proceeds are *now reflected* within the Borrower's cash flow.
- **The *Borrower's* Terms and Conditions Sheet:** This T&C will not as yet be included within the Lender's Package. This will be handed out later in the presentation as discussed later in the chapter.

The Invitation

Each Lender will be invited to the Borrower's business for a half-day meeting—preferably in the afternoon.* It is very important that this first meeting be conducted *at the business site*, not the Lender's office, because:

- The Borrower controls the visit.
- The visit is conducted without interruptions.

---

*The afternoon provides more of a consistent business time frame, avoiding late arrivals, coffee breaks, and lunch breaks. Refreshments, such as cold drinks, coffee, and cookies, should be available at all times during the meeting at a side table. Do not try to schedule one Lender in the morning and another in the afternoon. Invariably there are overlaps, early and late arrivals, and general confusion. This is not needed when establishing first impressions.

Lenders will be verbally invited by the president or senior officer of the company. If the senior officer of the company is not comfortable with inviting Lenders, the financial adviser or accountant may do so. Should a loan broker be engaged, the broker may wish to invite each Lender to his own independent meeting.

Provide at least a couple of weeks' notice, if possible, as Lender's calendars are usually backed up for about that period. It is worthwhile to suggest that the Lender bring along his credit analyst and, if available, the commercial loan department head. Attendance of the higher ranking loan or credit officers should be sought. Frequently, these more senior officers look forward to getting out of the office to visit new loan prospects with the Loan Officers. Give them the opportunity. Usually the more "takes" on the business the better. At some point in the future these individuals may have some say in the future of the loan request. They have been to the company and will remember both the efforts that went into the presentation and the business competencies exhibited.

When inviting the Lender to the company, provide only the bare minimum of information:

- Who you are and your status in the company.
- Size of loan request.
- Type of loan(s) requested.
- Purpose of loan(s).
- Repayment scenario.
- Timing of loan request (estimated time of loan closing). Give at least 60 days for a "normal" time frame. Actually closing could take up to 90 days, but an approval may be possible within 60 days.
- Explain that you are making afternoon presentations at your business site to interested *and selected* Lenders.
- Ask other senior lenders, credit officials, and analysts to attend.
- Arrange a specific appointment (1:30 P.M.) and provide directions.

Frequently, a Lender will say, "Well, I really don't have that kind of time. Why don't you just send in your package and I'll have a look at it?" The Borrower should not do this—it's a poor second choice. Prepare your response in advance. The Borrower should respond along the lines of, "Our on-site presentation is important to us and we expect it will be important to the Lender we select. This time away from your office also gives *us* time—time to evaluate the Lender who may win our business! It could be well worth your while."

The Agenda

Prepare a typed agenda for the presentation:

- A one-page agenda should be headed up by the names and titles of Lender guests first and then the attending Borrower's officers and personnel.
- Copy enough agendas so *all* participants will receive one.
- In this order, identify agenda bullet points: The Management Team, Company Summary, Product Lines (or Services), and The Market. Of course, if there are other unique aspects to the business, agenda items may be added.
- Current borrowing relationship (only in *generalities*—see the next section in the chapter).
- Borrower's terms and conditions sheet.
- Add a note on the agenda that supplemental reports provided, at the end of the meeting, will include a brief financial history, financial forecasts, and a Balance Sheet.
- Plant tour—conclusion.

Before each individual presentation of an agenda item, hand out only the appropriate segment sheet(s), as discussed earlier in the chapter. The guests then cannot read ahead to other agenda subjects.

THE MEETING

General Meeting Flow: The Lender will attempt to rush the Borrower to get to the details of the loan request (detailed within the Borrower's T&C). It will be much more advantageous for the Borrower to discuss agenda items in the order presented. The Borrower's T&C is on the agenda and will be addressed in good time. Questions will be welcomed at the end of *each* agenda topic:

- Introductions all around.
- Housekeeping: Restrooms, refreshments.
- Pass out agendas.
- Presentations by Management Team: Management Team, Company Summary, Product Lines (or Services), and The Market.
- The accountant presents a brief financial history, a current Balance Sheet, and cash-flow projections (which include approved loan proceeds).
- Current Borrowing Situation: The Borrower will *verbally* highlight the current lending situation, type of loans he now has, and the amount of debt outstanding. Why he is leaving the (unidentified) current Lender. The Borrower will not disclose his *actual* current Lender, the interest he is paying on the loan, or collateral advance rates. Of course, the *actual* situation rules—but such information is usually *not* divulged until a proposal letter is received and accepted by the Borrower. The potential Lenders should know only generalities about the Borrower's existing relationship.

The one important question the Borrower may be asked from the proposed Lender is "Why are you leaving your current Lender?" The Borrower's answer should be honest and diplomatic. If not under duress to do so, simply state that you do not have to leave, but as a growing company you must evaluate alternative financing proposals.

- The appropriate person will then pass out the Borrower's terms and conditions (T&C) sheet to all present. It should be explained, up front, that this is how the Borrower envisions a deal that *may* be acceptable. Time permitting, the T&C will be discussed. Usually the Lenders will home in on certain aspects of the Borrower's loan request. In the normal course of events, the Borrower may anticipate *verbal* T&C challenges from guests, but must not, at this very early stage, agree to anything. However, note all comments, as these may be valuable in T&C editing or later adjustments.

Once in a while the questi0n will be raised, "What are you going to do if you don't get the loan?" The answer to consider is that the Borrower may not get the loan from this prospective Lender, and the Borrower may not get the loan on the specific terms he would like, but he will get the loan. The Borrower recognizes that the Lender and the Borrower both have choices.

Now just a few questions for the Lender:

- Describe the loan approval process.
- What is the loan amount these Lenders can authorize?
- Who is on the loan committee, and how often do they meet?
- Do you loan to other industries similar to this one?
- Who would be the account officer?
- With what office would I work?
- Do I have to keep my operating and payroll accounts at your bank?
- What is the timing of a proposal letter, loan approval, and commitment letter

OK—Now *guide* the Lender back to the agenda:

- Plant tour.
- The Borrower may then suggest that the Lender take the entire package, evaluate the request, and get back to the Borrower. The Borrower, if asked, will provide a time limit of one week to gauge the Lender's interest—two weeks for a proposal letter.
- The Lender has now experienced a comprehensive overview of the Borrower's operations and collateral involvements. Importantly, the potential Lender has also met key members of management.
- It is time to seek the Lender's reaction. "So, would you like us to be a customer of your commercial loan department?"
- Conclusion: "Thank you for coming and we look forward to your positive response."

At the conclusion of the preceding scenario, the Borrower may now ascertain:

- A Lender's real interest in a relationship with his company
- Lender's place of authority within the institution
- Extent of personal rapport (*very important*)
- Problems to be resolved
- Risks to be mitigated

The information presented here, supplemented by Lender's personal observations, should enable the Lender to respond to the loan request quickly and intelligently.

Again, the Borrower should use the results of these preliminary meetings to prudently amend and edit the Borrower's T&C (for future Lenders), as well as meeting content, striving to address critical and relevant issues

If a Lender declines to proceed, the Borrower should request a turndown letter. This should include (and you should ask for) reasons for the turndown. Definitive turndown letters help the Borrower to improve his T&C sheet and Lender presentations, and may lead him to re-address business strategies, or even consider applying for certain supporting loan guarantees from other sources (Chapter 8).

Finally, a prospective Lender's response to the Borrower's terms and conditions sheet will reveal areas where one Lender may be non-responsive while another will consider the Borrower's requirements as reasonable.

Following a few of these perspective Lender meetings, the Borrower will begin to zero in on two Lenders with whom he feels most comfortable—those who passed the *Borrower's test.*

EVALUATING PROPOSALS RECEIVED

Preparing the Needs Worksheet and the Borrower's T&C, discussed earlier in this chapter, provide a road map representing a fairly accurate "overlay" to a Lender's favorable response (a proposal or term sheet).

Between these first Lender meetings and the receipt of a term sheet or proposal letter from perspective Lenders, the Lenders may request considerably more support data. This additional support data only takes these Lenders to the point of determining whether or not they wish to issue a term sheet or proposal letter to the Borrower. If a term sheet or proposal letter is successfully executed between the parties, even more support information will likely be needed during the Lender's conclusion of the approval process. If the loan is then approved, the Lender will normally issue a commitment letter. If a Lender says to a Borrower, "You know the terms of approval, let's save time and just go to loan closing," it is recommended that the Borrower wait a day or so longer and indicate the need for a commitment letter. *This commitment letter will detail the terms of the loan before the loan closing to avoid surprises.* Also, as stated previously in this book, make sure all loan documentation is reviewed by the Borrower, and his legal counsel, *before* the loan closing—not *at* loan closing.

If the response is a decline, follow the guidelines within the previous section for the next Lender's presentation. If a term sheet or a proposal letter is received from a number of perspective Lenders, it's time to separate the wheat from the chaff.

Real Experiences!

The family patriarch died after spending the later years of his life training his sons to take over his construction business. One son was now responsible for obtaining Lenders receptive to the business's need for expansion. This son had little actual business finance experience. While the father did build up some borrowing relationships, banks were not now willing to commit to the son for the larger amounts. Inasmuch as most commercial loan contracts are of a duration of one to three years, the Borrower could be "living" with the Lender for a long time. The son engaged a loan broker, who attracted a *number* of alternative Lenders as well as a couple of other banks.

The son spent almost one year trying to select a Lender for the business. This extended time frame was frustrating to these competing Lenders. Most dropped by the wayside. Finally he selected a Lender that was out of the son's geographical area and not normally recognized as a material contender in the marketplace. However, the patience (and instruction) provided by this Lender clued the son in that this was someone he could work with over time. The patient selection of this Lender paid off, as the business has since concluded a number of loans with this single Lender. Diligence in Lender selection provides multiple rewards.

A Comparative Loan Proposal Worksheet

A simple comparative worksheet usually does the trick fairly well. The following Loan Proposal Components & Comparative Analysis worksheet addresses the more customary components of a Lender's term sheet or proposal letter. This format also works for evaluating commitment letters. Items specific to your loan or industry may not appear and should be considered separately. However, the Borrower may wish to add such concerns at the bottom of the worksheet, to ensure they are not forgotten.

Loan Proposal Components & Comparative Analysis

(Fee comparisons at end of format)	*Borrower's* T&C	Lender "A"	Lender "B"
Date Received			
Overall Credit Line (all loans total)	$		
Maturity Date			
Response Required By (date)			
A/R Revolving Line(A/R Financing)	$		
Revolving Line of Credit Commitment (size and fee)	$		
Revolver Interest Rate	%		
360 or 365 day year (expressed in days)			
Prepayment Penalty (formula)			
Accounts Receivable Line	$		
Advance Rate	%		
Ineligibles (over X days): Usually 90 days or over	Days		
Other Ineligibles			
Other Ineligibles			
Collection Days (0–6) 3 Average	Days		
A/R Collection: Lockbox or In-kind			
Exclusions:			

Letter of Credit Availability (L/C)	$		
L/C amount carved out from A/R Loan Availability? (Yes or No)			
A/R Loan Caps (if any)	$		
Government A/R's (% or $ Limit?)			
Foreign A/R's (% or $ Limit?)			
A/R Insurance Requirement (Yes/No)			
A/R Insurance premiums	$		
# Of Audits per Year (1–4)			
Estimated Cost per Audit (Per diem + expenses)	$		
Inventory Line of Credit	$		
Inventory Loan Cap	$		
Raw Material Line of Credit	$		
RM Advance Rate	%		
Work in Process (WIP) Line of Credit	$		
WIP Advance Rate	%		
Finished Goods Line of Credit	$		
Finished Goods Advance Rate	%		
Ineligibles:			
Ineligibles:			
Machinery & Equipment Line / Loan	$		
Interest Rate (Fixed or Variable)	%		
Appraisal Valuation Type: Fair Market Value, Orderly Liquidation, or Auction?			
Advance Rate	%		
Maturity Date			
Amortization (Months)			
Monthly Payment (Interest + Principal)	$		
Balloon Payment?	$		
Prepayment Penalty? (Formula)			
Interest Only Option?			
Restrictions on M&E Purchases?			
Capital Expenditure Line of Credit?			
Real Estate Loan(s)	$		
Interest Rate (Fixed or Variable)	%		
Appraisal Valuation Type: Fair Market Value or Other			

Appraiser Selection (Lender/Borrower)			
Estimated Cost of Appraisal	$		
Advance Rate (Loan to Value)	%		
Loan to Value Requirement	%		
Amortization (Months)			
Monthly Payment (Interest + Principal)	$		
Balloon Payment?	$		
Interest Only Option?			
Prepayment Penalty? (Formula)			
Environment Inspection Requirement?			
Est. Cost: Transaction Screen	$		
Est. Cost: Phase 1 Site Assessment	$		
Survey Requirement / Cost	$		
Flood Search Requirement / Cost	$		
Septic System Inspection / Cost	$		
Asbestos / Lead Inspection / Cost	$		
Recording Fees	$		
Tax Escrow Account Required?			
Financial Loan Covenants			
Accounts Receivable Turn: Reflected as either # of times annually or in days			
Accounts Payable Turn: (Same as above)			
Inventory Turn: (Same as above)			
EBIT: Earnings Before Interest & Taxes	$		
EBITDA: (same as above but add Depreciation and Amortization)	$		
Minimum Net Worth	$		
Minimum Tangible Net Worth	$		
Debt / Net Worth (Sample: 5/1)			
Debt/ Tangible Net Worth (Sample: 3/1)			
Current Ratio			
Minimum Working Capital	$		
Working Capital Ratio			
Debt Service Ratio			
Interest Coverage			

Major Fee Comparisons			
Good Faith Deposit	$		
Commitment Fee	$		
Loan Application Fee	$		
Loan Origination Fee	$		
Non-Usage Line Fee	$		
Loan Broker Fee	$		
Legal Fees Estimate (Lender)	$		
Legal Fees ("Cap") (Lender)	$		
Legal Fees Borrower (Estimate)	$		
Audit Fees (Revolving Financing)	$		
Credit Reports / Background Checks	$		
Free Business Checking Account?			
Free Business Payroll Account?			
Charge Cards for Company Officers			
Lockbox Fees	$		
Prepaid Interest Due at Loan Closing	$		
Other General Comparisons			
Assignment of Patents			
Assignment of Life Insurance			
Assignment of CSV—Life Insurance			
Guarantees (Personal)			
Collateralized Guarantee (Home)?			
Guarantees Personal—Others:			
Guarantees (SBA, State, Local, etc.)			
Other Interest Only Accommodations			
Interest "Caps" and "Collars"			
Letter of Credit—Requirements			
Loan Participation Requirement?			
Mezzanine Loan Required?			
Officer Salary Restrictions?			
Shareholder Distribution Restrictions?			
Stock Pledge			
Capital Infusion Required?			
Estimated Loan Closing Date			
Loan Closing Location			

Explanations and/or suggestions for many of the line items in the worksheet are found within this book. However, I would like to address some selected items.

Response Required by Date: While the Date Received is important for record purposes, the "Response Required by" date is more important. Frequently within a term sheet or proposal letter there is a time limit within which the Borrower must accept or decline the specific offer. The time limit can be as short as one day, or a week or two. This varies depending upon the policies and aggressiveness of the Lender. If there is hardly any time to get it back to the Lender, it means he wants your deal "off the street." He does *not* want you to show his proposed deal to other competitors. This restricts the time required by the Borrower's to conscientiously interview, and analyze, other borrowing opportunities. Taking into account that accepting or declining is the Borrower's decision, and that the final result is living with one Lender for a number of years, the decision should *not* be made without due consideration.

Will this aggressive Lender disappear from the Borrower's landscape if the Borrower does not respond by the due date? Not really. Most all Lenders seek new business and recognize that Borrowers will necessarily negotiate with more than one Lender. It's just plain common sense. One aggressive Lender is not the only game in town. That type of Lender obviously wants the Borrower's deal. The Borrower simply must indicate that the time frame provided is not realistic to conduct a thorough review of opportunities. The Borrower will get back to the prospective Lender when he has concluded his evaluations.

Accounts Receivable (A/R) Revolving Line of Credit: This area pertains to a specific type of secured lending. It is frequently called "revolving financing" or "commercial financing." Briefly, this is where a Borrower may borrow, on a daily basis if he wishes, against certain pledged and eligible collateral. This financing mechanism is discussed in detail within Chapter 8.

Inventory Line of Credit: Usually within a component part of a larger line of credit (usually within revolving financing), an inventory line of credit may be specifically developed for the Borrower. Generally, however, not all aspects of the Borrower's inventory may be eligible collateral. Even then these individual components may carry much different advance rates. As mentioned previously, it is not unusual for a Lender to provide a zero advance rate toward the work-in-process inventory, because it is usually very difficult for a Lender (through auction) to get any realistic return on inventory that was in the production process when seized by the Lender. The Loan Proposal Components & Comparative Analysis worksheet requires the Borrower to identify the amount of the overall inventory line of credit that he seeks. The loan proceeds reflected within a forecasted cash flow may be partially derived from the eligible inventory collateral.

The following item, **Inventory Loan Cap**, is usually an area of surprise to the Borrower when it appears within a Lender's proposal. It means that no matter how much eligible inventory a Borrower has, and regardless of what the loan availability works out to be once advance rates are applied, the Lender will *not* loan more than "X" dollars against inventory. This cap protects the Lender against placing too much reliance on the inventory portion of the loan. Even segments of the inventory, such as raw materials, work-in-process, and finished goods may have their own individual caps. In my experience, Lenders get "burned" more on inventory collateral than most any other type of collateral. This is why lower advance rates and inventory loan caps may *both* apply.

Recognizing that the Lender most likely will be placing a cap on inventory, it is desirable for the Borrower to indicate (verbally or within the Borrower's terms and conditions) a cap amount he can live with. In the sample Borrower's T&C in this chapter, a cap rate is *not* reflected. Generally a Borrower would not volunteer information that he is amenable to a loan cap. If an inventory loan cap does become an issue, the Borrower, in order to achieve his forecasted cash flow, must ensure that the resulting cap amount is at, or exceeds, his forecasted *borrowings* from inventory. The Borrower should consider seeking a cap above his basic needs to allow for company growth and increased borrowing requirements. It is not infrequent for the Borrower and Lender to negotiate this item quite strongly. Also, it is an effective negotiating and leveraging point when working Lender proposals against each other. More on that tactic later.

Machinery & Equipment Line/ Loan: Generally a credit line is not sought against a specific piece of equipment, but rather a fixed loan amount is approved against all eligible equipment. This loan amount will be determined based upon appraised values and a realistic advance rate. The advance rate is based upon the makes and models, the age of the equipment, its current condition, and the current or probable market for resale (or auction). If the Borrower has plans to purchase *additional* equipment during the course of the lending relationship, a capital expenditure line of credit ("CapEx" line), explained earlier in this chapter, may be an appropriate consideration.

Real Estate Loan(s): Similarly, there is usually not a real estate "line of credit" but rather a specific real estate loan (which could actually include a number of properties). The *exception* may be the investor in investment properties, such as three- to five-unit apartment buildings. A financially strong Borrower who specializes in such properties could be approved for a line of credit to purchase qualified properties when they appear on the market. A line of credit, in this instance, would enable the Borrower to make immediate purchase commitments, rather than waiting for the Lender to process individual loan requests.

Financial Loan Covenants: The factors behind these covenants are more fully discussed elsewhere within this chapter. The Lender, it seems, will most likely include a financial covenant or two within his proposal that may not have been within the Borrower's terms and conditions format. As the Borrower analyzes these competing Lender offerings, he will be surprised at the covenants some Lenders have chosen to include and others have not. Also, there may be a wide range of precise covenant figures among competing Lenders.

Major Fee Comparisons: Some Lenders utilize different terminology for similar fees. Comparative analyses can usually clarify and reconcile any ambiguities. The whole idea, of course, is to *minimize Lender fees through negotiation*. One thing to remember is that a commitment fee should *not* be paid until:

- The Loan has actually been approved by the Borrower. Some Loan Officers tend to prematurely report to the

Borrower that their loan has been approved when, in fact, it really has not. These Loan Officers are just anxious, and as a result, serious misstatements have occurred. Confirm *approvals.*

- A *signed* commitment letter *has been issued* to the Borrower by the Lender.
- The Borrower, his legal counsel, and financial adviser(s) have reviewed and accepted all elements of the commitment letter.
- Those areas *not acceptable* to the Borrower must be further negotiated and reconciled *before* signing the commitment letter. If changes are agreed upon, a new commitment letter should be issued by the Lender with a new date, no pen changes.

Other General Comparisons: Of course, only those items that apply to the Borrower's specific loan situation are appropriate. Line items presented may also ignite further thoughts in the Borrower as to further "improving" his loan structure. Be careful—the Borrower does not want to give the Lender more ideas on how to restructure the loan. These comparative items *should not* be discussed, or negotiated, with the Lender until cleared with the Borrower's legal counsel and/or financial adviser.

Leveraging Lenders—Caution

Once the prospective Lenders are down to two, they most likely have each issued a term sheet or a proposal letter. Their offers have received comparative analyses by the Borrower and his associated professionals to determine the best deal. Following this, the Borrower may need to do some leveraging. Both proposing Lenders will have portions of their proposal that are more attractive than the other Lender's. *The Borrower's job is to work out the best deal!*

Without identifying the competing Lender(s), it is all right to contact a Lender and indicate that, for example, "I have another proposal that will increase my advance rate to 85% of accounts receivable, but you only provide 80%. Could you improve on that? Also, you indicated that you need my personal guarantee collateralized by my personal residence. The other Lender does not require this and my spouse, I am sure, will not go along with this. What can you do?"

This tactic works quite well—*to an extent.* Be careful of not doing this excessively, because one, or both, of these Lenders could simply give up on you and terminate the offer. Remember, for many of these changes, the Lender must go back to his approval authorities to obtain an additional approval for the new items. The Loan Officer's creditability may be lessened each time he must return to the credit committee for another exception.

It is possible that some of the arguable items within the Lender's proposal letter have been included as "try for" items. The Lender intentionally put these particular items within the proposal to see if the institution could get it. If not—no problem—the Lender will negotiate it away. But if the Borrower does not notice, or fails to ask that it be removed or modified, the Lender has increased its margin of comfort.

The Borrower should work with his legal counsel and financial adviser to determine where and when to leverage competing Lenders. It is not necessarily all said and done when the Lender issues his final clean *proposal* letter for the Borrower's signature. Once the proposal is executed by all parties, the Lender then completes his due diligence and approval process. The same leverage considerations may now be again exercised once a *commitment* letter is received by the Borrower. After all of his work, the Lender generally would not want to lose the deal because of one more "request" that he could probably live with. And, in "real life," such leveraged negotiations frequently go on right down to the wire (to the loan closing).

Of course, by the loan closing, the Borrower should have selected the preferred Lender. He may well have "traveled" with two Lenders right up to receiving the loan closing documentation. Both of the final Lenders may think that they have the deal. The Borrower then plans an early loan closing with what he believes to be his preferred Lender—as well as a later closing (days or a week later) with the runner-up. If something *goes seriously wrong* at the eleventh hour with the preferred Lender, the Borrower can walk out of the first loan closing. He has backup and can complete the loan with his "runner-up" Lender. There may be some prepaid fees or deposits to be forfeited, but this may be preferable to being locked into an unsatisfactory loan structure for the long term. *If the Borrower is working this dual-Lender arrangement he should work closely with his legal counsel and financial advisers, ensuring that all concerns have been satisfactorily addressed.*

When negotiating with the Lender, the Borrower must remember that the Loan Officer (LO) is simply doing his job. The LO does not usually have a vested interest in whether or not this single loan is approved and closes. The exception would be the amount of a year-end bonus based upon new business volume. His overall job description does include bringing in so much qualified new business during the year and maintaining a growing and profitable loan portfolio. His operational latitudes are really quite limited. He will strive, dependent on his experience and expertise, to accommodate the Borrower's wishes—those that do not directly oppose the institution's policy.

The Borrower should not anticipate a brick wall when making his requests. The Borrower should, however, come with narrative and/or data support justifying requests. Such a posture will not only support the rationale for the request but will enable the Lender to present the request in a realistic manner to other parties. I have never met a Lender that intentionally tried to "shoot down" a Borrower's loan request. Sure, questions of risk or creditworthiness will always be addressed, but it is not a contest between adversaries. The pure fact is that the Lenders need the Borrowers, and they do not wish to jeopardize a current or prospective relationship. See additional related information in Chapters 2 and 6.

CHAPTER 8

SPECIALIZED LENDING

"You know—this could *really* work for us!"

"The *Lender* is going to go through our company books?"

"I *can* finance a single invoice?"

Overview

You've heard the old adage, "There's more than one way to skin a cat." Likewise, in business financing, there are many financing "vehicles" through which to achieve your financing objectives. Whether seeking working capital, term loans, real estate or land loans, mezzanine borrowing, money to buy a business through a leveraged buyout, money to buy out a partner, financing a single invoice or all of your receivables, financing inventory, or financing materials to cover a new purchase order—there's most always a way, and usually more than one, to put together your loan.

Sure, some packages will cost more than others. The Borrower must carefully weigh the costs of financing against the forecasted benefits of the loan proceeds.

In this chapter we will discuss at length a few of the major specialized lending areas and just touch on others. Chapter 9 will then be beneficial insofar as determining and contacting selected categories of secured commercial lenders.

Note: When considering the following specialized finance alternatives, the Borrower should work closely with his accountant, financial adviser, and legal counsel. The following financing information is not intended to be a complete or an all-inclusive commentary on the financing types described. Through contact with companies that specifically provide such financings, complete information would become available. There are several differences between Lenders, their loan terms and conditions, and loan documentation.

Let's start off with one method, which can involve a significant amount of paperwork (Lender reporting). Sounds daunting, but the Borrower can receive money in his checking account for invoices (sales) he developed only the day before—sometimes even the same day. This can be a material improvement over the 30–60–90 days a Borrower usually must wait for funds. Also, loan advances may be frequently made available against selected components of the Borrower's inventory.

ASSET-BASED LENDING

Asset-based lending (ABL) is known by a few other names developed over time. These are commercial financing, revolving credit, revolving financing, receivables financing or, infrequently, evergreen financing. Unlike some other types of lending, there is usually no "cleanup" period required by the Lender during the ABL lending contract. Personal guarantees are generally required.

ABL is a secured line of revolving credit supported by the Borrower's fluctuating values of eligible accounts receivable and (more often than not) inventory.

While inventory is usually financed as a part of the overall ABL line of credit, *inventory by itself is seldom financed without receivables.* One reason is that if a Lender is *only* financing inventory, he would be "filed" under the provisions of the Uniform Commercial Code (see Chapter 1) as to inventory and proceeds of inventory. Proceeds of inventory are either cash or the creation of accounts receivable. Different Lenders with independent filings—one Lender against accounts receivable and the other Lender against inventory—could potentially clash as to which is entitled to inventory proceeds. One can see where the financing of receivables *together* with inventory can be practical, logical, and beneficial to the Borrower.

Advantages: The financing of accounts receivable (and inventory) has many advantages to a Borrower:

1. Accelerates cash flow (process usually permits *daily* borrowings).

2. Can improve the timely payment of accounts payable and other debt obligations.

3. Borrower (due to the accelerated cash flow) may now take advantage of purchase discounts.

4. Financing levels relate to current success of the Borrower; higher sales, increasing inventory, and growing A/R (usually

a good sign, but may be negative should delinquent A/R's be increasing).

5. Non-notification financing (Borrower's customers are not aware that receivables are being financed by a Lender).

6. Interest is paid on *only* the daily outstanding loan balance.

7. Cleanup periods are not required.

8. Lender contracts usually run up to three years.

9. Loan advances may be wired (daily) to the Borrower's account.

ABL is really an easy "sell." A Lender's loan advance can be in the Borrower's bank account as soon as an invoice is prepared and the product shipped to the customer. It really pretty much works like that.

Disadvantages: Of course there are possible disadvantages to a Borrower. The Borrower may not see these as real disadvantages, as benefits may far outweigh these concerns. Disadvantages, however, may be regarded as:

1. **Cost of Financing**—Why is the interest rate so high? Primarily because of the Lender's perceived, and sometimes actual, risks: the propensity for fraud, bogus invoices and shipping documents, conversion of customer payments, inventory values overstated to generate higher loan advances and, infrequently, duplicate financing with another Lender. Pricing is usually reflected as "X" percentage points over the prime interest rate. Some loans may be priced at the prime rate, but interest rates approved are usually higher. On the larger-dollar credits the index applied may be LIBOR (Chapter 5) rather than the prime rate. These indices are reported in *The Wall Street Journal.*

2. **On-Site Audits**—Frequent on-site audits (usually announced) may be conducted *by the Lender* quarterly, or less frequently. To address and minimize Lender risks, frequent audits are conducted on the Borrower's books and records (at the business site). Such audits are not to be confused with the year-end or other periodic audits conducted by the Borrower's accountant. These Lender audits primarily focus on the verification of reported collateral

values, eligibility, and quantity. Other aspects of the business are also reviewed at that time including, but not limited to, business performance, cash flow, new debt incurred, the timely payment of other debt, insurance premiums, and all taxes.

These audits may be considered an inconvenience to the bookkeeper, to company management (answering questions), and sometimes to the accountant. However, on the upside, audit discoveries by the Lender's auditors can in fact be of benefit to the Borrower. Mistakes in inventory costing and receivables errors are often discovered during the course of the audit. Audit results of consistent quality may also assist in developing higher loan advance rates, to the benefit of the Borrower, and reducing audit frequency.

3. **Collateral monitoring costs**—Audits are either conducted by the Lender's ABL personnel or are contracted out to firms specializing in these types of examinations. Per diem rates apply, per auditor, as well as associated expenses. Costs to the Borrower may be several hundred dollars per day per auditor plus expenses. The size and complexity of the business and the extent of the loan exposure to the Lender determine the number of auditors required, the audit duration, and audit scope. The Lender charges the Borrower for audits, plus expenses, as they occur, but may consider adding audit expenses to the loan balance rather than billing them directly.

4. **Reporting requirements**—Based upon the frequency of borrowings desired, the Borrower may be required to provide *daily reporting* as to the creation of new accounts receivable, the amount of daily receivable collections, other credits and debits to receivable balances, loan availability, and loan request reports. In addition, periodic accounts receivable agings, reconciliations, and inventory reports may be required. As in any other type of lending, periodic financial statements and forecasts are also required. Such controls are not hard to understand, in that the Lender is providing daily loan advances based upon the Borrower's reporting of daily supporting collateral values.

5. **Lender's Lockbox**—Customer's accounts receivable payments are usually directed to the Lender's lockbox—*not* to the Borrower. This provides the Lender with complete "dominion" over these A/R proceeds. The alternative is to have the Borrower receive payments as usual and then send these in directly to the Lender. These are called payments "in kind." *There are usually two Borrower concerns relative to a lockbox operation.* The first is that the Borrower's customers may be required to send their payments *directly into the Lender's lockbox.* Thus these customers may know that the Borrower is financing his accounts receivable. This does not usually sit well with the Borrower—and could be of concern to a customer. In fact, as a method to appease the Borrower in this instance, the address usually reflects the Borrower's name *but* includes the number of a post office box that the Lender actually controls. Secondarily, if the Lender gets the customer payments first, there may be some *time delay before the Borrower receives detailed payment information enabling him to post payments to his books.* Valid arguments. Again, the value of accelerated cash flow may outweigh such concerns. Usually the Borrower and the Lender can reconcile, or improve upon, these operating procedures. The Borrower also pays lockbox servicing fees.

Who Are the Prospects for Asset-Based Lending?

- Asset-based Lenders prefer *manufacturers and distributors.* This is because there is a definable product, determinable value, and proof of shipment.
- Some *commercial service industries* may also qualify, such as temporary employers, employee leasing firms, and trucking companies.
- Industries *not usually favored* are:
  - Contractors (progress payments)
  - Some metal fabricators (progress payments)
  - Hospitality and entertainment (business volatility)
  - General high tech (inventory valuation)
  - Medical receivables (proceeds may be diluted by third-

party insurance companies or others)

• Companies with limited earnings, rapid growth, or no growth. ABL will consider prospects with little or no earnings over a period of time, a deficit net worth position, or even a debtor-in-possession situation. Highly leveraged transactions may also be appropriate for an ABL relationship.

Asset-based lenders are flexible and *there are specialty asset-based Lenders* that may address industries indicated as "not usually favored" in the preceding list.

Certain businesses have cyclical trends that may discourage commercial bankers, or other conservative Lenders, from making loans collateralized by current assets. Accounts receivable may be high after a "season," but may be zero while inventory is being manufactured for the next season. "Seasonal over-lines" may effectively address such fluctuating loan requirements. Most ABL Lenders can effectively address seasonal considerations.

General Observations

The ABL Lender's due diligence evaluations place emphasis on:

- Borrower's integrity
- Management capabilities
- Quality and quantity of eligible collateral
- Business performance
- Within a difficult situation, that a positive turnaround is in evidence, or is forecasted, with a reasonable chance for success.
- Realistic business strategies

Real Experiences!

Asset-based Lenders' on-site inspections (or audits) are usually conducted during the normal business hours of the Borrower (sometimes unannounced). Examinations are performed primarily to satisfactorily reconcile the Borrower's

> *reported* (to the Lender) collateral to the internal records of the Borrower. During one examination the bank auditor was unable to reconcile the trade accounts payable balances reported to the bank to the company's general ledger. Being somewhat new to the game, and believing he must be wrong, the auditor reworked his reconciliations a number of times without success. Finally, at the end of the business day, after most of the employees had left, he questioned the owner of the business as to the discrepancy. The owner reported that after his bookkeeping staff left he frequently reduced the actual balances of the company's accounts payable. When asked why he did this, he stated that he believed his venders were overcharging him and that the supplies really were not worth that much. So much for management's integrity. Although the loan was not called, the frequency of audits was increased by the Lender.

In order to verify reported inventory balances, these especially trained ABL auditors frequently find themselves crawling in freezers loaded with chickens, counting Easter baskets, and well—you name it. In the instance of the chickens, an auditor's analysis revealed that, inasmuch as frozen chickens were always taken from the front of the freezer, the ones in the back had not moved for four years. Needless to say, the Health Department quickly followed up on the Lender's audit. In another instance, tall stacks of boxes representing finished goods inventory, when dismantled for the auditors' inspection, were found to contain empty boxes at its core. These exceptions are only a few of the inconsistencies found—providing good reasons for such Lender diligence.

Accounts Receivables, Slow Pay, and Excess Inventory

One purpose of revolving financing is to accelerate proceeds of slow-paying accounts receivable. These specialized Lenders seek accounts receivable in reasonably current shape. The more current the receivable account, the more of a loan may be generated (through higher advance rates). Lenders *generally* do not loan against receivables over 90 days in age from the invoice date. Some industries, however, *do* justify older account loan eligibility. Receivables based upon consignment sales or those involving employee receivables are not usually considered eligible collateral. Legitimate accounts receivable usually represent goods already shipped to customers—not those pending shipment.

To an extent—based upon the Lender's ability to obtain perfected security interests—government, municipal, and foreign receivables may also qualify as eligible accounts.

Further enhancing the asset-based Lender's capabilities are credit insurance, letters of credit, special Small Business Administration loan and guarantee programs, the Export/Import Bank, and state and local loan and guarantee programs.

Inventories

Most inventories lend them themselves to ABL lending. Raw materials and finished goods are generally the most acceptable inventory components for borrowing purposes. However, work-in-process (WIP) elements are normally considered ineligible. While it may be taken as part of the Lender's collateral "base," WIP is usually *not* available for lending purposes. This is because of its limited recovery (liquidation or action) value. Infrequently some small advance rate *may* be allowable against WIP due to an unusual circumstance or requirement.

All reported inventory components must be *owned* by the Borrower to generate loan advance considerations.

Lenders will seek to understand how the Borrower's inventory is valued. What is the history, and policy, for returns and allowances? They want to know how often a physical inventory is taken. What was the impact of the resulting book adjustments to inventory as a result of these past physical inventories? Periodic book adjustments may also reveal the accuracy of perpetual inventory records. What was the frequency of inventory turns during the past period? Is inventory properly protected and insured?

Lenders must know *all* inventory locations, whether facilities are leased or owned, and the name and address of the landlord. What is the nature of inventory in storage and/or at other locations, and the dollar amount at each location? Such information is necessary so Lenders may inspect their collateral as well as ensure they are properly filed (UCC-1) within the appropriate jurisdiction.

Lenders attempt to identify classes of inventory that may pose exposures when determining inventory advance rates. Some of these may be:

- Technical risks
- Product warranties
- Perishables and shelf-life considerations
- Customer specific
- Vendor specific
- Borrower specific
- Appraisal requirements
- Seasonal products
- Fashion trend items
- Commodity items
- Vendor allocated products
- Items on consignment
- Obsolete items
- Slow- moving items
- Inventory in transit
- Inventory out to subcontractors
- Living inventory
- Customer-owned inventory
- Hazardous materials

Real Experiences!

Ineffective management and faulty inventory controls critically wounded this plumbing supply house Borrower, forcing his asset-based Lender into action. Management of this 50-year-old business revolved around the elderly founder. Over the past few years he had put his adult children and their spouses in most all of the responsible areas of the business. He came in periodically to "see how things were going."

During a recent Lender's collateral audit, the auditors were unable to reconcile the actual quantities of inventory reported to the Lender to company books. Further, due to alleged inventory purchases (which increased loan availability), an unusually high cost of goods resulted in the company suffering continuing and increasing losses. Finally, after unsuccessfully trying to reconcile the situation and being *unable to determine its collateral position*, the Lender first exercised its demand rights and later showed up on the premises to take possession of its inventory and other collateral. The Lender then contracted for trucks and labor. Trucks were backed up and the inventory loaded for transfer and subsequent auction. Accounts receivable records were also removed by the Lender.

This was on a Friday. The next Monday, the elderly owner's son-in-law (an employee of the plumbing business) opened up an *identical* business on the other side of town with a *complete* inventory. As best as the Lender could determine, the son-in-law had no prior sources of funds with which to purchase this large amount of beginning inventory. This owner had no choice but to close his half-century-old business. Effective management is always the most important part of a business's success—even when considering the employment of family members.

Inventory financing can be a risky business. Lenders, of course, seek to eliminate as much of this risk as is feasible. Asset-based lenders do seek to provide inventory financing whenever possible. After determining *eligible* inventory, advance rates may be as low as 15% to 45% of the eligible amount, while 50% seems to be a customary advance rate against average inventory risks (raw materials and finished goods).

Leveraged Buyouts

Many leveraged buyouts may also be effectively financed through asset-based lending. The buyer (in addition to his own contributed cash) frequently needs additional funds with which to complete the financing aspects. The financing of the current assets being purchased, such as the accounts receivables and inventory (utilizing an ABL Lender), can be a good part of the answer. Also, some ABL Lenders will go forward with the buyer and continue to provide working capital (ABL lending) into the life of the relationship. As a note, the same ABL Lender, to make up other required portions of the deal, may further provide loans against machinery, equipment, and real estate. It is noted that *other* Lenders may also participate in such a transaction. There are other funding sources that may become involved, such as quasi equity holders if such additional funds are needed. These Lenders (mezzanine lenders, subordinated debt holders, and loan participants) are discussed in Chapter 9. The ABL audits (initial "survey" examinations) are especially valuable to potential business buyers. The audit's in-depth scope may further support an accurate determination of values and, not infrequently, may result in price adjustments to the sale.

The Borrowing Base Certificate

By any other name, this is *one of the most important* collateral and loan recapulation schedules within the ABL process.

As one can see by the following example for the stated period, the details of collateral additions and reductions are presented. Also, differences between eligible and ineligible collateral are identified. Total loan availability is then applied against the current loan outstanding and the new loan availability is established. The new loan position is then re-established. *This Certificate is utilized any time (even daily) that the Borrower wishes a loan advance against eligible collateral.* Frequently, and depending on the extent of the relationship, a Borrower may "call in" for a loan advance and then fax the supporting Certificate after the fact.

An example of the Borrowing Base Certificate follows:

Date: _3/17/XX__
To: ABC Commercial Bank, NA

BORROWING BASE CERTIFICATE
Customer: Unique Manufacturing Company, Inc. Certificate # 144

1) Accounts Receivable Control:
(Line 5 of previous Certificate dated 3/10/x) $ _ 1,365,741_____

A) New Sales (Period _____3/17/XX__________) $ __ 154,732_____
B) Other additions (Explain on reverse) _________________

TOTAL ADDITIONS: $__ 154,732______

2) Reductions to Accounts Receivable since last Certificate:

A)	Cash Receipts	$_ 126,297_______
B)	Credit Memos issued since last Certificate	_____ 142_______
C)	Other reductions since last Certificate (Audit Adj.)	_____ 274_______
D)	**TOTAL REDUCTIONS:**	$_ 126,713_______

3) Accounts Receivable Control (Line 1 plus Total Additions minus 2D)	$1,393,760_______
4) Adjustment to Accounts Receivable Control	________0_______
5) **ADJUSTED ACCOUNTS RECEIVABLE CONTROL**	$1,393,760_______
6) Total Ineligible Accounts (Line 5 of previous "Recapulation," Dated 2/28/xx_)	___ 97,563_______
7) Eligible Accounts Receivable (Line 5 less line 6)	$1,296,197_______
8) Accounts Receivable Availability (80% of line 7)	$1,036,958_______
9) Inventory Availability (Line 13 of previous "Recapulation," Dated 2/28/xx_)	$_ 368,000_______
10) Other Availability____________________	________0_______
11) Other Availability____________________	________0_______
12) Holdback for Letters of Credit, Acceptances or Other (minus) (AJK- Germany)	___ 30,000_______
13) Total Gross Availability: The totals of 8, 9, 10, 11 and less line 12 OR the Line of Credit of $1,500,000; whichever is less.	$1,374,958_______

LOAN POSITION

14) Beginning Loan Balance (Line 18 of previous Certificate, Dated _3/10/xx)	$_ 876,016_______
15) Plus: Borrowing(s) advanced since last Borrowing Base Certificate	___ 35,000_______

16) Less: Payments remitted against Line of Credit since Last Certificate ___126,297______

17) Adjustments to Balance ________0_______

18) NEW LOAN BALANCE (Line 14, plus 15 less 16, plus or minus 17) $__784,719______

19) Net Availability (line 13 minus Line 18) $__590,239______

CERTIFICATION:

Borrower hereby Certifies that they are not in default under the Loan and Security Agreement, or any of the Borrowers' liabilities or subsequent agreements, between Lender and Borrower. No remittance has been received, or returns and allowances granted to any debtors whose accounts have been assigned to Lender, other than previously reported. We hereby assign to Lender all accounts which came into existence since our last Certificate and all rights, title and interest of the undersigned in and to the goods represented thereby and all monies due or to become due thereby.

___3/17/XX_______ ___________________________________

Date Authorized Signature, Title

As the reader scans the preceding Borrowing Base Certificate, some clarifications need to be made. *Not all line numbers are addressed:*

1. The previous Certificate, #143, is not shown. The total accounts receivable balance is brought forward from the prior Certificate.

1.a. New Sales, in this case, is a weekly number. The Borrower has chosen to borrow weekly but can usually change frequencies at his discretion.

5. The total *current* balance of accounts receivable is determined.

6. These ineligible accounts (over 90 days in age, foreign, employee, and so on), *may* be calculated on a monthly basis and is supported by a monthly aging of accounts receivable. ABL Lenders usually require only monthly updates regarding these ineligible items. A separate backup schedule, frequently called a "recapulation," details such monthly changes within each ineligible category. It may be attached to the month-end Borrowing Base Certificate.

7. This is the updated total of eligible accounts receivable *before* the Borrower applies the approved advance rate.

8. The approved advance rate of 80% of eligible accounts is applied.

9. Inventory availability comes from a separate supporting schedule and usually reflects the inventory values at the end of the reporting month, or quarter, or whatever period has been agreed upon between the Borrower and the Lender. Most companies do not take inventory monthly, so other period-end amounts may be satisfactory. Also, in some cases, if physical inventory numbers are not available for the period, the Lender may accept an adjusting computation considering elements of the cost of goods sold.

13. In no case can the Borrower borrow more than the approval credit line regardless of the amount of eligible collateral. This Line of Credit of $1,500,000 is reflected on the Certificate to remind the Borrower than he cannot exceed this amount.

14. Again, from Line 18 of the *prior* week's Certificate, the *former loan balance* is shown.

15. During the prior week the Borrower has requested and received a loan of $35,000 against his line of credit. Funds were wired into his operating account.

16. This reflects the amount of funds that the Lender received in its lockbox representing customer payments during the previous week. Sometimes the Borrower will call the Lender for this number to place on his Borrowing Base Certificate. He may not as yet have all the detail from the Lender as to the prior week's collections should a lockbox be used.

19. After deducting the amount of the new loan balance from the total gross availability, the result is the amount the Borrower has available for future borrowings. This remaining loan "availability" is over and above the loan already identified as the New Loan Balance. With all of the daily changes to collateral, one can see how the net loan availability frequently changes.

Types of ABL Audits

Generally, there are three types of ABL audits:

Initial New Business Survey (at the Borrower's Site): This provides the Lender with the *preliminary* opportunity to review the Borrower's books, records, and collateral. Also a tour of the plant (hopefully in operation) is conducted. This initial audit may take a day or two, or a week or more, dependent upon the size, complexity, the number of business locations and the cooperation of the company. Considering the expense involved for the Borrower, usually all cooperation is offered and a number of documents and/or schedules are prepared, or made available, in advance for the auditor(s).

Takeover Audit Requirement: A takeover audit is held at the Borrower's site a day or so before the scheduled loan closing. The purpose is to determine the balances of eligible collateral at the closing date (or at a date reasonably close to the loan closing) so initial loan advances may be supported and everyone has a common starting point.

Continuing Audits (for the Life of the Loan): As mentioned previously, these are usually conducted quarterly and are by and large announced. These may frequently tie into physical inventory times, or the preparation and/or issuance of annual or periodic financial reports.

During the life of the loan, collateral is usually monitored on a daily basis by the Lender's analysts, account executives, or Lending Officers, as well as periodically by the auditors. Their responsibilities address the monitoring of the daily flow of invoices (sales), receivable proceeds from the Borrower's customers, requests for daily loan advances, and any other significant "events" in the life of the relationship. *In essence, ABL controls the entire cash flow of the Borrower—on a daily basis.*

In preparation for an *initial* ABL audit the Borrower must have available certain records and documents. Some documentation may have to be prepared—most items should already be on hand. Different Lenders may require different documentation.

1. Three or more years of annual (year-end) financial statements (complete with accountant's Notes).

2. Most recent interim (monthly or quarterly) financial statements; usually internally prepared.

3. Interim financial statement (comparative purposes) for the same period one year ago.

4. Most recent financial projections with assumptions and/or a business plan.

5. A schedule of company debt (exclusive of accounts payable). Show creditor, type of loan, maturity date, account number, initial balance, current balance, and current monthly payment. Identify supporting collateral.

6. Accounts receivable aging by customer and invoice date. Aged by invoice date, columns will include those receivable balances that are 0–30 days, 31–60 days, 61–90 days, and over 90 days in age.

7. Accounts payable aging (similar breakdown as #6).

8. Inventory description and a dollar summary by category.

9. Identify all inventory locations with amounts and components at each.

10. Have available all bank statements for the past year.

11. Company history, union affiliation(s) if any.

12. Leases for facilities or equipment, rental agreements.

13. Financial statements of personal guarantors (use Lender's format).

14. *Current* Lender's most recent Borrowing Base Certificate and monthly interest billing statement.

15. Company brochures and/or product information.

16. If applicable, most recent machinery and equipment appraisal and/or listing.

17. If applicable, most recent real estate appraisal.

18. If applicable, most recent Environmental Site Assessment report.

19. Detailed statement regarding any litigation, bankruptcy, environmental, product liability, or OSHA issues.

20. Reasons for seeking new financing.

21. Identify the principals of the company, percentage of ownership, and provide brief management profiles.

22. Copy of Letter Agreement with the loan broker or consultant, if applicable.
23. What is the Borrower's *preferred* loan structure?

Again, though this list seems long, most items are readily available. Remember, this would be the auditors' *first* time at the business. Things tend to proceed quicker as auditors become familiar with the business and develop their internal working papers.

Real Experiences!

During a recent asset-based audit of a distribution company, the Lender's auditor (a member of the bank) was confused over some entries within the general ledger of the company. Approaching the full-charge bookkeeper, he said, "You know, there's something here that I just cannot understand." The bookkeeper, without waiting for the auditor's clarification, opened the second drawer down on her desk and replied, "I knew you would find out. Here is our second general ledger, which shows exactly where the company *really* stands. The one you are looking at was prepared especially for the bank. Oh, and here's a pile of payables that never were posted to the books." Needless to say, the Borrower received a 30-day letter to find another Lender. This auditor also found the value of keeping quiet after his initial comments. The lesson came too late for this Borrower—keep it clean.

Management Note: Do not let the commercial finance auditors leave the premises without an "exit interview." Auditors may leave with misconceptions absent clarifications by management—and such misconceptions can often jeopardize the loan request. Questions for management to ask the auditors:

- Were findings satisfactory?
- What specific points were unsatisfactory?
- Were our company books and records maintained properly?
- What part of the books and records or of the operation did you not understand?

- Were our personnel helpful and receptive?
- Do you have any recommendations for the company?
- Are you going away with any unanswered questions?
- How long before the audit report will be completed and delivered to the Lender?
- May I have a copy? (Probably not—but it's worth a try).

Finally, there are *two types of asset-based Lending:* conforming and non-conforming. *Conforming* indicates that all of the control "bells and whistles" apply: frequent reporting, on-site collateral audits, and so on. *Non-conforming* means that a Lender has taken a security interest in selected current assets without the associated operational controls. A Lender may feel that the creditworthiness of the Borrower precludes such controls (and associated Borrower costs) and could possibly alienate the Borrower. Or, simply, the Lender has no control capacities but still wants the loan on his books.

FACTORING

Factoring is frequently a recommended alternative to asset-based lending. It is apparent that an ABL approval basically rests upon the creditworthiness of the Borrower, the quantity and quality of the overall collateral, and in the Borrower's integrity. However, there are avenues through which cash flow may be aggressively enhanced through the financing of *selected* accounts receivable or invoices—not necessarily the entire Borrower's accounts receivable portfolio (although factors will consider that as well). Sometimes factoring is regarded as last-resort financing. *Not necessarily true*—it can be unto itself a valuable and effective financing tool.

Factoring is defined as the *purchase*, at a discount, of a single invoice or multiple of invoices by a Lender. An "advance" is then made by the factor to the Borrower, representing a major portion of the value of the invoice. This type of Lender is known as a "factor." Factoring has been carried out worldwide for hundreds of years, including in Colonial America. From trading ships around the world agents, or "factors," accelerated trade and the flow of funds through their monitoring and funding of commercial transactions.

Loan advances to the Borrower by the factor, from 70% to 90%, may be available against an invoice's value. The remainder of the invoice, once paid by the account debtor, is remitted to the Borrower less a factor's fee. If, following a purchase, the account debtor is unable to pay, the factor may assume the financial consequences. See the sections about non-recourse and recourse factoring later in the chapter.

Advantages accruing to a factored Borrower are:

- Accelerated cash flow resulting in improved working capital
- An ongoing source of funds
- Improved credit evaluations of existing and new customers
- A decrease in bad debts, which may lessen credit losses
- Enhanced credit protection
- Customer collection efforts by the factor
- Possible reduction of Borrower's A/R administration expenses
- Complements business expansion

Factoring services may include, but are not limited to:

- Financing of accounts receivable—specific invoices, all invoices within a single account debtor, or an entire portfolio of receivables
- Accounts receivable controls
- Bookkeeping functions
- Account credit evaluations for Borrower's existing or new customers
- Receipt of accounts receivable proceeds
- Collection services and late notices

Industries that commonly utilize factoring as an effective financing tool are:

- Transportation
- Textiles and apparel
- Manufacturers, wholesalers, and distributors
- Seasonal businesses
- Seafood industry
- Furniture industry
- Temporary employment firms
- Staffing firms: medical, professional, and technical

- Security services
- Other qualified service businesses
- Qualified start-up businesses

Traditionally, factors have not provided *inventory financing*. However, considering both the consistent competitive pressures on such Lenders and the availability of in-house experts, some factoring firms do now offer inventory and equipment financing along with letter of credit arrangements.

A benefit that accrues to *both* Borrower and his customer is the possible improvement in the terms of sale. Let's say that a Borrower has terms of "Net 30 days." With a factoring arrangement, the Borrower may give to his best customers—or new ones—terms of "Net 60 days" or better. The customer may not be aware of the fact that the Borrower is receiving his money for these factored sales within days of his billing. The Borrower has a greatly improved cash flow and his customers have a very competitive payment period. The Borrower should weigh the costs of such factoring arrangements against the financing benefits.

Is timing an issue? It should be noted that the timing of a loan closing of an ABL loan and a factoring arrangement are considerably different. ABL usually requires significant Lender due diligence, an extended credit and approval process period, and significant loan closing documentation. Appraisals, environmental issues, and field audits may additionally slow down the process. Experience shows that an ABL deal may close no sooner than 60–90 days from the initial Borrower contact. There are exceptions to any rule, but that is generally the time frame. Factors, however, already have the credit information on many of the Borrower's customers within databases and can make informed determinations quickly. A factoring contract may usually be closed within two to three weeks.

REALITY CHECK

If it is going to take *too long to close* a needed asset-based credit line, consider closing on a more timely factoring arrangement. Negotiate a limited or zero prepayment penalty. Once the factoring agreement is closed, and your *immediate* funding requirements have been met, consider again opening the application for asset-based lending. When dealing with larger Lenders (who have both services), such a move may be accomplished through the same Lender at reduced cost.

The Process

Once a Borrower completes an order (or services rendered are completed) and the goods have been received by the account debtor (Borrower's customer), the Borrower transmits the invoice to the factor.[[Jeremy: from here forward I changed this to lowercase with tracking turned off. Not capped in Webster's.]] An acceptable shipping document may preclude the actual product delivery. The factor, following his review of the predetermined customer credit limit and loan advance criteria, forwards the acceptable invoice on to the account debtor. *Prior to the actual mailing* of the invoice to the account debtor, the invoice may be imprinted with the factor's identification, and payment instructions included. An advance is then processed, with funds sent to the Borrower. This advance is usually made within a day or two of the factor's receipt of the invoice. There are variations to this process.

Factoring loan advance rates generally range from 70% to 90%, depending upon customer quality, accounts receivable history, and identified risks within the Borrower's operation or within the industry. In unique situations, advances may reach 100%. Advance rates may be different for each accounts receivable customer, or may be the same for all qualified customers within a portfolio. This determination is made by the factor and agreed to by the Borrower.

The invoice balance stays open with the factor until the invoice is paid by the customer. Payments from account debtors are usually routed to the factor's lockbox. Any other communications included within the incoming mail, *other than* invoice proceeds, are then forwarded to the Borrower. The collection period may be quick; often within 30 days or, in some cases, 90 days to 120 days or more. The factor, in accordance with the terms of sale, may provide reminder and collection services on behalf of the Borrower. Once the factor does receive payment from the account debtor, the factor then remits the remaining balance (within days of receipt) to the Borrower, *less* the loan advance and the deduction for the factor's fee.

It is important for the Borrower to be able to transmit information on a timely basis to the factor. This may involve imaging the invoices and shipping documents. The factor also provides the Borrower with periodic accounts receivable agings, collection, status reports, and the like. Some factors provide such reports via the factor's secure Web site in real time.

Factors may also seek a *minimum volume* (monthly or annually) of invoices to be processed through a single Borrower. Some have no such requirements.

Non-Recourse Factoring: The process thus far is that the factor "purchases" an invoice, or a multitude of invoices, from a Borrower. There are *two types of purchase considerations*, one of which will apply to the Borrower. The first is non-recourse factoring. This signifies that the factor has no further recourse against the Borrower in case the Borrower's customer does not pay the invoice because of credit problems. Once the invoice is "sold" to the factor, it is gone forever. Borrower fraud and product disputes can be the exceptions. Inasmuch as all credit risk now rests with the factor, non-recourse factoring may be somewhat more expensive than recourse factoring.

Recourse Factoring: A recourse arrangement may be less expensive for the Borrower. Under a recourse contract the factor, once an account doesn't pay, may charge back the amount to the Borrower. The Borrower must buy back this previously financed invoice. Such a factoring agreement may also require that an invoice must be "put back" (returned) to the Borrower once a specific period of time has passed; 90 days, for example. In practice, if the Borrower is factoring a number of accounts on a continuing basis, the Borrower may not have to actually cut a check to the factor to buy back the factor's invoice. The factor simply reduces the next factoring advance to the Borrower by the defaulted amount. The Borrower is then free to continue to attempt collection activities on the specific invoice in question. Once proceeds do come in, if they ever do, they belong in total to the Borrower. The Borrower may also, on his own, commence collection activities against this customer. The Borrower should work with his legal counsel when contemplating such collection activities.

Spot Factoring: It is common, and usually more profitable, for a factor to seek an arrangement in which all, or a reasonable portion, of the accounts of a single Borrower are factored. However, in some cases, factors will consider factoring one single invoice from a Borrower. It may be of a large dollar amount and from a Borrower's customer with an excellent commercial credit rating. Other special considerations may also make it feasible for the factor to consider such financing. When a single invoice, from a single Borrower, is factored, it may be referred to as "spot factoring."

Factoring Costs

Cost components may be broken down in two distinct areas: the interest charged on borrowed funds and the factoring fee (or commission).

1. Interest Rate: The cost of borrowing (through periodic "advances") is computed against the average monthly balance of borrowed funds utilizing a published interest rate index. An example would be the prime interest rate as quoted in *The Wall Street Journal*, plus a percentage.
2. Factoring Fee: The *factoring fee* may be based upon the amount financed, number of invoices factored, average invoice size, and the average collection period.

Maturity Factoring: The factor performs the *entire* customer credit and collection process for the Borrower. Proceeds of receivables are sent to the Borrower (monthly, or other acceptable periods) based upon actual collections. This type of factoring may, in effect, eliminate a Borrower's *interest expense* because a factor's commission is charged instead. *Collected* funds are sent to the Borrower by the factor based on *agreed-upon intervals*. This method of factoring usually applies to *creditworthy accounts*; collection periods are generally within the Borrower's terms of sale.

General: The factor, because of an identified risk, may require that the factoring client establish a cash "reserve" with the factor. This may be funded up-front or through the application of a small portion of the periodic advances against invoices.

There may be an administrative fee of $1.00 or more for each invoice factored. Depending on the volume of invoices anticipated by the factor from the Borrower, there may also be one-time setup fee.

For some Borrowers, factoring works so well that *all sales* are run through a factoring operation. Taking this a step further, and considering a program that charges a 3% discount against the Borrower's overall annual factored sales, a Borrower could accordingly experience a 3% decrease in his gross margin. Some businesses traditionally have very low profit margins. A factoring arrangement of this nature may have an unfavorable impact on a company with marginal profitability. Most likely the *factoring of only selected invoices or customers*, who are well rated, may be the best avenue. The factor is well equipped to analyze the best-case scenario for potential Borrowers.

It is somewhat unusual to find factoring services within a commercial bank. However, some of the larger banks that offer ABL may have an in-house (or own) a factoring operation. Smaller banks may also "subscribe" to outside vendor services, enabling them to provide factoring services. There are many Lenders who specialize *only* in factoring. These are usually managed by factoring professionals who have been in the business for many years. Many of these long-term factoring companies have excellent established reputations. Chapter 9 describes how to make contact with such factors.

PURCHASE ORDER FINANCING

What Is Purchase Order Financing?

Purchase Order Financing (POF) is a lending program used to *finance the purchase of inventory or components* that are required by a Borrower to fulfill a bona fide customer order. The Borrower may not currently have the cash (or other financing availabilities) to address the purchase of the materials required to fulfill (or manufacture) purchase order requirements.

Advantages of purchase order financing:

- Frees up and preserves cash flow for other operations
- Enables the acquisition of the necessary raw materials, finished goods, assembly components, or parts to fulfill a purchase order
- Enables a Borrower to compete when orders larger than normal are received
- Allows Borrower to address purchase orders that may otherwise be lost
- Helps to protect potential profits
- Provides quicker Lender response over other types of secured working capital lending arrangements
- Allows Borrower to consider enhanced product lines and growth into new markets
- Possibly reduces "over advances" granted by the current lender
- Allows Borrower to stay with his current Lender (asset-based lending, factoring, or conventional) rather than leaving to employ POF

Who Uses POF?

- Manufacturers
- Distributors

Note: POF is available to most industries, with the exception of construction and businesses involved in sales on consignment. Again, there are exceptions to every rule, but these industry exclusions seem to be most recognized.

Early Actions

The following should be completed before a Borrower applies for POF:

1. A candidate for POF should be successful in acquiring a purchase order from a strong new or existing customer.

2. The POF Lender must approve the strength of the purchase order originator.

3. Borrower must determine a reliable supplier to provide the materials to complete the PO.

4. Borrower must prepare a draft order to the supplier for POF review.

What's important to a POF Lender within the purchase order?

- That the purchase order is non-cancelable.
- What are the important dates, such as delivery and shipping?
- What are vendor requirements before manufacturing and delivery?
- Is the customer (purchase order originator) a new or existing customer?
- Does the ordering customer represent a creditworthy source?
- If a foreign manufacturer or distributor is involved, is the vendor an experienced and legal provider? Can it meet customer timing and specifications? What are shipping, insurance, and U. S. Customs considerations?
- Purchase Order issuers may also be qualified by factors. A factor may ultimately finance the invoice (once purchase order is complete), permitting payment to the purchase order finance company.

The POF Lender will also be interested in the Borrower's capacity for performance and purchase order compliance. This purchase order could be unusually large; even though raw materials or components may become available through POF, can the Borrower in fact process and complete the order? Has another vendor been used in the past for the same requirements? If so, why is the Borrower now using a new supplier? Recognizing that a factor most likely will be the initial source of repayment, are there, or should there be, other repayment considerations (i.e., guarantees)?

The Process

POF Lender will advance to the supplier (or vendor) funds necessary to fill up to 100% of the order. Such an advance may involve direct payment to the supplier or obtaining letters of credit on behalf of the Borrower. Once the initial purchase order is completed, an invoice to the Borrower's customer is produced. The POF Lender may then either factor that invoice himself or do so through a third party. The resulting factoring payment will be used to pay out the purchase order advance and fees. Any remainder, which may include a portion of profitability, would go to the Borrower.

The Cost

A POF Lender's loan (advances) pricing depends on the transaction. These funding fees generally fall in the range of 2%–4% per 30 days. Additionally, certain management fees may be included based upon the total value of the purchase order. Applicable costs related to the purchase order transaction may also be required to be paid by the Borrower.

Specialized purchase order lenders are few in number. However, these few are generally key contenders in the industry. See Chapter 9 for sources.

There are certain *pre-approved* purchase order financing programs, which are similar to lines of credit. The purchase order is submitted for approval. Once approved, funds are provided to the Borrower to assist in the funding requirement to fulfill the customer order.

A purchase order financing Lender can materially assist the Borrower throughout the entire purchase order and fulfillment process.

MEZZANINE LENDING

We recognize that sound (profitable) operating companies may be able to successfully arrange for both short- and long-term financing covering their working capital, equipment, real estate, and growth financing requirements. *Once a company's financing requirements exceed its capital, as well as its ability to attract conventional Lenders, it may be time to consider outside investors.* The investors' contributions to capital would normally dilute the ownership of the company. Such dilution may not be acceptable to the current owners. There are options.

At this point, mezzanine financing may become a viable vehicle whereby additional funding could be obtained without substantial owners' dilution.

Dissimilar mezzanine Lenders seek different relationship profiles. In practice, mezzanine lending usually focuses more on the "bread and butter" type of business rather than high technology or rapidly developing companies. Turnarounds and real estate development generally are not considered.

The term "mezzanine" is derived from the fact that (on the liabilities side of the Balance Sheet format) this financing is neither reflected as pure debt nor as pure equity. It is not on the top shelf (current or long-term debt) nor is it on the bottom, classified as owners' equity. It is rather displayed in the middle, or in the "mezzanine," of accounting classifications.

Mezzanine debt is usually unsecured and subordinated to senior-debt financing. It may exist with a term of up to 5 years or more. There may be financial covenants associated with this subordinated debt. Mezzanine Lenders may also rely on the senior secured Lender's default provisions. Mezzanine Lenders may, or may not, seek a seat on the Borrower's board of directors; most seek board observation rights.

Mezzanine Lenders commonly seek:

- A seasoned management team
- A history of profitable operations
- Established cash flow to address debt service
- Satisfactory books and records
- Acceptable historical financial statements
- A scenario of tiered financial forecasts with assumptions
- Return on investment anywhere from 10% to 25% (or higher)
- A realistic "exit strategy"

Remember that this layer of debt is actually *both debt and equity* concurrently. These specialized lenders (or investors), following their substantial due diligence, loan funds to the company with an "equity kicker" attached. In many cases such funds are regarded as redeemable preferred stock. These equity kickers enable these investors to exercise *pre-established options* to buy into the company (equity purchase) if they wish to do so upon maturity. Exit strategies are paramount to these investors. In the beginning, most mezzanine Lenders really do not want a piece of the company. They only seek to have their position repurchased. However, with a substantial "winner," stock conversion may be the right choice. During the period of time to maturity, there may or may not also be an interest rate factor associated with the debt portion. Sometimes loaned funds are interest free for a few years, and then an interest provision may kick in.

Mezzanine lending is usually an expensive way to go. Such lenders seek the bigger dollar investments with little probability of loss.

At maturity, the (premium) final payment becomes due to the mezzanine Lender. If the complete debt, along with the premium, cannot be paid, agreement provisions may detail how this debt, or a portion of it, may be converted to common stock. Other options may also be addressed.

SBA LOANS AND LOAN GUARANTEES

Many of us have had some experience with the Small Business Administration (SBA). It may have been for a small business loan, an equipment or real estate transaction, or simply a discussion relative to a business situation with the no-cost consulting group SCORE (Service Corps of Retired Executives). Additionally, the SBA-related Small Business Development Centers (SBDCs) are located nationwide to answer questions and conduct training courses. For a detailed review, criteria, and qualifications for programs offered by the SBA, go to the administration's Web site at *www.sba.org*. We will only cover some of the fundamentals within this section. Also, be sure to discuss the relevance of an SBA loan program or guarantee with your accountant or financial adviser.

The reader is put on notice that federal programs, such as the SBA's financing and loan guarantee programs, are subject to frequent amendments. Please contact the nearest SBA district office or the SBA Web site for complete and up-to-date information.

For *our purposes* we are discussing the 7(a) Loan Guaranty Program and the 504 Certified Development Company ("CDC") loans. These programs can be of value to businesses that are being squeezed by their current Lender; that is, where cash flow may no longer meet working capital needs or debt service requirements. Collateral may also be regarded as insufficient by the current Lender. Possibly special large-asset purchases may be on the horizon, or an acquisition opportunity has developed. The 7(a) program will be discussed first.

7(a) Loan Guaranty Program

The 7(a) program is the primary assistance program, and the most popular, for small business, and is extremely flexible. "Small business" is defined by both the number of employees and annual sales revenues. This program provides *a benefit to a Lender* in that a *portion* of his loan can be guaranteed against loss. Lenders actually make the loans and, in conjunction with an SBA approval, a loan guarantee is issued. Such guarantee considerations may induce the Lender to approve a loan, or restructure one, which would not otherwise be approved. Both the SBA and the Lender *share* in the risk of loan loss.

Possible uses of loan proceeds:

- The purchase of real estate (land or buildings)
- Expansion or renovation of facilities
- New construction financing (commercial buildings only)
- Leasehold improvements
- Purchase of machinery and equipment, furniture and fixtures
- Purchase of inventory
- Short-term working capital
- Business acquisition

Generally the Borrower cannot refinance existing debt through the SBA. However, there are some exceptions. A Borrower should discuss such needs with an SBA Lender. Also, SBA loans cannot address the repayment of funds to an owner or the payment of delinquent federal or state taxes.

The SBA Lenders

While not all banks participate in the SBA lending programs, most banks do. Also, selected alternative Lenders (such as federal credit unions, commercial finance companies, and others) may also take part in these SBA programs. Lenders are referred to as either a "Preferred" Lender or "Certified" Lender. Preferred Lenders provide a faster track to loan approval because they themselves are authorized by the SBA to approve and close the loan. Preferred Lenders may also do most of the loan servicing and have liquidation authority. Preferred Lender candidates, based upon their demonstrated expertise over time, are nominated by SBA field offices. Certified Lenders perform applicant analyses, sending their completed applications to the SBA for approval.

The Process

The Borrower applies to the Lender for the loan needed. It is important for the Borrower to know in advance the basic loan requirements of the Lender and the SBA. Most of these "preliminary" qualifications can be obtained from the Lender. The Lender then utilizes his normal credit and loan approval procedures. If the Lender determines that this loan cannot be made within the institution's own credit criteria, the Borrower may be a candidate for an SBA guarantee. The Lender must certify to the SBA that he is unable to make the loan without an SBA guarantee.

The Lender will then apply (submit an application) to the SBA for approval of a loan guarantee program. The application, with supporting schedules, is substantially a credit analysis with recommendations by the Lender. The SBA then conducts its own credit review and renders a decision. *This is true unless the Borrower is working with a Preferred Lender.* As mentioned, a Preferred Lender may approve the entire guarantee relationship. The SBA may also seek additional information directly from the Borrower. Once the SBA guarantee is approved, the Lender may close the loan. Loan payments are made to the Lender.

The SBA has its own set of criteria to qualify a potential Borrower as "eligible." Some of these include adequacy of:

- Collateral
- Cash flow
- Owner's equity
- Business plan (if applicable)
- Management capability ("Statement of Personal History" will be required from each owner)

Other important qualifiers:

- The type of business
- Business size restrictions
- Must be a for-profit company
- Use of loan proceeds
- The Borrower must not already possess sufficient assets to cover the financing requirement sought
- Debt service coverage (loan repayment ability considering all other debt)

Once the SBA approves the guaranteed portion, it also will establish certain financial and non-financial loan covenants. Loan repayment structures and amortizations will be determined.

It should also be noted that all who own 20% or more of a business are required to personally guarantee the SBA loan. As is common to most loan transactions, there will be associated costs and fees. There may also be *important loan prepayment considerations*. These costs and fees are similar to those discussed in Chapter 5.

SBA 504 Certified Development Company Program

This program addresses Borrowers seeking long-term, fixed-rate financing for large fixed assets such as:

- Purchase of real estate and land
- Construction of new facilities
- Renovations of existing facilities
- Purchase of machinery and equipment

The 504 loans, as with others, may be initiated through a commercial Lender whose institution works with the SBA. A certified development company (CDC) may also work with the Lender, assisting in loan approval. An important consideration affecting the approval of these loans is both job retention and job creation. SBA collateral usually involves those assets being financed. The Lender generally will provide 50% of the financing, and the CDC 40%; the Borrower is required to have at least 10% equity. The 504 program *cannot* be used for working capital or inventory purchases, consolidating or repaying debt, or refinancing. As in the 7(a) program, personal guarantees will be required from those owning over 20% of the borrowing company.

SBA "LowDoc" Loans: This program addresses the smaller business loans—a maximum of $150,000 (at this writing). The Borrower must have an excellent credit history. The program is touted as fast and takes much of the red tape out of the loan process. Check with the SBA, as minimums and maximums change frequently. A response within the LowDoc Program can usually be received from the SBA within 36 hours of application submission. The application is only two pages; the Lender completes the first page and the Borrower completes the second (reverse) page. The Lender then submits the application to the SBA for approval. Loans are expected to be satisfactorily collateralized by the business, and possibly also by the owners, but *a lack of collateral is not necessarily a reason for a turndown.* This type of loan may also be addressed for business start-ups.

What if the SBA is called upon by the Lender for its guarantee? It should be noted that if an SBA guarantee is "called," the SBA would only reimburse a Lender for that portion of the loan which is guaranteed. The Borrower would still have a legal obligation to the primary Lender for any remaining unpaid portion of the loan. However, if the Borrower's situation is not too difficult, the Lender may consider a "term out" (create a short-term loan) for the small remainder still owed.

Other Specialized Lending

The following categories of specialized lending offerings are generally available to most borrowers, acknowledging certain criteria and application requirements. To address these financial offerings, the Borrower should rely on his accountant, financial professionals, and his current Lender. An excellent professional commercial lending association source, the Commercial Finance Association and its membership of commercial lenders, may be contacted through the association's Web site at *www.cfa.org* (see Chapter 9).

STATE AND MUNICIPAL FINANCE OFFERINGS

Most states and counties (or other political subdivisions) offer financing for businesses currently operating within their borders or as an incentive for "foreign" (out-of-state) businesses to move to their localities. The Web site of each governmental entity usually lists contacts and links to programs that are offered.

Such programs may be identified by names like these:

- Economic Development Commission
- (State or Regional) Economic Development Corporation
- Department of Economic & Community Development
- (State) Business Development Corporation
- (State) Development Authority
- Office of Business Development
- Finance Authority
- Community Development Finance Corporation
- Community Capital Corporation

Generally there are expected to be benefits accruing not only to the operating business but to the local government. Local benefits may be realized in several areas: creating jobs for local residents, enabling a local company to continue operations, enhancing tax revenues, addressing social responsibilities, and positioning area businesses for the global economy.

The *business loan offerings* are not unlike most commercial banks or fixed-asset Lenders:

- Term loans (equipment and real estate)
- Term working capital
- Real estate mortgages: Acquisition, renovation, construc-

tion, and permanent financing (owned-occupied property)
- Lines of credit
- Investment capital
- Equity capital (early stage)
- Loan guarantees
- Performance guarantees
- Loans and guarantees for technology-based business
- Specialized agricultural and energy conservation loans
- Special loans to assist businesses in specific communities
- Venture investments

Benefits to a Borrower from contacting such governmental entities are:

1. Targeted loan programs
2. Flexible and attractive interest rate packages
3. Accommodating debt amortizations
4. Flexible loan terms and conditions
5. Dealing with local Lenders with local connections

These state, regional, or local Lenders may also participate with conventional Lenders (even your current Lender) to make an overall transaction work. Loan participations enable your current Lender to retain your primary business relationship. This additional supplemental lending (usually of a unique nature) is obtained through governmental or local sources and does not generally increase the exposure of the primary Lender.

EMPLOYEE STOCK OWNERSHIP PLAN (ESOP)

Essentially an ESOP is a unique way to sell a company, buy out a retiring owner, or upset a hostile takeover. *For the purposes of our discussion* we are regarding a company in financial difficulties. When a company has exhausted its sources of working capital (and Lenders' credit), the ESOP is frequently used as a last-ditch effort for business survival. The profile of such an ESOP candidate may be one of a history of losses, a deficit net worth, and a Lender(s) seeking to recover loans without delay. These *current Lender(s) may seek repayment* either through another take-out Lender or through liquidation and sale of its collateral.

As indicated by the title, this ownership program enables participating employees (including management) to "purchase" all, or a portion, of the company. These new shareholders generally expect to have a voice in the company's direction and are personally motivated to rescue their company (and their source of employment) from its current state.

The ESOP is described as an employee benefit plan in which the employees (to include management) own the shares of the company. These shares are held in an ESOP Trust. The trust itself may borrow money from Lenders to facilitate the ESOP transaction and for ongoing business finance purposes. This trust can only invest in the company's stock.

A replacement Lender will usually be needed to fund the ESOP and provide fresh working capital. There are Lenders that may address this situation, but usually with caveats that may be much more stringent than that of the former Lender.

The ESOP Trust executes a Promissory Note and the company further guarantees payment to the Lender. The trust may then purchase the stock from the former shareholders with its newly borrowed funds. Over time the company contributes funds to the ESOP Trust (or through other mechanisms), enabling it to pay off the Lender's loan. As the loan is paid down, stock is issued to the employees.

An ESOP is a transaction of intense negotiations with many associated parties. All too often the company involved may also be one of the major employers in town. The local or regional press usually publicizes the transaction.

The former management may, or may not, stay on in the "new" company. A new business plan is usually required, not only to map a reasonable path to recovery, but to attract a replacement Lender. It is important to have ESOP employees be a part of the business plan development. As "owners" of the company they now expect to be part of the process—and *that is important* within this environment.

While it is possible to regain productivity, improve efficiencies, and lower employee turnover, there is no assurance that operations will be profitable. However, if success is in the cards, employees of an ESOP may be well rewarded for their investment through enhancement of the company's value.

The ESOP is not a quick fix. There are many ongoing management, legal, accounting, and tax issues. *Because of these issues, it is imperative that the buyers and sellers work with knowledgeable legal counsel and Lenders who have a history of addressing ESOPs.*

DEBTOR-IN-POSSESSION (DIP) FINANCING

It is essential that the Borrower utilize legal counsel and financial advisers before initiating actions concerning DIP financing.

A business bankruptcy need not be the end of the road. There are usually identifiable reasons for such a circumstance. Not all of the reasons may have been in the company's control, and not all of them may be of a magnitude to "kill" a company. Bankruptcy may be voluntary (at the Borrower's election) or involuntary (initiated by creditors and a court petition).

If it can be established that there is a strategy that has a reasonable chance of success in returning a company to prosperity and financial stability, as well as addressing creditor requirements, the owner's recovery efforts may be worthwhile. A plan of reorganization addressing these issues must be approved by the bankruptcy court. This plan is prepared by the Borrower with the assistance of his legal counsel, financial advisers, creditor information, and potential Lender(s). It follows, of course, that DIP financing can be accomplished only under the approval of the bankruptcy court.

Asset-based Lenders are especially adept at providing DIP financing. This financing can provide funds to address both the required working capital as well as addressing other reorganization plan requirements. Much like the asset-based criteria described earlier in this chapter, eligible assets are the foundation of this secured financing. Working with an asset-based Lender (determining loan availabilities up front), it is possible to assess the potential practicality and success of preliminary creditor arrangements, as the Borrower develops his settlement package. If the Borrower's current Lender is unwilling or unable to provide DIP financing, the Borrower may, in concert *with recommendations from his financial advisers,* contact an asset-based Lender.

It is noted that the Borrower cannot emerge from bankruptcy until the DIP Lender is paid. Once the DIP Lender is paid off, the Borrower most likely will continue to have need of a Lending partner as the business continues.

There are many *other financial vehicles* through which to address both mundane and unique business financing challenges. Your accountant and financial advisers are aware of most. While a few of the more prominent have been discussed in this chapter, there is no lack of variations or creativity of Lenders who seek to address business financing requirements. And that's good news!

CHAPTER 9

EFFECTIVE SOURCING OF BORROWED FUNDS

"There are so many Lenders—how do I choose?
And why bother?"

"The bank is sharing my loan with how many lenders?"

"Maybe I do need an 'alternative' Lender."

"A broker for what?"

Depending upon the creditworthiness of the Borrower, and his eligible collateral, sourcing new or replacement business borrowings can be an extremely quick exercise or a time-consuming and daunting endeavor. It can be especially tough on the Borrower who is not aware of the numerous funding sources available. In Chapter 8 we covered many types of financing that may be relative to a Borrower's situation. *In this chapter we'll discuss the mechanics of locating these potential Lenders.*

TRADITIONAL LENDERS

Commercial banks and thrift institutions (savings banks) continue to be the traditional sources of business lending. These traditional Lenders are also referred to as "mainstream" or "prime" Lenders.

In the past, the source of funds for almost any business use was the neighborhood bank. While selection of a bank for personal use has not changed too much—close proximity being the prime issue—the sourcing of *business loans* has completely changed over the years.

While the bank down the street may still exist, its commercial banking capabilities cannot come close to matching those of the larger state, regional, and national banks. However, these smaller banks, through specialized subscriber services and affiliations with larger institutions, may still offer commercial loan opportunities.

There are basically four types of traditional commercial banks:

1. A *state bank* is chartered by the state and subject to state banking regulations. State banks have access to the Federal Reserve services and can become members of the Federal Reserve System. State bank supervision is the responsibility of each state's banking department and the Federal Deposit Insurance Corporation (FDIC).

2. A *national bank* is chartered by the federal government. National banks are supervised by the Comptroller of the Currency, a member of the FDIC. National banks came into existence in the 1860s, when the government began developing a uniform national currency. Currently, national banks represent about 30% of U.S. commercial banks, but hold more than two-thirds of all deposits in FDIC-insured banks.

3. A *thrift institution* (aka savings bank and savings & loan associations) primarily accepts deposits and makes home mortgage loans.

4. An *independent bank* (aka *community bank*) is a locally owned and operated commercial bank. Its market is within its community and it is not affiliated with a multi-bank holding company.

Credit unions will be covered later in this chapter under Alternative Lenders. This is because several credit unions are emerging from being traditional consumer Lenders into being *competitive* commercial Lenders.

By their nature, one expects a "commercial" bank to be a full-service bank. These institutions, based upon their size, may provide to their business customers an array of business products, including:

- Free business checking accounts
- Business loans (secured and unsecured)
- Specialized lending services (asset-based, factoring [see Chapter 8])
- Commercial real estate mortgages
- SBA loans and guarantees by certified or preferred Lenders
- Cash management services
- Payroll services
- Business credit cards
- Letter of credit services
- Trade financing
- Foreign exchange
- International banking
- Precious metal services

- Leasing programs
- Tax depository services
- Insurance services
- Brokerage services

That's the real advantage of going with the larger traditional lenders. They really can do it all!

Of course, the Borrower who does not precisely fit within a bank's credit policy—one whose collateral may not be quite satisfactory, whose risk rating does not excite the bank regarding future business, whose type of business is something the bank doesn't do—may seem to be out of options. This is where the alternative Lender comes into the picture. Frequently, a bank will "participate" in a lending relationship with an alterative Lender (see explanation later in this chapter). This way, the home bank may retain the primary banking services while letting another Lender do all, or a portion, of the commercial lending requirements.

The alternative Lender will usually rise to the occasion when a traditional Lender says, "We cannot do this," or "It cannot be done."

ALTERNATIVE LENDERS

Alternative Lenders *do not include* commercial banks or savings banks per se; however, divisions or wholly owned subsidiaries of commercial banks may be considered alternative Lenders due to the nature of the subsidiary or its product offerings.

Alternative Lenders primarily include:

- Independent commercial finance companies
- Specialized commercial finance companies
- Divisions or captives of industrial or insurance companies
- Divisions or subsidiaries of commercial banks

For our purposes, we will also include within alternative Lenders selected credit unions, the Small Business Administration (SBA), and state, regional, or municipal development corporations.

The profile of an alternative Lender differs greatly from a commercial or savings bank. Many are not regulated in the manner of commercial banks. While some have industry peer groups that provide annual reviews of loan portfolios and operations, some others may be self-regulated through periodic internal reviews. This is not to say that professional standards are not adhered to or that the highest ethics are not in evidence.

Alternative Lenders are frequently staffed with former seasoned bankers as well as commercial finance specialists, attorneys, and in-house accountants. Their operating departments may rival those of the larger of commercial banks. Dealing with alternative Lenders may provide:

1. **Quick access** to the decision maker. Many do not operate through a formal credit committee. Most provide rapid credit approvals. New-business personnel are aggressive and, in my opinion, are *frequently* more experienced than their banking counterparts, the new-business Loan Officers. The sales staff usually has *direct access* to credit approval authorities, thus enabling quick *preliminary* loan qualification at the highest level. Senior management of an alternative Lender may know a good deal about the loan prospect as well as which direction the loan structuring will take *before* the loan approval process is even completed. This can be a real plus for the Borrower.

2. **A host of financial products** are available: Asset-based lending, factoring, and various types of term loans, real estate lending, purchase order financing and others. Some will have unsecured loan components. All seem flexible on terms and conditions; interest rates and advance rate flexibilities are readily apparent. Of course, all are consistent with good credit and collateral management.

3. **Capacity** may be a drawback. While most alternative Lenders can address loans from $250,000 to $5,000,000, only the largest (and there are some) can loan into the mega-loan deals up to $100,000,000.

4. **Riskier credits** are usually adaptable to selective alternative Lenders. These loans typically are below $5,000,000 and may

go down into the $100,000 range. While the alternative Lender may approve such loans, interest rates will definitely address risk exposure. If a Borrower *with a credit risk issue* is sensitive to interest rates, he may have to reconsider the reality of his situation.

5. Of course, alternative Lenders may have *restrictions*. There may be collateral advance rate limitations or possibly loan caps placed within eligible components of inventory. The size of machinery and equipment (M&E) term loans as compared to the entire credit facility may need to be "balanced." There will be appropriate financial and non-financial loan covenants. Most have no depository capacities (as commercial banks do) and no letter of credit capacities (unless they are bank affiliated). Usually there are no, or limited, cash management programs, but many do use lockboxes for Borrowers' customer payments. *Much of this is really not too much of a problem as many alternative Lenders permit the Borrower to continue working, to an extent, with a commercial bank of their choice.*

6. **Hot buttons**. What gets the attention of an alternative Lender?

- A pass-off from a bank—it may be a poor bank deal but it can actually be a *good* deal for the alternative Lender.
- Direct contact by a potential Borrower, rather than through a Lender, broker, or consultant.
- No broker involvement. No loan proceeds dilution (more on this later).
- Borrower has no price sensitivity. Usually the last concern of a Borrower in troubled times, when he absolutely needs the loan, is the interest rate. Sure, there are limits (sometimes regulated limits), but these can usually be satisfactorily resolved. *Alternative Lenders must, of course, be paid for their risk taking.*

The Borrower will note when reading the term sheets or proposal letters received from alternative Lenders that they may appear very aggressive in nature, much more so than commercial banks, considering their focus on their targeted market. The reader will remember that we discussed collateral enhancements in an earlier chapter. Alternative Lenders also seek collateral enhancements, and usually ask for more than expected. Again, the Borrower's exceptional risk may be the issue. Alternative Lenders expect their due, and in return can usually perform well for a Borrower.

There are certain business situations that may indicate the need for an alternative Lender:

- Unfavorable trends. Banks do not like to take on, or live with, a continuance of poor performance. This is especially true when they see little chance for recovery.
- Borrower is in a forbearance situation with his current Lender.
- While not yet in a forbearance situation, the commercial bank's attitude indicates to the Borrower it may be time to review his options.
- Risk rating issues continue to be voiced by the current Lender. Certain risk ratings may no longer be regarded as viable credits for the bank.
- Inability to rectify financial covenant violations.
- Collateral deterioration.
- Other commercial banks the Borrower has contacted show little interest in "bailing out" a competitor.
- Due to internal bank situations, it is suggested that the Borrower finds another Lender.
- Seasonal business. Too difficult for the bank to provide needed financing.
- Borrower is in too volatile an industry for the commercial banker.
- The Borrower is growing too fast and may blow through the approved credit line or the bank's lending limit.
- Bankruptcy.
- Borrower has been assigned to a loan workout department.

All of these represent an alternative Lender's "field of dreams"—lots of new business opportunities. Alternative Lenders' sales personnel frequently visit the loan workout departments of commercial banks, for obvious reasons. Only two or three "booked" referral contacts from these banks can result in a good year for business development representatives of alternative Lenders.

I have found that collateral advance rates are not greatly improved when dealing with an alternative Lender. This may be compensated by the Lender's unique loan structures (addressing needs) that a commercial bank would not consider. Most alternative Lenders are well seasoned in collateral analysis. Also, continued collateral monitoring procedures may be more stringent or frequent than they are for a commercial bank.

Interest rates, like those of commercial banks, are most always tied to the variable prime interest rate. Some alternative Lenders will use the LIBOR index, but these loans must be of a good size. Alternative Lenders may charge from prime + ½% to prime + 8% or more (higher rates are infrequent). The total loan yield is really the key for the Lender. If a lower rate must be quoted to obtain this loan, the fee structure may take up the slack. *Again, there usually is a significant risk for the alternative Lender.* Remember, the bank does not want to do this deal, nor commit to any significant credit line extensions.

From time to time a "bankable" credit is done by an alternative Lender. And sometimes, a Borrower does not recognize his own creditworthiness. I've also seen instances in which the Borrower has had an established relationship with an alternative Lender and would not think of moving his business elsewhere. I believe it is all due to the flexibilities and experience levels of such Lenders and their reluctance to "pull the plug" on *any* Borrower.

Fees charged by alternative Lenders are similar to those discussed in Chapter 5.

Loan documentation is not dissimilar to a bank commercial loan. I have found the financial covenant section somewhat simpler, and with fewer covenants, than when dealing with a commercial bank. This is not true in all cases, but is a common observation.

When dealing with alternative Lenders, *personal guarantees* are almost always required. As discussed in Chapter 5, owners of 20% or more of a business usually must provide such guarantees. Spouses may also be requested to provide their guarantee. The guarantee may have to be additionally collateralized by personal real estate or other personal assets. It really depends on the adequacy of the basic collateral coverage that will be available to the alternative Lender.

Timely performance is usually excellent. Alternative Lenders are known for their rapid new business reviews, approvals, and loan closings. It may be that a loan opportunity may be impacted by a forbearance fee deadline, vendor pressures, or competitive alternative Lenders. They are used to working under such pressures—a plus for the Borrower.

Real Experiences!

This large East Coast Borrower had, during the past two years, turned down *two* loan proposals from the same alternative Lender. Both times he decided to remain with his existing bank, where he was "more comfortable." At the beginning of each loan search, the Borrower indicated to the alternative Lender that he definitely wanted to see what they could provide and that he was dissatisfied with his current bank relationship. Exasperated after putting much work into these two proposals, the alternative Lender had pretty much decided this was definitely a bank-oriented Borrower and no additional time should be expended on this prospect. Still, the alternative Lender sent a short letter regretting the loss of the deal and indicating that if he could help in the future, the Borrower should call.

In less than one month the Borrower did call, saying he had the opportunity of a lifetime. He wanted to buy an existing profitable business but had to have a Lender's commitment in two days. His current bank had begun working on this, but he was sure it could not handle the required time frame. He was right—and his bank also told him *no one* could move this quickly. Inasmuch as the "unsuccessful" alternative Lender already had significant credit information from the two previous *lost* deals, all it really had to do was to review the most recent business financial data. Alternative Lenders usually do not have a maze of credit committees or layers of credit approvals. A commitment letter *was* issued within two days, addressing a multimillion-dollar business purchase with a closing scheduled within weeks. At the time of the closing, the bank was still trying to put the deal together. The bank is now concerned that the Borrower, because of the alternative Lender's unique performance, may give them his other two material loans. Do not assume, just because a Lender is *not* a commercial bank, that it does not have the expertise, or the will, to invest the time it takes to address special loan situations.

LOCATING ALTERNATIVE LENDERS

Working with well-known, reputable, and respected alternative Lenders and their industry associations, as well as seeking referrals from other professional sources, can keep a Borrower on the straight and narrow. When questions arise on such issues of Lender qualifications, capacities, and the like, contact your attorney or a professional lending association for clarifications.

Identifying alternative Lenders may be accomplished through preliminary contacts with professional Lender associations. A particularly good source is the Commercial Finance Association (CFA). Contact the association at:

225 West 34th Street, Suite 1815
New York, NY 10122
(212) 594-3490
www.cfa.com

Founded in 1944, CFA represents the financial services industry. Members include both traditional and alternative lenders—commercial banks, their financial subsidiaries, captive commercial finance companies belonging to major industrial companies, and independent commercial finance companies. Member capacities and capabilities can address Lending requirements of almost any size in just about any industry. The Web site reflects the membership, lending specialties, loan sizes, and contact information. The Web site also provides for initial loan inquiries through its "Need a Business Loan?" page.

There are CFA chapters regionally throughout the United States and

Canada, with affiliates around the world. Its membership of Lenders address the types of loans listed below, as well as others not listed:

Asset-Based Lending	Term Lending
Factoring	Mezzanine Lending
Accounts Receivable Financing	Loan Participations
Inventory Financing	Floor Planning
Purchase Order Financing	Healthcare
Machinery & Equipment Loans	Import-Export
Real Estate Loans	Leasing
ESOP Loans	Construction
Letters of Credit Financing	Leveraged Buyouts
Debtor-in-Possession Financing	SBA Loans
Seasonal Lending Requirements	Bridge Financings

A Borrower's professional contacts may also be familiar with the Turnaround Management Association, business and industry associations, and area chambers of commerce. Members of these groups are frequently aware of alternative Lender contacts.

There are other organizations with entrée into commercial lending sources:

The Small Business Administration (SBA) provides business loans and loan guarantees through its 504 loan program and its 7(a) Loan Guaranty Program (see Chapter 8).

The SBA works closely with its originating commercial Lenders (to include alternative Lenders) through its network of "Preferred" and "Certified" Lenders. Through the Small Business Development Center (SBDC) program, the SBA also provides lending information, contact sources, and guidance at numerous national sites. There are 63 SBDC offices, at least one in every state. The SBA's Web site is *www.sba.gov*. SBDC's Web site is *www.asbdc-us.org*.

Federal Credit Unions: There were some 5,776 federal credit unions in the United States as of December 2003. These are nonprofit savings institutions that historically have made personal loans and provided other consumer banking services to persons within their field of membership.

Many credit unions, abiding within the National Credit Union Association (NCUA) rules and regulations, may now also provide commercial loans to their business members.

Such lending products may include secured commercial loans, including term loans, lines of credit, and commercial real estate loans. Depending on the size of the credit union, and the extent of its commitment to developing this line of business, a Borrower may find many of the lending products that are offered within a commercial bank.

Credit union commercial lending personnel are as experienced as any found in banking. In fact, most of them have material commercial banking backgrounds. They, like their banking counterparts, are interested in expanding their loan portfolios. Where the situation allows, credit union Lenders can be flexible with their terms and conditions. Following are some of the special requirements and other items of interest regarding credit union lending:

- A Borrower *must* become a member of the credit union. This is true whether the Borrower is a sole proprietorship, corporation, LLC, LLP, or a trust. Also, guarantors, shareholders, and directors may be required to become members. This is an easy and inexpensive requirement and is frequently accomplished at the time of a commercial loan closing.
- Credit unions cannot participate loans with commercial banks, but may participate with other credit unions (see Loan Participation later in this chapter)
- Credit unions do not enter into joint ventures.
- Credit unions may be able to charge below-market rates on loans while paying higher rates to member savers, as they are exempt from certain taxes.
- Credit unions' field of membership eligibility has been expanded during past years. Most likely a Borrower can find a credit union where he will be qualified for membership.
- Commercial loan relationships may be restricted to certain market areas.

Credit union regulations and requirements do change from time to time, so a Borrower should become aware of the current offerings by visiting those credit unions in his area that provide commercial loans. It can be well worth the time involved.

For a listing of those credit unions (the 100 largest credit unions by city and state) that *may* provide commercial loan products, go to the NCUA Web site at *www.ncua.gov*. Go to Reports, Plans & Statistics, then to the 2005 Year End Statement, Table of Contents and then to Table 22.

State, County, and Municipal Development Corporations: In Chapter 8 we discussed the many and varied loan and guarantee offerings provided by local and regional development corporations. To further identify these loans and guarantee resources that may address a Borrower's situation, go to the Web site for the National Association of Development Organizations (NADO) at www.nado.org. Go to the Economic Development Finance Service (EDFS) links (click More on EDFS), click Links, and then click on any of a long list of over 100 development organization contacts. For example:

- **Department of Agriculture Rural Development; Business and Industry Guaranteed Loan Program:** Loans and grant programs for the private sector and community organiz ations through financial assistance and planning.
- **Angel Capital Association:** A peer-to-peer organization for early-stage venture investments.
- **Coalition of Community Development Financial Institutions:** Click "Need Capital" for offices by state.
- **National Association of Development Companies:** Companies certified by the SBA to provide the SBA's 504 Loan Program. Directory provided.
- **National Association of Small Business Investment Companies:** SBIC programs for venture capital equity funds and term loans.
- **National Venture Capital Association:** Connection for start-up and early-stage capital.
- **Association of Small Business Development Centers:**

More of an information site for smaller business, but does address accessing capital, with a special section for veterans.

Technology Capital: Due to the extensive nature of this subject, I will highlight only one state organization. The Borrower can identify other technology loan funding sources from private and public technology sources at *http://www.eere.engery.gov/inventions/energytechnet/resources.* Once at the site, click down to Funding Sources, search All Records, click Loan Fundings, and then click All States.

The Technology Capital Network (TCN) is hosted by the Massachusetts Institute of Technology (MIT). This program is open to Massachusetts investors and entrepreneurs. This is the nation's longest-established venture capital network. Within the Web site it is mentioned that the network provides introductions of entrepreneurs to private investors. For more, go to the Web site: *www.tcnmit.org.*

The Export-Import Bank of the United States (**"Ex-Im Bank"**) assists in the export of American products through loans, guarantees, and insurance programs to businesses. Most programs are available to *any* size U.S. business. Ex-Im Bank provides a Working Capital Guarantee Program and Export Credit Insurance. Credit insurance diminishes risks of non-collection in foreign countries; political risks may also be covered. The Working Capital Guarantee Program provides guarantees to banks that are willing to lend to exporting companies. This guarantee may be secured by a Borrower's foreign accounts receivable and/or inventory destined for foreign customers. The Small Business Administration and the Export-Import Bank now have a co-guarantee cooperative program. Contact the Ex-Im Bank at *www.exim.gov.*

The Turnaround Management Association (TMA) was established in 1988 and has over 7,000 members with 34 chapters worldwide. TMA is the only nonprofit association dedicated to corporate renewal and turnaround management. Among its membership, some *14% are Lenders, bankers, and workout officers*. This resource may assist Borrowers in identifying Lenders who are experienced in debtor-in-possession financing. Contact TMA on its Web site at *www.turnaround.org.*

Internet Loan Sourcing: There is a large universe of Web sites offering business loans. Loan sizes addressed appear to be relatively small, with most loans under $100,000. There are some that offer larger loans, but they really seem to be Web-based loan brokers. These sites, in addition to providing their own loan criteria, offer assistance in preparing financing requests and business plans.

There are also what is termed "peer-to-peer" loans. These seem well suited for those who seek a small amount of start-up capital (or working capital)—up to $25,000—and have been rejected by a Lender. These sites seek to match Borrowers and Lenders in a bidding format. Two of these peer-to-peer sites are *www.prospper.com* and *www.zopa.com*. Generally, peer-to-peer lending is considered to be a risky business. Higher interest rates are typical because of the Lender's risk.

Other sites enabling expanded searches for commercial loans are:

www.smallbusinessloans.com
www.ibank.com
www.inc.com/guides/finance/23039/html

ABOUT LOAN BROKERS

As the reader can appreciate, there is a considerable amount of preparation time required prior to the point of actually approaching potential Lenders. Simply the array of such Lenders, both traditional and alternative, can be daunting. Also, unique to each of these Lenders are their internal credit and collateral qualifiers as well as their appetite for risks.

How should a Borrower approach this important issue? Should a Borrower attempt to canvass all apparent potential Lenders, or simply go to those Lenders who are in his comfort zone (considering locality or familiarity)?

Focusing on only those specific Lenders who most likely would be receptive will significantly increase the chances for a timely success. And *timing* may be the deciding factor if the Borrower is under pressure to refinance with another Lender. The experienced commercial loan broker performs an extensive search for *qualified* Lenders; Lenders he believes will address a Borrower's *specific* situation. The loan broker performs most of the legwork including elements of search, evaluation, and coordination. The commercial loan broker, for a fee, does this in an accelerated and focused fashion, more so than is usually achievable by a single Borrower.

The commercial loan broker is most likely a financing business professional with many years of successful experience. He may be from the field of banking or alternative lending, or may be a certified public accountant, lawyer, or business consultant (or a combination of these). Usually there are no formal state, professional, or academic requirements for presenting oneself as a commercial loan broker. These brokers will have readily available professional references, which may include not only the clients they have directly served, but the commercial lenders who may have benefited from the broker's referrals. Brokers may be sourced through professional business associations, commercial lenders with whom the Borrower may be familiar, accountants, business consultants, or commercial attorneys. It is advisable to contact at least three loan brokers, meet with each, and then make a decision. The Borrower's accountant or other advisers may also assist in this selection.

The Borrower may wish to simply place the Lender search directly in the hands of his direct professional affiliations. The Borrower most likely has an accountant, a legal adviser and, in many cases, a business and/or financial consultant. Each of these may have none, some, or considerable experience in Lender searches, and the resulting successes may have been graded from minimal, to satisfactory, to excellent. Are your business professionals really ready to spend all of the time required in working with a number of potential Lenders? Do they bring the Lending experience to the table that a qualified commercial loan broker could? Of course, as in dealing with any source of business assistance, the results can be varied—and that's why *validation of a broker's professional qualifications is important.*

Services of a commercial loan broker may involve:

- Initial consultation with the Borrower to identify needs and expectations.
- Reviewing supporting financial documentation that may be needed to develop information for potential Lenders.
- Evaluating, or assisting in the development of, the Bor-

rower's *suggested* loan terms and conditions.

- Executing a broker's contract with the Borrower.
- Developing a "Borrower's financing package" for potential Lenders. The broker may be responsible for executing a number of these presentations, either via mail or direct Lender presentations.
- Assessing the necessary materials with the Borrower's accountant, lawyer, and/or consultant(s).
- Incremental distribution of the Borrower's financing package to *targeted* Lenders.
- Responding to potential Lender questions and requests for additional documentation.
- Continuing liaison with the Borrower as to progress achieved.
- Once proposals or term sheets are received, assisting the Borrower in comparative evaluations.
- Upon receipt of a commitment letter(s), evaluating content and coordinating its execution.
- Attending to any pre-closing Lender requests and Borrower queries.
- Attending the loan closing.

A loan broker cannot *guarantee* a loan placement. He only offers his *best efforts*. A caveat to that effect may be within his broker agreement.

Real Experiences!

There are few guarantees in life. A successful broker's performance is *not* one of these. In most cases, an experienced commercial loan broker is able to attract an appropriate Lender who can address an explicit loan request. The broker's agreement usually states that the broker will use his "best efforts" to attract a Lender. Frequently the broker's fee is *not* based upon a successful loan closing. Some agreements interpret a broker's success *only* by the issuance of an executed proposal or commitment letter to the

Borrower, a proposal letter that *substantially* reflects the same loan terms and conditions that the Borrower was seeking. Be sure you know the basis for "success."

A Borrower made the *assumption* that a loan would be *agreed to and closed* by the end of the broker's 90-day exclusive engagement contract. Unknown to the broker, the Borrower made firm commitments to vendors for materials, labor, and supplies to be delivered to his company. The Borrower told all of his providers that payment would be made on or before the date of the end of the broker's contract. Unfortunately, due to the nature of the industry, the broker was unable to attract a Lender. Needless to say, when the broker notified the prospective Borrower, the roof fell in. The Borrower ranted and raved, threatening a lawsuit for breach of contract. The Borrower said to the broker, "You guaranteed me a loan by the end of our contract. I 'went to the bank' with this. My company is absolutely depending on this loan." The prospective Borrower called his lawyer. The lawyer wrote a letter to the broker reiterating the Borrower's concerns and wanted all broker retainer fees returned.

Responding through his lawyer, the broker referred the Borrower to that portion of the agreement that promised *only* "best efforts." Certainly on a sour note, the broker and Borrower parted ways. There were neither lawsuits nor a return of fees thus far paid. A loan broker, no matter how experienced, is *not* a magic bullet. A loan broker can, however, be of *great help* in attracting loan funds and multiple Lender proposals—but nothing is *ever* guaranteed. And you *can* take that to the bank!

The **broker's agreement** is a principal document that the Borrower should fully understand so there will be no problem arising at the loan closing. Broker agreements most likely will contain the following elements.

Exclusivity: The loan broker will usually request an exclusive broker period, providing the broker with the necessary time to attract a satisfactory Lender. The Borrower agrees he will not make application elsewhere during this period for the needed loan. This period may be 90 days (sometimes less) or up to one year. *The magnitude or complexity of the deal would determine the period of exclusivity.*

It is unusual for a loan broker to agree to a non-exclusive agreement. By not being exclusive, other brokers could be working on the same deal at the same time. Also, the Borrower may be independently soliciting other Lenders while the broker also seeks Lenders. Sometimes these attempts intersect (different representatives in contact with the same Lender), which will not only cause embarrassments, but may seriously jeopardize a broker relationship—or kill the deal altogether. The brokers refer to this as being "blindsided."

At the end of the period, if the broker has not been successful, it is up to the Borrower to decide whether to renew the exclusive agreement, not renew the agreement and search out a Lender by himself, or seek to engage a new loan broker. *Review the ramifications of these terminating actions with your legal counsel and financial advisers.* It is customary, even though the agreement has been terminated, that should the Borrower later (usually within one year of contract execution) close a loan with a Lender developed through the earlier services of the broker, the broker is still entitled to his fee. Such a provision may be within the broker's agreement.

Lenders Sourced: The Borrower should instruct the loan broker as to Lenders not to be sourced. There may be an unfavorable history or prior personality conflicts with certain Lenders.

Fees: The loan broker's fee is usually expressed as a percent of the approval loan–*not* the initial funding, but *the total approved credit facility*. This fee usually runs from ½% to 2%. Again, the difficulty and the estimated time involved in successfully placing the loan will impact the fee. I've seen fees as low as ¼% and as high as 3%.

From time to time, a Borrower may engage a broker that derives fees from *both* the Borrower *and* the successful Lender. Some Lenders will pay these additional broker fees to attract business from brokers. Inasmuch as the successful Lender may wish to "recoup" this additional fee expense, the Borrower may then be subject to a higher proposed interest rate on the loan. If such additional Lender fees, payable to the broker, are hidden from the Borrower, the broker may be regarded as not dealing in good faith. This "double dipping" by certain loan brokers is discouraged by some lending professionals.

And finally, there are times when the broker seeks *only* a finder's fee *from the Lender—nothing* from the Borrower. This seems to occur frequently in the case of specialized machinery and equipment loans.

Most loan broker agreements are clear cut. Some of the preceding specifics were presented only to reflect variances one may encounter. The Borrower should, of course, expect to pay a reasonable fee for comprehensive deal sourcing and successful loan placement.

Payment of Fees: The broker's fee is *usually* paid *at the loan closing* from the loan proceeds. In some broker contracts the fee is considered earned once a Lender's commitment letter has been issued to the Borrower; the loan does not necessarily have to close. This arrangement protects the broker in case the Borrower decides, *after* receiving a commitment letter, the Borrower wishes to go somewhere else, to a funding source where the broker may not be entitled to his normal fee. This could be a potential Lender that the Borrower has established a preliminary contact *without* the use of Broker services. The broker's obligation to find a Lender who would issue a commitment letter has been fulfilled, and payment may then be due to the broker. The loan broker will frequently attend the loan closing and expects to receive his check at that time. Alternatively the broker, with an authorization letter from the Borrower, may have his fee wired into his bank account.

It is the experience of some brokers that if the fee is *not* paid at the loan closing, loan proceeds are then quickly exhausted through the payment of payables and other Borrower obligations. It also follows that the Borrower, now that the loan is consummated, may feel that the broker's fee is excessive and seeks to negotiate a lower fee. This is an unfortunate situation, especially so if the broker *did his job*. The Borrower may well be advised to pay now—he may need this broker again in the future.

Deposits: From time to time, a broker will require a modest up-front, nonrefundable deposit. This may cover the broker's initial costs. Also, such a deposit may provide the broker with an indication as to the level of the Borrower's commitment to the arrangement. This fee is usually later *credited* against the total broker's fee due at loan closing. If a loan does not close and/or the contract is terminated, this earlier deposit is considered *earned* by the broker.

The preceding elements should be discussed and/or negotiated with the prospective commercial loan broker. The Borrower's legal counsel or accountant may wish to participate in such discussions.

LOAN PARTICIPATIONS

It is often the case that a Lender does not wish to extend additional financing to a Borrower because the amount of internal "exposure" (potential for loss) is too great. Other reasons may be:

- Too much specific industry concentration within the institution
- The loan request would put the Borrower over the "house" lending limit
- Fear of losing the entire relationship
- The Borrower's *specialized* lending requirements cannot be provided by the current lender

Commercial banks usually participate with one another, but alternative Lenders may participate as well. Most alternative Lenders can participate with another alternative Lender or a bank.

A loan participation usually works quite well for all three parties; the primary Lender, the participating Lender, and the Borrower.

- **The Primary Lender** usually retains the normal banking functions of the Borrower, the "relationship" if you will.

He may also, but does not have to, hold a part of the loan transaction(s). It can happen that the primary Lender will retain only certain types of loans. Then the participating Lender will seek to do only the working capital or real estate portion of the loan requirements. There is almost no end to the participation arrangements that can be negotiated.

- **The Participating Lender** now has a "new" loan on his books. A primary Lender may call a potential participating Lender to see if he is interested in accepting requests for loan participations. Alternative lenders frequently have their sales representatives calling upon commercial banks, indicating that they are receptive to such loan participations.
- Most important, **the Borrower** has *achieved the total funding needed.* He does not have to leave his primary banking relationship; his operating accounts and other banking benefits remain in place. His bank is also relaxing inasmuch as a determined portion of the loan is now with another Lender. Yes, the Borrower may have to work with two different Lenders, but they do strive to work as partners.

In practice, the two participants are required to work in collaboration, sharing credit and business information. Covenant violations and the like are usually jointly agreed upon. Each participant must be consistently aware of the entire business situation, so joint and appropriate actions may be taken as needed.

In smaller two- or three-party participations, one of the Lenders would be identified as the *"lead Lender."* Usually this is a Lender with over 50% of the loan, or one who is responsible for most of the credit and collateral controls. Usually material changes to the credit facility are not made without the permission of all loan participants. The lead Lender may charge the other participants a "management fee" in the area of ¼% to ½% of the participant's loan share. This may affect the Borrower's overall interest rate, or the fee may be absorbed by the participating Lender(s).

A loan participation may also be referred to as a "blind" participation. In such a case the Borrower is *not* aware that his primary Lender has *already* placed all, or a portion, of his loan with another Lender. The Borrower will have no idea that the loan is participated; only the funds, in part or in total, are actually being provided from elsewhere. The Lender has made the determination that the Borrower is not required to be aware of this participation. A blind participation cannot happen when both partners in a participation have different reporting or covenant requirements—the Borrower will become quickly aware of dual requirements. Most often participations are *not* of a blind nature but are, from the beginning, known by the Borrower.

Programs requiring many participants and involving very large loan amounts are called "syndications." When one views a number of these syndication loan structures, there appears to be a "fraternity" of strong lenders who seek to subscribe to portions of these mega-loans. More formally, this set of participants may involve correspondent banking networks—banks that frequently work together.

A participation is not really as complex as it may seem. It does enable a transaction to be accomplished—*usually to the benefit of the Borrower.*

DEBT LAYERS, STRIPS, AND HURDLES

Within some of the larger loan transactions, it is not usual to have more than one Lender, or different types of Lenders, involved in *selected* portions of the Borrower's debt. These Lenders' debt may serve different functions and may be driven by different needs. These debt portions are considered "layered" by their *priority* of debt. Lender **debt layers** may be further defined by their priority, or position, within the collateral hierarchy.

Generally, Lenders are interested only in a specific layer of debt—such as real estate. A layer of debt may be also be envisioned as a line item of debt within the liability section of a Balance Sheet.

- **Senior Secured Lender:** The *first and highest priority* is the senior secured Lender. These Lenders usually have a *first position* in key or *all* assets of the Borrowers. They almost always have a priority interest in the current assets of accounts receivable and inventory. All other Lenders are usually subordinate to this Lender. Also, this Lender frequently provides most of the loanable dollars. The senior secured Lender will be well collateralized, may charge modest interest rates, and will usually write loans on a demand basis.

- **Term Lenders:** May only loan against certain elements of fixed assets, such as machinery and equipment. This Lender, to improve his position, may take a *secondary (backup) position* or security interest in the senior secured Lender's collateral. This Lender's specific loan is also well collateralized, charges moderate rates, and is usually on a term basis.

- **Real Estate Lenders:** Same as term lenders, but exclusively dealing in real estate. May take junior positions (also as a backup) in the other Lender's collateral.

- **Subordinated Debt:** This layer of debt is usually the most junior of all debt. Holders of this debt—owners or officers of the Borrower, and possibly trade debt (former accounts payable) holders—will not get paid until everyone else has been satisfied. There may or may not be collateral involved, or interest payments authorized. But again, subordinated debt holders' collateral priority would be very low. See more on subordinated debt in Chapter 5.

- **Mezzanine Lenders:** Almost the lowest in priority collateral positions—if they take a collateral position at all. While they may be the highest-priced Lenders, their additional and expensive funds may be needed to make a loan structure work. Mezzanine Lenders may be involved in "equity kickers" (provisions to acquire an ownership position). They need little collateral, require higher interest rates, provide many loan structuring advantages to both the Lender and Borrower, are accustomed to long-term arrangements, and usually do not require personal guarantees. See Chapter 8 for more on mezzanine Lenders.

Other Lenders, more so on the larger of financial transactions, seek a **strip** or a portion of *each* layer (or category) of debt involved in the transaction. This would be, in effect, taking a ruler and drawing vertical lines down the liability section of the balance sheet. *Each* Lender could then have a portion of the senior debt as well as other layers of the debt structure. This way the Lenders involved in the transaction may, to an extent, share in *all* collateral and possibly receive a higher average return on their investment. Subordinated and mezzanine debt portions are excluded from strip considerations.

Each Lender attempts to achieve its own investment return requirements by effectively being represented in *selected* debt layers or strips. Lenders refer to the attaining of their desired elements as reaching their **hurdles**.

A small-business Borrower need not anticipate the strips scenario, as usually a single Lender would be interested in only one element of his debt structure.

CHAPTER 10

GETTING YOUR SHARE IN DIFFICULT TIMES

"The Lender is going to be my pal?"

"Just what we need—a party!"

"Hey—I'm all for a video!"

"I'm beginning to like this."

What's a difficult time? The Borrower is unable to get a commercial loan.
What's a difficult time? No one is paying attention.
What's a difficult time? Nothing is happening!

There are times when it seems that loanable funds are nowhere to be found, at least at terms agreeable to a Borrower. Then again, there are times when it seems as if the Lenders are consistently calling, visiting and sending advertisements offering flexible and attractive deals. They have money and they can't give it away fast enough. Methods seem unfocused and advertisements too good to be true.

Both scenarios can be frustrating to a Borrower. Most Borrowers seek a steady and confirming relationship with a Lender. This would be a long-term relationship where the Borrower is recognized, appreciated, and respected as a customer of the Lender. The Borrower wants to be—*and needs to be*—more than a number or a risk rating. Business survival may be dependent, in the long run, on how the Borrower is *perceived* by his Lender and the lending organization.

Real Experiences!

This potential bank borrowing customer brought a long history of business success and a solid work ethic. The bank was trying to win a piece of his extensive business holdings. He was in the property development business long before the bank was making construction loans. He was gruff and really didn't see the need for all of these loan applications and forms. He said, "In the old days we did these things on a handshake—my word was good! You think I'm a crook?" He finally, after many disputed versions, signed off on a bank proposal letter to finance a small development.

The Borrower arrived at the local attorney's office for the loan closing. The meeting was attended only by the lending officer and the bank's outside legal counsel. The Borrower's arm was in a cast because he had recently fallen at one of his properties. He would not employ his own attorney because, as he stated, "I've been doing enough of these things. Why should I pay an attorney when the bank's attorney has gone over everything? You think I was born yesterday?" A very short way into signing the loan documents he exclaimed, "I didn't agree to this. What do you guy's think you're doing?" The loan officer and the bank's attorney tried to explain that these were just the legal phases required in secured lending. "Either you take that sentence out of the agreement or I'm out of here. I don't need your money that bad!" The loan officer asked him to relax. The Borrower abruptly walked out of the conference room and began pacing up and down in the waiting room. The bank's attorney said he could remove the disputed phrase, but it was really standard "boilerplate" and he was reluctant to eliminate it.

A call to the bank headquarters by the loan officer resolved the issue. The bank really wanted this new customer, not only for this loan, but the potential of additional new business. The offending section was deleted. All returned to the conference room and the closing continued. It was not without other less potent confrontations, but the loan was finally closed. The lending officer called the Borrower the following day and told him he was mailing over some copies of the loan documents. The Borrower said, "Don't mail them, just bring them to my house first thing in the morning." A little uneasy, the loan officer went to the Borrower's house. The Borrower was worth a considerable sum and the officer expected a large residential property, but instead he found a small, unassuming house. The Borrower's wife answered and directed the officer to a table in the kitchen. The wife poured coffee and offered little cakes. The Borrower came in and the officer thanked him for the hospitality of his home and for inviting him there. Following concerns as to the broken arm, business was discussed. A longer discussion followed about the Borrower's family, business history, and the loan officer's background. Since the first contentious loan closing and this out-of-the-way meeting by a loan officer, this relationship flourished. The Borrower would deal with no one else from the bank, and future meetings were *always* made in the Borrower's kitchen. A long-term relationship was established and flourishes still.

There are many who feel that the numbers of lending organizations are decreasing overall as the mega-Lenders acquire state Lenders, regional Lenders purchase state Lenders and the acquisition frenzy goes on. *New* banks are appearing to serve geographic niche markets. Because of their size, they are too small to provide significant commercial lending products. They seem to grow for awhile but, once a few branches open and a deposit base is developed, they sell out (or "cash out") to a larger institutions.

In all of this confusion it is difficult for a Borrower to stand out within a commercial loan portfolio. When times do get tough, either for the Borrower, within the Lending institution, or with the national economy, it will be the Borrower who has *maintained a solid relationship* with the Lender who will then be reaping the benefits of "relationship management."

In our world of business finance there is more than manners or etiquette to the exercising of effective relationship management techniques.

"Effective" equates to a relationship conducive to supporting, not detracting from, the continuing extension of credit. A relationship of trust, consideration and, on the lending level, abiding by loan covenants, builds a solid foundation.

Even though a sound personal relationship is maintained, the Borrower should not expect to be bailed out of difficult circumstances due solely to this personal relationship. *But*—maintaining a positive personal relationship will never hurt your standing. If a decision is really "on the fence" it can, of course, make the difference!

It is through the *application of effective relationship management techniques* that loan requests may be approved, credit lines extended, loan defaults *not* declared, and flexible lending accommodations made when other commercial Borrowers are suffering due to lack of Lender response.

REALITY CHECK

The Borrower's objective is not to be just another business loan but rather to be the *preferred* business Borrower. This Borrower will not only have the compelling likelihood of attaining his needs but can also enable his Lender to achieve his objectives. This Borrower *will* stand out!

FINANCIAL MANAGEMENT RELATIONSHIP TECHNIQUES

Put Your Lender "On the List": It is important that your lending officer (LO) reflects credibility when discussing your loan, loan request, or your industry before the credit committee. *Make him an expert* in your business. Provide him with a *complimentary subscription to your trade publication*. He will absorb much of this and retain selected articles within your credit file. Also invite your Lender to *trade shows* and, if your loan relationship is a large one, invite him to your *annual industry association meeting*. This annual function can be an expensive affair but the Lender will not forget this opportunity and new relationships which will invariably be opened up to him. Less expensive would be regional chapter meetings of your trade association. When the LO now appears before the Loan Committee he will be well versed in your industry, which can only benefit the Borrower's cause. Out of 100 Borrowers less than 5% take such constructive actions to educate their Loan Officers.

Create Your Own Quarterly Analysis: Generally all Borrowers must submit periodic interim financial statements to their Lender. End of story—no! *Do some of your Lender's work within your periodic submissions.* Compare your performance results to the same period last year and present to your Lender both the dollar and percentage variances (a comparative analysis). Determine whether you are, or are not, in compliance with financial loan covenants. Then note *each significant variance (favorable or not)* and write a short explanation about each. You are telling the Lender, in advance, about the variances, highlighting the positives and mitigating the negatives. The Lender thus knows you are aware of, and are addressing, variances. *Also, you will not be caught "cold" on Lender telephone calls regarding such variances.* Compare your results to key ratios and coverage common within your industry. How do you stack up? Use the "RMA Annual Statement Studies"; this may be the same publication your Lender uses. Also, your industry association may also be able to provide industry comparative ratios.

Additionally, through a short narrative (bullet points are fine), tell your quarterly story:

- *Highlight quarterly new business successes*
- If there has been a significant lost account or purchase order—explain
- New deals in process
- New personnel
- New products or production procedures
- Accounting changes and computer control developments
- Trade shows
- Possible upcoming financial needs
- Other achievements

This information, coupled with the above analysis, will provide a *complete overview of the last quarter*. So much so, that much of the information will find its way *verbatim* into the Borrower's credit file. Now, how many Borrowers provide that kind of information to their Lender? In my experience, less than 5%. You are making the LO's job much easier—and probably more accurate. You know that your business will be one of his favorites, and you are telling your story *your* way!

Real Experiences!

A large manufacturer of diversified products for technical industry applications was having trouble getting a working capital loan from just about any Lender. Losses had been continuing for some time and the net worth of the company was just about down to zero. Long-term prospects, as touted by the owner, were excellent if the Lenders would only be patient and make an attempt to understand the industry. The owner's current bank, in order to reduce their risk, was unsuccessful in seeking a loan participant or in attracting a replacement alternative Lender. The Borrower was not impressed by interest rates required by Lenders that did show some interest. The owner did not want a mezzanine loan or an equity infusion of capital as his ownership could be diluted. But what he did do, which was ultimately successful, was to keep *all* Lenders he had talked to over the past years informed. *Every* quarter he provided these Lenders with a copy of the complete periodic financial statement with notes. A short cover letter reflected highlights for the period and future probabilities.

He concluded the letter, "If our performance is approaching your standards for commercial lending, I would appreciate discussing loan potentials with your Lending Officers." This went on for a few years until a Lender, detecting the emergence of favorable trends, made a secured commercial loan to the company. The jury is still out as to whether the company will prosper but trends remain positive. As all of these prior Lenders knew something about the company, they followed his quarterly information. The Borrower's persistence and consistency in providing information, made all the difference.

OK—Let's enhance your visibility.

You are a business person and deal with a number of business associates outside of your business—vendors, suppliers, customers and professionals (accountant, attorney, business consultant, financial adviser, insurance agent, etc.). So once every two months or so, host **"A Luncheon for 4"** at a *good* restaurant. Not at a center table but a booth. You'll invite two "outside" business associates, your Lender and yourself. The purpose is *not* to discuss your borrowing relationship but to –

- *Expand the horizons* of your LO (loan officers are always prodded to get to know people and expand their business relationships).
- Demonstrate that you are *well connected* to the business community.
- Exhibit an interest in *developing possible business leads* for your LO.
- Establish that there is *more to you than a loan number.*

Considering the diversified business relationships at the table, conversations are never dull—new ground is *always* broken! You pick up the tab. In two or three months do it again with your LO *and a different agenda of guests.*

Attend a Meeting: Find out if your LO is a member of a local service or community club (Kiwanis, Lions, Rotary, etc.) or business groups (Chamber of Commerce, Business & Industry Association, etc.).

- Call your LO indicating your interest in visiting his club (as a potential member or simply as a guest—be honest here). You may indicate you are interested in the club's community or national work and in their program presenters. Or more simply you are just interested in networking. Most clubs urge their membership to bring guests. This 1-2 hour time with your LO, *in a non-business atmosphere*, can go a long way in building a special relationship.
- If *you* are a member of a local club invite your LO to your meeting *as your guest* when a good program is planned—and introduce the LO to the membership. The LO will recognize the opportunity to develop further business contacts as regards *his* objectives.

Dinner Clubs: Clubs such as local country clubs, city clubs, golf courses, etc., are excellent, and sometime unique venues, for one-on-one opportunities with your LO. Many of these facilities also serve breakfast. The outcome is usually a quiet and uninterrupted atmosphere.

Stay out of the bank cafeteria lunch rooms or the local diners—too many interruptions. Admittedly, the better clubs of this nature may be somewhat expensive but they could also serve as a base for your "Luncheon of 4". In some instances you must be a member of the club with luncheon bills signed for and billed at month end. So check out procedures beforehand. You may consider joining such a "club" so the venue would always be familiar and available.

Exception: The executive dining room (main office) of your Lender, where many senior Lenders *always* lunch, may be an opportunity for the Borrower to meet the most senior lending officials. Exchange business cards as appropriate—may *need* these later. Follow up with individual notes indicating your pleasure at the introduction.

REALITY CHECK

Do not go to a local civic or dinner club to discuss switching Lenders with a prospective Lender. Your current Lender may be there and deduce what is happening. They do all generally know one another. *Many* embarrassments over this one. Such meetings should best be held at your company—*in a controlled atmosphere*. See Chapter 7.

Open House: Consider an open house at your business—*annually.* Considering the seasons and summer absences, late spring or early autumn seem to be the best times. The work and costs involved really do not justify more than *one* annual event. Invite your suppliers, customers, professional associates and employees and your Lender(s). It is dvised that you consider inviting your LO's superiors, one or two levels *above* his position. Make sure all are invited ("RSVP") *separately* by name. Also consider inviting (your choice) spouses. Lots of "goodwill" for all. You will have an opportunity to demonstrate your business operations as well as introducing Lenders to your office and supporting personnel. Ensure name badges are available at the welcome table for both the Borrower's personnel and *all* invited guests.

This may run from 11:00 AM–3:00 PM ("walk-in") with RSVP announcements mailed well in advance. *Follow-up calls made the day before* the function to the RSVPs and those others who have accepted *will* enhance attendance. When on the phone tell them they can bring a guest. It all helps.

A product presentation, tour, samples or promotional items are offered and a small buffet (catered) or hors-d'oeuvres with beverages (nonalcoholic) may be appropriate. I have even seen Borrowers who are in trouble benefit from such an annual event. And if there's no other way, an Open House will usually bring senior lending personnel (decision makers) to the event. Don't infringe on people's personal time for an Open House: do it during business hours. That gives more incentive for guests to attend.

If a service business or the business operational site is not conducive to an Open House, consider a first-class hotel meeting room (it may be a small one). Be generous with your product and service displays, samples and cuisine. Badges again are appropriate.

The Class Act—An Annual Recognition Dinner: The business year may almost be over but it's time for one more function that can be very beneficial to the business. The year may have provided some disappointments, but there were also successes which should be highlighted. There were some individuals who really "made the year" for the business; whether selected customers, suppliers, professional associates (accountant, attorney and financial consultants), Lenders or special employees, who went "that extra mile." Their bills may have been paid and your appreciation expressed.

But this additional expression of your sincere gratitude can provide multiple and lasting benefits. Of course, *you are planting seeds for the future.*

This recognition function need only be as expensive as you wish. The ideas presented below are the middle of the road approach. This can be done for only six people, sixteen or forty-six. It usually need not involve a "cast of thousands." *It is suggested (where costs are not prohibitive) that spouses are also invited.* This further solidifies the relationship aspects.

Select and commit to a hotel's *private* dinner and meeting space (through the hotel's sales department) at least 45 days in prior to the date of the desired "recognition diner." This will be an evening sit-down dinner meeting with business dress. *Frequently* the room is cost free when multiple dinners are purchased and bar service is made available.

A hotel is recommended in case a few of your guests require sleeping rooms. Such guests will have all travel, room, and associated expenses paid by your company. Set up a company "Master Account" where all guest charges will be applied—including breakfast the following day for those staying overnight. *Excess* room space can be booked in advance and, once the guest list is confirmed, rooms not required may be cancelled.

Generally it is best to use round tables (seating about 10 persons each). Conversation will be easier than at smaller square tables and comments may be shared with more than just a few people at a time. Personally examine the suggested room to see if it will accommodate the number of tables needed. If only a half a dozen people are involved the hotel will still have an appropriate-sized private room, either off of the main dining room or within the area of conference rooms.

The hors d'oeuvres (in the reception area) and dinner are usually served in the same room but may be separate if desired. If it is in the same room, have an area where participants may mingle before the sit-down dinner commences. Generally an open bar with a bartender is contracted and will be open prior to and following the dinner.

After about thirty minutes you may ask the participants to take their seats. The President, or another management member, will welcome guests with appropriate comments. Brief introductions from the podium should be made. Introductions will include members of company management (hosts) and guests.

The table(s) will have place cards so guests will not be confused as to where to sit. Further, name badges will be prepared (to include company affiliation) and made available as they enter the dining area. Alternatively, a small table with a table cover and one chair may be located outside of the dining room with badges displayed. The table could be manned by a company member. Some larger functions may hire hostesses for this service but it is usually not necessary. Sometimes spouses of top management may welcome guests and present them with their badges. Set all of these items up at least two hours before guest arrivals.

Forty days prior to the function, send out invitations to all—including management and employees (if any) attending. A sample invitation outline is presented below. An "RSVP" response would further establish the function as an important affair. Also, a selection of dinner alternatives, three or four with a vegetarian option, will be included within the envelope. Twenty days prior to the function, management members should follow up by phone to those who have not responded. Ten days before, additional invitations may be sent out to *new* possible attendees, should the initial response not be as large as anticipated. Finally, seven days prior, secretary calls to reconfirm *all* guests.

BECKER PLASTICS, INC.

Is Pleased to Invite You to its
NEW HAMPSHIRE
200X APPRECIATION DINNER

We value your business and now it's time to show it.
- at -
THE RIVER VILLAGE INN
("The Colonial Room")
NASHUA, NEW HAMPSHIRE

Thursday, November 19, 20XX
5:30 to 8:30 PM

Open Bar &

Hors D'oeuvres	*5:30—6:30 PM*
Dinner	*6:30—8:00 PM*
Closing Comments	*8:00 to 8:30 PM*

Invitees include
Our Customers and Suppliers
Professional Associates
Our Management & Staff

A completed guest list (for management's use) will then be prepared which includes the name, company or professional affiliation, and phone number of the individuals. At this time badges and place cards, for management, guests and their spouses, will be prepared. Frequently a guest may ask if a list of all attendees is available. They may wish to network at a later time. Such a list should be prepared with names, affiliation, addresses and phone numbers. Don't forget management members in attendance. This list could always be reduced in size and placed on the dinner plates.

On the day of the function, confirm all hotel requirements, sleeping room assignments and room set up to include bar area and Badge display. Place cards should be positioned on the tables. Senor management may wish to have the seating arrangement on a single piece of paper for overall reference. An enlarged seating plan, placed on an easel near the entrance, enables rapid seating rather than having guests milling around searching for seats.

Table decorations or small gifts for guests (presented upon departure) are at the option of the business. A very small box of chocolates, etc., may be placed at each place setting. Usually the hotel sales staff can take care of most of these items. A sign in the hotel lobby should direct your group to the dinning area. Last, but not least, insure management members have their business cards.

Many detailed helps have been presented above. This is because a "class act" will not only be appreciated by guests but will enhance the business profile. I've seen these functions really develop additional business (even for guests) and result in personal bonding really not anticipated. Too, spouses enjoy the special evening out and are a part of their spouse's business activities.

Objectives of all these various venues receding are to get your loan officer into a relaxing situation that is:

- Under *your* control.
- On *neutral* turf.
- Beneficial to his understanding of your business and its needs.
- Enables your loan officer to network.

A more *personal bonding will take place* and you'll be much more than a number on a loan portfolio schedule. Don't discount the possibility that you may really become friends with your commercial Lender.

More ideas:

- Keep your current (and potential) Lenders on your promotional direct mailing list. Former Lenders may be considered as well if a positive relationship exists.
- Don't forget those special days; birthdays, anniversaries, promotions, graduations, etc.
- If close to the Lender's secretary or administrative assistant send flowers or consumables on special occasions or as a "Thank You" gesture. Values under $25.00. Not recommended for credit or operations personnel.
- Publish a periodic newsletter—size appropriate for the business. There are firms that will provide newsletter services (focused articles and timely data). Your company provides the fill-in company specific information and data.
- Take advantage of your public relations. Send to the Lender your published tombstones, newspaper articles, information on promotions, new business contracts, etc.
- Invite your Lender (and family?), along with key credit analysts, to your company's annual holiday or summer (picnic) affair.
- Buy one share of your Lender's stock. You'll not only receive an annual report that will tell you who's who and how your Lender is performing but you will be invited to the annual Stockholder's Meeting. If the distance is not prohibitive, consider attending. You'll meet senior officers—get their business cards and put them on your mailing lists as well.
- Have a company video? You can tell your "story" the way you want it told. You usually cannot personally present your story before a credit committee but they *most always* view submitted company videos (an important captive audience!).
- Host an annual employee and family picnic. You don't have to travel 50 miles. Simply in back of the plant or in a local

park setting. Possibly some games for the kids. This family affair does wonders for worker moral. And yes, again invite those professionals who are close to the company—including your Lender.

And don't forget these basics:

- Make loan payments on time; If not able - communicate with LO
- Comply with loan covenants
- Timely and accurate reporting
- No surprises to your Lender
- Return Lender calls promptly
- No "short notice" appointment cancellations
- Provide new business referrals to your Lender

Whether you are a large or small Borrower, when the next money crunch comes, when loanable funds are not readily available, or when you've had a disappointing quarter—all of your efforts can pay off by having your needs satisfactorily and timely addressed.

There is a litany of financial relationship management techniques. No one, of course, should fail to recognize that basic, *business financial performance is always paramount.* We all recognize many of these financial management techniques but so few actually put them into practice. But to those few who do–commercial borrowings and special accommodations may come much easier.

Doing all of the above is certainly impractical for any Borrower. Some tactics may be cost prohibitive. Some Lenders may not respond as expected. However, by doing those selected activities *appropriate* for *your* situation, your name can be on your Lender's "short list" of preferred Borrowers.

Remember: Do it—others won't.

CHAPTER 11

CLOSE TO HOME

"But—I'm not *going* anywhere!"

"Of course I can handle all of these jobs."

"Oh sure—I'll hire a CFO!"

"I need an (advisory) board of directors?"

THE MANAGEMENT TEAM AND SUCCESSION

Business direction and the viability of future leadership could be in jeopardy without an effective management team in place and a *defined* plan of management succession addressed. Such could be the case of the death, absence, or incapacity of a key officer(s).

It is well recognized that the most important element in any business is the strength of its management team. In a difficult situation an *effective management team* has the potential to succeed—sometimes in the most hopeless of cases. Even in a financially sound business, a poor management team can run it into the ground in short order. I've been in credit committee meetings where, after all is said and done, and the approval could go either way, the chairperson will say, "Tell me about management." Management can make or break a deal.

Do you have *your* "dream team" on board? Maybe yes and maybe no.

Build a management team—generally it is best not to be regarded as a "one-man band." Your team may involve full timers, part timers, consultants and yes—even relatives.

A team of a moderate size company may include these positions *(and one person may fill more than one slot)*:

- President
- Chief Executive Officer (CEO)
- Chief Financial Officer (CFO)
- Chief Operating Officer (COO)
- Sales and Marketing—VP
- Human Resources—VP

It is imperative that the few persons comprising the management team be adept and possess the appropriate credentials. Credentials may not only address formal education but successful business experience in the business being undertaken. Certainly the chief executive officer and the chief operating officer must know all of the "nuts and bolts" of the specific business. This usually holds true for the person in charge of sales and marketing—although there are sales professionals who seem to do well in many different environments. The disciplines of chief financial officer and head of human resources frequently focus on the nature of their specialties rather than the actual running of the business.

There are *seasoned professionals* who provide the chief financial officer proficiencies on a *contract basis*. Some of these "temp" professionals I have known have been with their client companies for years. These temporary CFO's prefer to operate within the consulting arena—and many have accomplished impressive results for their company clients. They are paid salaries (or retainers) commensurate with their experience level and successes, but would not cost as much as a full time CFO. Companies who have not grown to the level of requiring such full-timers, enjoy the benefits of such professionals, and do so at considerably lower cost. The CFO billets (and other selective positions) can often be effectively filled with such proficient "team members."

Real Experiences!

A Dallas Borrower was more comfortable (and proficient) in running the company than confronting financial statements, developing forecasts, evaluating financial trends and strategies, and negotiating with Lenders. A financial consultant (fee based or under retainer) or a "temporary" CFO could be the answer to restoring financial proficiencies. An alternative Lender in California was on the fence as to whether to approve a turnaround loan to this electronics firm. While the overall customer list was impressive, the Borrower's performance was not. What with purchase order cancellations, depression within the industry, and the prospects of layoffs, the Lender was in doubt as to the company's real potential—if any. However, the Borrower had recently hired a "temporary" chief financial officer. The CFO's credentials and client lists were verified as satisfactory by the Lender. Also, the loan request was accompanied by detailed "best and worst case" financial forecasts with detailed assumptions, all prepared by the temporary CFO. These revealed that, in any event, the bank was well collateralized by both current and fixed assets. The loan was subsequently approved and funded.

Things then proceeded from difficult to worse. The bank requested a meeting to discuss possible courses of action—their action. This, and follow-up meetings, were since held at the Borrower's place of business (an excellent tactic). Before the Lender had a chance to enumerate his requirements, the Borrower, along with his temporary CFO, indicated that the company plans had not changed; challenges were being addressed as presented within the earlier worst case scenario. Collateral was *still* satisfactory and the Lender's position was not in jeopardy. The Borrower by himself could not have orchestrated such an effective presentation. The Borrower did present the sales and marketing highlights. These enumerated new purchase orders which were received, the potential of *new* business, the cancelled orders which may be revived, and the potential for an overall industry recovery. Handouts for the Lender's reference were also provided. The Borrower's presentation took up almost all of the available Lender's time—planned as such. When the Lender's actions were finally discussed, most were immediately and favorably resolved.

The industry did *not* recover for another year. Minimal orders were processed and layoffs did occur. But at each of the following quarterly, and sometimes monthly meetings, the Borrower and his CFO had reasonable explanations and forecasts. All were presented professionally. Unfavorable actions from the Lender were delayed until a turnaround finally developed. Most all predictions regarding the new customers, order releases, and a return to profitability finally occurred. Most production personnel were rehired. *After many years* this "temporary" CFO *still continues* to assist the company in most financial and borrowing negotiations. This CFO has also been recommended by the Lender to other management teams. It is believed that this particular company would not have survived if they did not make such a "temporary" commitment.

Additional professionals may include the turnaround manager, who actually takes over the operation of a troubled company until certain objectives are achieved (see Chapter 9). The objectives may be a return to profitability, managing a company in a reorganization posture for the benefit of the creditors, or possibly a Lender has highly recommended such a professional to provide a situation analysis.

A professional such as a loan broker (Chapter 9) or financial consultant may be contracted for, on a short-term basis, to accomplish refinancing of the company debt, raise additional equity or prepare a business plan.

There are all kinds of help available to the small or medium size business—competent help that can put the company on par with management talent that larger companies enjoy. *It is very important that professional references (to include referenced clients) be verified.* Review the engagement contract with your attorney (and accountant, if necessary) covering the terms of engagement, the duration and scope of services, and the pricing of services to ensure conditions are understood by all parties.

The management section of your business plan or a management profile must sufficiently tout the expertise of those holding key positions. As stated before, the management of a company is of paramount interest to a commercial Lender. *Regardless of the quality or quantity of collateral, a loan approval will go nowhere without competent management.*

> **Succession Management:** It is imperative that a plan of succession management be in place and made part of the business plan. This information will be required by Lenders. The management style of the President, even though he may have a number of subordinate officers, could be that of sole control, without authority given to key management members. Even with a leader who successfully delegates responsibilities, an unexpected tragedy, death or incapacitation, may occur. The company is suddenly without designated management leadership. These inherent dangers will be recognized by a Lender. Who will do his job—will all scramble for it—a member of his family? Without established continuity of management, confusion reigns and a Lender may well deem himself "unsecured." Professional and explicit planning is required here. Utilize the professional resources of your legal adviser and financial consultant(s) to develop a *formal* succession management plan.

A Lender may also seek "key man insurance" on those officers in critical management positions. These insurance proceeds are used to source, interview and attract new management members, provide initial salaries, signing bonuses, travel costs, etc. Proceeds may also be used by the Lender to payoff outstanding loans. See Key Man Insurance and Proceeds" in Chapter 5.

A Board of Directors—Why Not?

Regarding the development of a board of directors, there seems to be more success if the board is really an "outside" board—from outside of the company. However, it is normal for a limited number of board member(s) to be company officers. An outside board brings impartial viewpoints, experience from different professional or management disciplines, may help to attract investors and loans, and may even develop new customers. *An operating board of directors simply adds credibility to a company, and overall management capabilities are greatly enhanced.* A board, among other duties, may appoint operating officers, approve new projects or company strategies and report to shareholders. Board members are usually paid per meeting and have certain legal exposures as a board member. The Borrower's legal counsel should be consulted in any area involving the formation or operation of a board of directors.

An alternative approach is creating an advisory board of directors. This is an informal meeting of those persons who may provide constructive advice for the company. Formal meetings may not be held, meeting stipends or expenses may not be paid, and the company is not bound by recommendations of this group. There is usually little legal liability regarding advisory board members. Again, even for this less formal Board arrangement, contact your attorney for implications and procedures.

CHAPTER 12

YOUR WINNING FINANCING PACKAGE

"You're kidding—what's wrong with my envelope?"

"I can hire someone to do my business plan—right?"

"I see my future here."

". . . and they liked my plan—great!"

In Chapter 7 the Borrower learned how to prepare his own terms and conditions for review by prospective Lenders. This document has now been presented to prospective Lenders, either directly by the Borrower or through an engaged loan broker. The Lenders have now responded—some with their own versions of their terms and conditions. After some comparative analyses, the Borrower has selected at least two of the most promising responses and, upon the Lenders' request, will now provide *additional* financial detail within a **Financing Package**.

The financing package, again containing a copy of the *Borrower's* terms and conditions, is a compilation of relevant business and financial documents, and is likely the single largest package the Borrower will ultimately provide to the interested Lenders.

The Outline—The "Press Kit"

Yes, in a way the Borrower *is* placing a media advertisement. The "media" are the potential Lenders, and the press kit (the financing package) is the loan request, a combination of pertinent documents. Is the package complete and attractive? Does it differentiate itself from the current stack of other loan requests on the Lender's desk? Will the Borrower will receive recognition as to its professional presentation, or will the reviewer think "Don't waste your time on this one"?

We've all seen press kits provided by local newspapers and magazines. They are very well coordinated, from the binder to the arrangement of the general and specific data to the cover letter and glossy public relations information. To a great extent these concepts may be reflected within a Borrower's financing package.

Preparation need not be an expensive process. Inasmuch as the Borrower may put out anywhere from only a few to a dozen or more identical financing packages, the costs, weight (mailing), and "glitz" should be reasonable. Basically, it should look professional. We have already covered most of the content requirements in previous chapters and now are putting together the components of the physical package.

The Mechanics

The cover is not the first thing the Lender will see that represents the Borrower's package. What is the first, then? It's the envelope. *Why worry about the envelope*? I would like to think that someone put some thought into the address: proper name, title, department, institution, and street address. If a Borrower cannot even get the Lender's identification or spelling right, how much effort was taken regarding the package contained inside?

Take the time to call the potential Lender's office. If you would rather not talk directly to the Lender at this time, call during lunchtime. The phones will be covered but the Lender will most likely be at lunch or on the way to a meeting. The secretary will confirm the Lender's name and its spelling, the person's title, and title of the department. Make sure you have the proper mailing address. Many times a commercial loan department may operate in a location other than the Lender's headquarters building. Also, many larger institutions will have *mail codes* (ask for this), which are placed after the department name. This will show attention to detail—right up front—and guarantee an accurate delivery.

Make sure the Borrower's return address is correct. Frequently a business will already have preprinted adhesive mailing labels reflecting the business name and address. These should be OK to use. Otherwise, print out a return address label and place it on the envelope rather than just writing this information directly on the envelope. And be sure the envelope is 1) strong enough to safely contain the information through the mailing process, and 2) large enough for the material to comfortably fit. If it's going to burst open, it will burst at the worst possible time—in the post office. Many financing packages actually arrive in flat boxes of various sizes, addressing both strength and capacity. If the package is going to be hand delivered, mark "Hand Deliver" in the upper right-hand corner.

A single postage meter strip, rather than a rainbow of colored commemorative stamps, reflects a professional mailing. This may be a small point, admittedly, but after all of the work performed relative to the financial information, why not go all the way? If you do not have a postage meter, mail it at the post office and make sure the clerk stamps it "First Class." That's a good way of designating your package: first class.

Should potential Lenders visit the Borrower's business, it is *not necessary* to put the on-site local presentation documents in an envelope; however, do consider having similar-size envelopes available for Lenders so they can easily carry off their accumulation of documents.

The Cover: Selection of an outside cover, or an indexed binder, should again reflect a professional appearance. Avoid bright colors. If using a binder, rather than a faux-leather cover, use one with a clear plastic pocket on the front and spine. This way you can slide in your own prepared cover information. Make sure the binder size is at least a half an inch larger than needed. The Borrower doesn't want his information bursting through the rings every time it is opened.

There will be a table of contents. The corresponding index pages should have a plastic tab so the entire presentation doesn't get too frayed as it is utilized. There are a number of formats available at most business supply stores, some with computer templates.

A **cover page** reflects the basic information about the deal:

Dearborn Manufacturing, Inc.
1826 Industrial Drive South
Lawrence, Massachusetts 01856

LOAN REQUEST

WORKING CAPITAL
EQUIPMENT
REAL ESTATE

$2,800,000

Date Submitted
June 1, 20XX

CONFIDENTIAL

Some Borrowers will try to control the number of copies put out to Lenders by indicating a copy number on each cover page. The control aspect is understandable, but a Lender getting copy #13 knows that this request is most likely being shopped all over the place—not a good signal to send. Just keep a control log at the place of business *without* identifying cover pages with a number. Also, do not identify the recipient Lender (other than on the outer envelope). Invariably some financing packages wind up with the inappropriate Lender, and now a Lender knows 1) who its competition is, and 2) that the Borrower is dealing with more than one institution. Too many embarrassments happen, possibly impacting credibility. Watch the small points.

The reader should note that not all of the elements of the following table of contents are necessarily applicable to every financing package. If some elements of the financing package are not completed as yet (for example, still with the accountant), it's all right to leave them as part of the table of contents but indicate within the management cover letter that they will be arriving under separate cover.

DEARBORN MANUFACTURING, INC.

Financing Package
Table of Contents

Management Cover Letter
1

This one-page letter, on company letterhead, acknowledges receipt of the Lender's request for further information. It may also indicate items not included with the package, and the reason why they are not. For items not as yet prepared, indicate the expected time of arrival. Similar to the Borrower's terms and conditions, this letter will also indicate the Borrower's primary and secondary contacts at the company. The cover letter should be signed in the original with an "Enclosure" identified as the "Financing Package."

Borrower's Terms and Conditions (Copy previously provided)
2 thru x

If the Lender has previously been presented with the original of the *Borrower's* terms and conditions, it is appropriate to include *another* within the financing package marked "COPY." These types of informative documents frequently disappear into the miscellaneous files of the Lender during due diligence. An extra copy of this important document doesn't hurt.

Business Plan
Pages xx thru xx

Do you really need to prepare a business plan? Does it need to be a part of the financing package? Think about it this way: Do you really need to show your potential Lender that you know and can support the direction of the company? The answer is, of course, *yes*!

The business plan will constitute the remainder, *and be the primary part*, of the financing package. In order to be manageable, a plan should not exceed fifty pages (fewer is better).

THE WELL-DEFINED BUSINESS PLAN

A well-thought-out business plan is not only important in the short term to attract a Lender or investor, but in many businesses it becomes a "living" document—updated annually—that is especially valuable to the small business. Considering the topical subjects within a plan, preparation provides time for reflection that may temper, adjust, or accelerate former business goals and strategies. The annual updating approach acts as a management tool, additionally fostering both internal and external communications. The various department managers—sales and marketing, accounting, production and distribution—as well as management and the company's outside professionals, all have a part in the revision of plan segments. Also, inasmuch as the competition, markets, and industrywide conditions constantly change, so must the plan.

Many companies will hire a firm, or individual, who prepares business plans. These plans are usually very well done, presentable to Lenders and investors. Also, the Borrower is relieved from the responsibility of drafting an entire plan. Of course, there will be much interview time required by the preparing contractor as he discusses his requirements with members of management. Depending on the purpose, the scope required, and timing, a business plan may cost from $500 to $10,000 or more—with some taking weeks to prepare.

Free counseling services, to assist in the development of the business plan, may be available to the Borrower locally through the Service Corps of Retired Executives (SCORE), an extension of the Small Business Association (*www.sba.gov*).

The size and cost of a plan does not carry much weight with a Lender. Rather, the *effectiveness* of the plan (to include the executive summary—see the following) will rise or fall on its thoroughness and accuracy.

The Borrower may decide to prepare the business plan himself with the assistance of his accountant and attorney. Such internal business plan preparation by the Borrower must be to the level of comprehensiveness sought by a Lender. The Borrower's accountant or financial adviser will not only have suggestions but may make recommendations regarding the use (and selection) of outside assistance. The key elements of a business plan are presented in the next section.

While a full-blown plan may be the "norm" for some businesses, consider, in responding to a Lender's *initial* request for information, a *smaller version* of the plan. This may be adequate and not overwhelm a Lender. Anything over fifty pages may be too weighty for a Lender. I have had business plans provided for which, due to the amount of the *supporting* documents, appendix items were bound in a separate package, thus making the plan appear smaller. It is an easier read when the Lender realizes that half of the package is referenced supporting materials. Within the plan text, defining information by bullet points or highlighting key information in **bold** is usually more reader friendly than is lengthy text. The extent of information, or lack thereof, should be evaluated by the Borrower's accountant.

Additional business plan structures, samples, and links may be found within the SBA's Web site, at *www.sba.gov*. On the home page, go to the upper right-hand corner and type "business plans" into the yellow box, and then click "go." You will be directed to an area of material business plan information, helps, and alternatives.

Segments of a business plan were already discussed in Chapter 7, within the section titled Put Prospective Lenders to the Test. In that instance, the Borrower's management put together a business presentation and component handouts for visiting Lenders. As you will see, some of those handouts actually could match up with, or at least contribute to, selected business plan requirements.

Business Plan Components

The business plan should have its own cover page, similar to the title page of the financing package.

Dearborn Manufacturing, Inc.
1826 Industrial Drive South
Lawrence, Massachusetts 01856

BUSINESS PLAN

Developed in conjunction with a Financing Request

For

WORKING CAPITAL
EQUIPMENT
REAL ESTATE

$2,800,000

June 1, 20XX
CONFIDENTIAL

Table of Contents: Develop a table of contents reflecting each subject segment numbered within the business plan.

The Executive Summary (a *critical* first impression) **Page xx**
Usually only *one to three pages*, this summary encompasses the entire business plan and is meant as *a quick read.* This document is regarded by most as the *most important element* of the business plan. Frequently, the reader will not get past the executive summary if it demonstrates, early on, that the Borrower is not providing suitable information. Then the plan may be bounced back for a rewrite—or the Lender may simply move on to the next deal.

Again, the executive summary should be prepared *following completion* of the overall business plan. At that time management will have accumulated enough information from which to develop an accurate and concise executive summary.

Only a *brief, succinct narrative paragraph on each of the following* items may be needed within the executive summary. The reader then quickly learns, through this precise synopsis, what he needs to know:

- Name and location of the Borrower
- Business origin
- Nature of the business
- Regulatory or licensing requirements
- Management and ownership
- Products and services
- Patents or copyrights owned
- Market and competition
- Financial performance
- Financial forecasts (it may be advisable, in order to reflect further creditability, that forecasts reflect the best-case, worst-case and most-likely case scenarios as addressed in Chapter 1).
- Financing sought (amount and purpose of loan, type of loan(s), collateral available; refer to the Borrower's terms and conditions sheet previously provided to Lender *with copy included within appendix*
- Loan closing time frames sought, with flexibilities, if any
- Reasons for leaving your current Lender
- Environmental issues, if any
- Special risks and mitigating circumstances, litigation pending, other potential changes

Remaining Business Plan Components

Within an actual business plan, information provided is much more comprehensive than within the executive summary. Following the executive summary, the business plan may be presented in sections as identified in the following text. All pages of the business plan will be numbered as a separate unit. Flexibilities are, of course, allowed within a business plan presentation. The plan here is presented as a guideline only. Your accountant or financial adviser may assist with content and flow.

The Company

Indicate the business name, type of corporation, divisions and affiliates, company history, and past mergers, acquisitions, and divestitures. Further indicate the nature of the business or services, stage of business development, and market position. If you have a mission statement, include it in this section.

Financial Proposal

Discuss in a *narrative format* the funding sought, proposed loan structuring, available collateral, significant covenant considerations, guarantees, and subordinations. Again, reference the *Borrower's* terms and conditions as already provided and included. As appropriate, provide information relative to (potential) equity participations, warrants, options, and conversion rights. *Discuss important timing issues and flexibilities.*

Use of Funds

Recap the major usages. Who is being paid off—and why? What will be the benefits, if any, to cash flow, existing debt service, and accounts payable? Will officers or owners of the company benefit personally from the newly borrowed funds? Will subordinated debt continue to exist? Indicate that the financial forecasts and the pro forma Balance Sheet reflect data *as if the loan closed under current assumptions.*

Financial Summary and Projections

Discuss the financial results of the past two to three years. Expand on these numbers by a *narrative* presentation of *prior* difficulties and the mitigation of problems. Cover the material elements of the new financial forecasts plus the rationale for the improved financial numbers and assumptions employed. What is the company going to do if the numbers don't materialize? Consider presenting the worst- and best-case financial scenarios, and address solutions.

The financial statements and schedules relating to the preceding will be placed and referenced within the appendix.

Management, Directors, and Organization (*prime* interest to Lenders)

A singe "profile" paragraph (not a complete résumé) *on each key executive* to include education, former position(s), current responsibilities, compensation, incentives, and stock ownership. Compensation and benefits may be presented with financial forecasts.

Identify key board members, employee workforce data, productivity

Concerns, incentives, training, and area labor availability. Provide an organizational chart, and comment on union relationships as may be appropriate.

Briefly identify your associated professionals: Your CPA, attorney, insurance agent, and other financial and business consultants. If a loan broker was used, indicate his identification as well. For each professional, include the full name, firm name, key contact (where appropriate), address, phone, fax and e-mail information.

Manufacturing

Identify the production methods, operations cycle, production capacity, level of integration, subcontractors, significant supply sources, shipping methods, raw materials availability, and warranty servicing. Comment on the type of machinery and equipment used in the business processes *and future requirements*. Is existing manufacturing capacity adequate? Are there any material Occupational Safety and Health Administration ("OSHA") violations or events? These would be job related safety and related issues.

Research, Development, Engineering, and Design

Provide information on state-of-the-art technology and processes within the company. Indicate copyrights or patients owned or pending.

Facilities

Provide a narrative description of the existing physical facilities. Include off-site manufacturing and/or storage facilities. Who holds the mortgage(s), if any? Provide mortgage detail. If facilities are leased, who is the Landlord and what is the duration and expense of the existing leases? Are there any plans for improvements or a move? Provide a facility layout (within the appendix) if diagrams included in an appraisal are not definitive or up to date.

Computer Technologies

Explain the extent of computer technologies used in various business operations (to include inventory control). Indicate the updates required, appropriate timing, cost of updates, and whether or not costs are included within the financial forecasts.

Services

If the business is a service business, identify service description, markets served, labor intensity, and contingent servicing liabilities. If a franchise, describe the training provided by franchisor, marketing assistance, and inventory programs of franchisor. Provide descriptive data on real estate leased or owned. Also indicate the franchisor's required royalties or percentage requirements of gross (or net) income. Include a copy of the franchise agreement within the appendix.

Markets and Competition

Discuss market segments and potential barriers to entry. What is the Borrower's market share? Is it growing? Are seasonal or cyclical markets involved? What are the Borrower's customer profiles? Who are the major competitors, and what are their strengths and weaknesses? What are the critical assumptions?

Marketing Plan

Is the business satisfactorily addressing served markets? Identify the strategic issues and responses. What are the sales strategies and tactics? Are distribution methods satisfactory? Provide some detail as to advertising, pricing, credit, and collection policies. If a service business, explain within the Plan the effective delivery of services and/or proximity to customers.

Credit Facilities Information

Provide detail on current capitalization; terms on lines of credit outstanding and on term loans; mortgages; leasing agreements (real estate and equipment); banking relationships; loans due to officers; subordinated debt; status of required taxes; insurance; and detail of prior equity financings. Has the company ever filed for bankruptcy? What were the reasons and the outcome? Why is the company leaving the current Lender?

The Industry

Describe the industry, indicating its history, trends, and changing technology. Are there unique exposures (to the business or to the Lender) within the industry? Are there job bonding requirements, special billing arrangements, or seasons unique to the industry? Are certain financial ratio outcomes peculiar to the industry? Is the business a member of, or does it participate in, an industry organization? Copies of relevant industry articles may be referenced and included within the appendix.

Critical Factors

Identify social, economic, political, or environmental issues. Are there licensing or regulatory requirements or concerns?

Legal Considerations

Identify contingent liabilities, litigation pending or proposed, and any local/state/federal licensing requirements.

Implementation Planning

Provide implementation schedule(s) and time lines as may be appropriate. Identify the assignment of responsibilities, monitoring of progress, and the process of effecting plan changes.

Following the business plan, the final portion of the financing package is the **appendix**. The appendix includes supplements and supports to the package and to the business plan. If this develops into considerable bulk, these items may be contained in a separate package labeled as "Appendix to Business Plan." The separate sections of the appendix may be referred to within the plan by letters of the alphabet. The Borrower may add or make deletions to this list depending upon his specific situation. Many are "need to have" items, and a few are "nice to have." Some may not be available until a later time, but will be assigned a letter within the appendix. A fly sheet within that appendix should acknowledge the absent item, indicating the reason for its absence and the expected time of receipt.

The appendix contains:

- *Borrower's* terms and conditions sheet
- Historical financial statements (2–3 years with notes)
- Financial forecasts *with assumptions* (1–2 years)
- Current and pro forma cash-flow analyses (first year by month, second year by quarter)
- Post-closing Balance Sheet
- Current aging of accounts receivable
- Current aging of accounts Payable
- Debt schedule (creditor identification, account numbers,

type of debt, collateral, total amount due, payment schedule, debt maturity; is debt current?)
- Personal financial statements of owners (Lender prefers own format)
- Personal financial statements of Guarantors (Lender prefers own format)
- Personal income tax returns of owners (complete)
- Personal income tax returns of Guarantors (complete)
- Real Estate appraisal (current or former—plot plans as applicable)
- Rent rolls
- Flood plain document
- Facilities layout (include off-site manufacturing and storage sites)
- Appraisal—machinery and equipment
- Environmental Site Assessment
- Complete résumés of key officers
- Insurance schedules (indicate current loss payees)
- Franchise agreement(s)
- Company PR, photos, etc.

Note: Prior to a loan closing, Borrower will be required to provide articles of incorporation, bylaws, corporate resolutions, and other pertinent legal agreements and opinions. Your attorney may assist you with this.

We've brought together considerable information and spent much time developing strategies and tactics within the business plan. Again, consider completing your executive summary *following completion* of the business plan. Underline those key sentences or ideas within the plan that contribute to the development of a concise executive summary. This procedure is really the most effective use of time.

Usually the only "tweaking" required within the financing package when sending it to different Lenders is the envelope and the management cover letter. Within the plan, and associated documents, refer to the *prospective* Lender as "the Lender" or "the Loan"—*not* by specific Lender name. Confidentiality is to be maintained throughout the plan distribution process.

CHAPTER 13

THE FINANCIAL MANAGER'S "WATCH LIST"

"I do appreciate this recap."
"I thought you would."

There can be no complete or definitive checklist as to things to actually "do" in addressing all of the exposures and covering all of the situations to which a Borrower may be subject as a result of business borrowings.

However, I have, by chapter, highlighted what I feel to be a Management Watch List. The list reflects guidelines to positive actions (along with selective thoughts) that could make the difference, possibly a *major* difference, in maintaining the financial health of a business that leverages its growth through commercial borrowings. Future disappointments may be eliminated, or at least diminished, through application of many of these basic considerations.

To ensure that basics are covered on a continuing basis, don't try to do all of this by yourself. Assign selected "watch list" responsibilities to other business associates, *but do make sure they get done*!

If you have skipped ahead in this book, some of these comments may not be completely understood or appear constructive. Everything is explained in the book!

The chapters identified here may include additional and specific information pertaining to each summary comment.

Chapter 1: Your Lender's Reasonable Expectations

Automatic Loan Payment Arrangements: Consider the "loss of control" aspect when authorizing a Lender to charge your account for business loan payments. Considering the grace periods available and the time for check clearance, this could be translated into an effective cash-flow strategy.

Business Management: In spite of the materiality of the business Lender to a business Borrower, it is best to *remember that the business is run by the owners*—not the Lender. Lenders are not business consultants. They do not wish to be, nor should they be, allowed to fill that position. Should they try, it may be time to find another Lender.

Financial Statements: Are the types of *periodic financial statements* prepared by the business accountant satisfactory to address the Borrower's current level of borrowing *as well* as future growth plans? Does the type of financial statement type also address the requirements of the Lender? Usually the specific type of financial statement required by the Lender is within the loan closing documents.

Forecasts: Financial forecasts are not management commitments. When preparing, provide definitive assumptions along with a variance qualifier. Save the "work paper" details of these assumptions for use within future forecasts.

"Informal" Agreements: If borrowing on a demand note basis, should there be an additional "informal" agreement with the Lender as to when the Note is to be "called" (or paid), get it in writing, signed and on the Lender's letterhead. Any informal or extra conditions should *always be documented.*

Legal Review *Prior* to Signature(s): *Do not sign Lender's documents without first reviewing with legal consul. Do not accept the "OK" of the Lender's lawyer.* Exercising this right of attorney review may further enable a Borrower to develop additional time (as may be needed) as documents work their way back and forth during editing.

Lender Fees: Lender fees should *most always* be challenged. Throughout this book, fees are well covered. Fee justifications, along with countermeasures that may result in fee reductions or complete fee elimination, are reviewed in this chapter. (See "Fees" in the Index for additional information.)

Lender Communications: This chapter indicates the importance of timely and accurate communications between Lender and Borrower. A financial reporting log should be established to cover such things as covenant compliance, correctness of company financial statement reporting, delivery of personal financial statements required from owners and loan guarantors, and other sundry reporting requirements. Also include items promised to the Lender, the promised delivery date, and date sent. Follow up twice a month. A check-off system should be adequate to ensure that the Borrower is *always* on time.

Going to miss a loan payment? Notify the Lender *in advance*. Whether slow accounts receivable or botched cash flow is responsible, advance notice can usually mitigate problems before they happen.

Loan Closings: Ensure that loan closing costs will not unfavorably impact loan proceeds needed at closing to pay off other Lenders, payables, attorneys, fees, and so on. If closing costs hold back too much of the closing proceeds, consider having these closing costs *added* to the loan balance. Closing costs should be determined prior to the actual loan closing.

Loan Covenant Monitoring: Monitor *monthly* your own financial and non-financial loan covenants to determine potential violations. If in violation, correct and communicate with your Lender *per recommendations in this book.*

Loan Defaults: It is a good idea to know what the Lender's "rights and remedies" to a loan default situation are *before the fact.* See your loan agreements. The Borrower *also* has rights when in default. Loan defaults and actions to consider are discussed in some detail within other chapters.

UCC Filings: Maintain *your own copies* of all Notes and borrowing documentation (to include copies of UCC1 Filings). These will be valuable (on-site) in many instances during your borrowing relationship.

Periodically check UCC records at the office of the secretary of state or commonwealth. Is the existing business debt and associated information properly reflected? If an old debt is reflected, get rid of it. Anyone reviewing a company's information may be misled as to the extent of company debt or its composition. See chapter guidelines.

Chapter 2: Recognizing the Danger Signals

Lender Fatigue: Ever get the feeling your Loan Officer is "tired" of your business and/or its problems? If so, it may be time to consider switching Lenders. Read this chapter and Chapters 7 and 8.

Lender "Seasoning": Insist that for a Lender to "win your business," you *must* work with a seasoned Lender. A comfort level would be a level of vice president (not assistant vice president) or above with over five years *within commercial lending*, not operations, auditing, or marketing. Should your Loan Officer have had job experience with other Lenders in the past, it is *not* a detriment, as the Loan Officer's experience levels have been broadened.

Loan Covenant Violation: Facing a loan covenant violation because of one short-term situational anomaly? *Save money and time.* Have your

Lender amend the existing loan document with a Letter Agreement. A Letter Agreement is frequently the answer to a short-term problem. Benchmark a return to the *normal* lending parameters. A Letter Agreement may also be less expensive than *restructuring* a loan.

Loan Officer Contact: Know how to contact your Loan Officer at any time, whether at home, at the office, or on the road. *Make sure* you have exchanged business cards. Ensure that someone else besides the company CFO or president has the contact numbers for the Lender (to include Lender assistants and key credit personnel). Also, if the Loan Officer has a specific "mail code," make sure it is on all correspondence and outer envelopes.

Loan Restructuring: When Lender seeks a loan restructuring in the *midst of the relationship, negotiate all phases* (to include costs) of the restricting process. *Normally* restructuring is done only upon the maturity of the current approved loan. When done in the middle of the life of a loan, there are usually reasons that *should* concern the Borrower. Find out what these are, and include your accountant and attorney in necessary strategic planning and negotiations.

Play for maximum time before the execution of loan restructuring documents. Use this time to preserve and/or strengthen your current position (or commence the process to obtain a replacement Lender). Read Chapter 7.

Ratio Negotiations: *Negotiate* your business financial and non-financial covenants. This includes the financial ratios that you agreed to abide by within your loan documents. Justification may be your *average industry ratios*, past and present financial statements, and your financial forecasts *with supporting assumptions.*

Reporting Requirements: Your business may be unable to comply with the Lender's reporting requirements on a timely basis due to lack of internally qualified personnel—or simply because of time constraints. *Negotiate* a change in due dates. Alternatively, engage a part-time bookkeeper or controller (for two or three days following the close of a month) to permit time to complete requirements as promised.

Risk Ratings: Also discussed within other chapters (see Index), risk ratings are almost a universal scale by which the creditworthiness of business borrowers, within a lending institution, may be measured. Know the *risk rating* assigned to your business and how to *improve* it.

Risk ratings may be updated frequently by the Lender. As is the case with a personal credit rating, the Borrower does not need a surprise when asking for additional loan(s), special existing loan changes; such as interest rate considerations, covenant considerations and so on. At least quarterly, identify the risk rating and ask the Lender for a schedule of rating information. The rating is *first* established by the Lender during the initial credit and approval process for a new borrower.

Chapter 3: The Borrower in Trouble

Trust Is Mutual: If you don't trust the Lender, or the Lender doesn't trust you, this could develop into an *irreconcilable* and unproductive situation. It may be the right time to commence sourcing a replacement Lender. Chapter 7.

Loan Covenants (Tightening): Are loan covenants being tightened by your Lender? Revisit and understand the composition of the alleged violated covenants. Sometimes even Lenders are not quite sure how to figure these out. Such actions could *later* result in an "easy" (and unjustified) covenant violation—so beware. Get the Lender's reasoning for any changes *in writing*. The Borrower should then counter with solid logic and evidence that covenant tightening is *not* the answer. Provide another solution, and bide your time.

Cash Accounts: Watch your cash accounts—*diversify* your deposit institutions when to do so is *not* a violation of current financial covenants. This action can reduce the impact of Lender "offsets" against the business accounts *in its institution*. The Borrower will at least have some cash in banks elsewhere.

Collateral, Request for: Beware of Lender requirements for collateral enhancements. Get a *supporting letter* from your Lender. If you are not satisfied with the Lender's justification, mount a rebuttal. Such collateral enhancements, which impact your "*other* available collateral," may trigger loan amendments, which could translate into additional legal costs. Even the Lender's legal costs will be passed on to you. Don't agree to anything until meeting with your attorney, accountant, and/or financial adviser.

Collateralization of Your Personal Guarantee: *Fight this hard*! Your home, investments, and other assets could be placed at *additional* risk. Should the Borrower wish to pledge these personal assets as collateral elsewhere for personal reasons, he would be then be unable to do so. See Chapter 5.

Appraisal Updates: If updated appraisals are requested by your Lender, that's another warning signal! Again—obtain the Lender's reasoning *in writing*. Also keep a copy of the most recent "complete" appraisal(s) (and environmental reports) at the business site.

Delaying Tactics: When difficulties develop, the Borrower needs time to plan and execute strategies. *Each* Lender request, suggested loan amendment, Letter Agreement, or critique *must* be supported in writing by the Lender. Then the Borrower must have his attorney, accountant, and/or financial adviser(s) review the documents, and inform the Lender that he is doing so. These Lender letters may then be red lined and returned to the Lender—for further negotiation or correction—resulting in *more time* for the Borrower to plan. Always receive a fresh *clean* letter (not pen changes), and involve your attorney.

Forbearance Fees: A forbearance fee may be a prelude to the serious action of a Lender "calling" the loan. Commence to keep a ***daily* log** of all Lender contact and resulting actions. Communicate happenings to your attorney.

Negotiate strongly against the *amount* of a forbearance fee. More than not these fees are "blue skied" and can be reduced—or eliminated! See more on Fees in the Index.

Loan Workout Department ("Special Assets"): In the loan workout department? Most likely you will now have a *more* experienced Lender. The Borrower's full cooperation, honesty, proficient legal representation, and *aggressive participation* in essential business recovery tactics are critical for his survival. Again—*never* sign anything without your attorney's approval.

Chapter 4: Pitfalls Out of Your Control

Industry Acceptance: Make sure, *before* the fact of completing a loan application or putting up application deposits, that your industry is acceptable to a prospective Lender. Not all are—or the Lender may have had a *recent* loss working with this industry. Even a Lender's new-business representative may not know of an *internal* industry problem. Such a situation could be an almost automatic rejection. Find out early!

Approval Authorities: Do you know your Loan Officer's *loan approval authority*? What are his superiors' authorities? Is the Lender really too "junior" to effectively address the Borrower's needs? Only borrow from a Lending Officer who has the clout to do the job! Who actually approves the loan?

Lender Proximity: In spite of this "tech" age, excessive distances from your business Lender is *not* a good idea. Your physical presence can be extremely influential and supportive of your needs. Proximity to your Lender can gain your Lender's singular attention—the ultimate communication. So, if a distant Lender offers only a slightly better deal, is it really worth the potential loss of essential visibility?

Lender's Annual Report: *Get a copy* of your Lender's annual report. It will list the senior lenders of the institution and their specialized functions. It can come in handy in a number of social and business situations.

Acquisition (One Lender by Another): If *your Lender is acquired* by another Lender, read this chapter. If *your Lender acquires another Lender*, you're OK, but should still read this chapter. The upheaval experienced by the institution's commercial borrowers can be unnerving and jeopardize Borrowers' cash flow.

Regulatory Considerations: If your lending institution is having difficulties with bank regulators, read this chapter and meet with your legal counsel. While the lending agreement may remain in force (for a period of time) you may be forced into a new lending relationship.

Environmental Considerations: Environmental inspections and/or remedial solutions may slow down loan approvals and/or impact loan closings. They may not have to—*there are alternatives.* Read about related Letter Agreements in this chapter.

Don't count on your Lender's ability, or desire, to purchase Lender's *environmental risk insurance* (the Borrower pays the premiums). While it may ease the concern over certain of the Borrower's environmental exceptions, it is frequently unavailable. Some insurance companies have discontinued offering such coverage to commercial Lenders. It was good while it lasted, because it enabled loans to get done. It doesn't hurt to look around.

Purchase and Sales Agreement (Real Estate): *Before* signing a Purchase & Sale Agreement on real estate or land, ensure that the buyer has a "subject to" clause: "This agreement is subject to a satisfactory [satisfactory as determined by the buyer] environmental site assessment." Or the Borrower may add issues of appraised value, land surveys, asbestos and lead inspections, or whatever else may be an important issue. This action may enable an "out" for the buyer in case of serious and potentially expensive, or irreconcilable, exceptions. The buyer should work with his attorney.

Chapter 5: What You Don't Know About—But Should

Credit Committee: If a larger business: The Borrower does *not* usually get to make a presentation before the credit committee. *Only* the Lending Officer is present representing the Borrower. However, if the Borrower's company has a video about its operation, the video is usually viewed by the credit committee. A business video, which should be updated every so many years to include new customers, vendors, and employees, can be a valuable addition to the many types of company presentations—and it could possibly even influence a loan approval decision. A video enables a business to tell its story *its way*—and so could be a justifiable investment.

Fees: Most "required" Lender fees are not. Many are simply what the market will bear. *Challenge fees.* Possibly leverage the fees, or lack thereof, against other Lender(s) that you are considering.

If *total loan closing fees* are significant enough to reduce the net proceeds at loan closing to less than what is required, ask the Lender that closing fees be *added* to the loan balance. At least the Borrower may then have the net amount of loan proceeds expected.

Collection day fees are a real moneymaker for a Lender. Your loan payments *may not be applied* until days after receipt. See chapter for details.

Some Lenders will seek *a loan commitment fee* upon executing their commitment letter. Try to defer this fee, which averages about 1% of the approved credit facility, until the actual loan closing—when funds may be more available to pay the fee.

The *forbearance fee* is a serious Lender action and may involve a significant fee. However, the amount of the fee is frequently *arbitrarily chosen* by a Lender. This fee should be subject to Borrower negotiations. See "Fees" in the Index for additional information.

Negotiate the loan prepayment fee (penalty) *before* accepting the Lender's terms and conditions. Many variations of this fee are available and, considering the Borrower's future departure plans, should be negotiated in the Borrower's favor.

Fee Duplication: If working with a potential of *two* replacement Lenders, do considering paying selective *duplicate* deposit or good faith fees. This way you may be considered a serious Borrower by both parties. These duplicate fees may enable approvals and commitments from both Lenders. These are *not* loan closing fees. These tactics should be accomplished *before* a loan closing. Such strategic expenses may well be worth it if one Lender backs out at the eleventh hour—or the Borrower wants "out." Using this mechanism, a loan can then be closed regardless of which Lender "folds." In some cases fees may even be returned by the aborted Lender—especially if it seeks the Borrower's business at a later time.

Interest Charges: New loan? Are loan closing expenses overwhelming to the extent of reducing the loan proceeds anticipated and needed? In order to manage cash flow for the first few months of the new loan, ask the Lender for an "interest only" period (such periods may extend 3, 6, or even 12 months). In this case, the Borrower would pay *only* the interest due; the loan principal portion would *not* be reduced. If paying interest only *still* would jeopardize cash flow for a period of time, ask the Lender for a one-year moratorium on interest *and* principal. Many Lenders will do this at the beginning of a relationship. Make it part of the loan's terms and conditions (*before* loan approval). The Borrower's cash flow forecasts should justify this procedure.

Know your interest rate. It is *variable or fixed*? Would different indices enable better planning or improved cash flow? Is your Lender computing your interest rate on a short 360-day year? If so, you're paying more than if you were on a 365-day year. Details and examples are in this chapter.

Close a real estate or term loan close to the end of a month. Prepaid interest costs may thus be minimized.

Is your loan a large one—over $1,000,000? You should consider the benefits of interest rate caps and collars. See the chapter.

Key Man Insurance: Key man insurance is touted as a must when structuring business succession strategies. However, *be careful*—the Lender may have the *first* use of insurance proceeds. Learn the actual process. Even some Lenders do not know what happens when key man insurance is operative. Read the chapter.

Legal Fees: When preparing for a loan closing with a new or existing Lender, work to get a cap on the Lender's legal fees. Read up on this.

Remember, the Borrower's attorney fees are *not* usually included in the Lender's closing costs. These are paid separately by the Borrower.

Do not use the Lender's attorney as yours. He only has the best interest of the Lender at heart—not yours. Engage, and pay for, your *own* attorney. There are too many things that can go wrong in a commercial loan—don't pinch pennies in regard to your legal protection.

Loan Approval: Even if your Lending Officer says that your loan has been approved, *do not make any preliminary promises* of payment(s), or payment dates, to any party. Do not hand out post-dated checks. Wait until the Lender's check is in hand, or funds have been wired into and *received* by your bank.

Loan Broker Fees: If the Borrower is *not satisfied* with the *loan broker's fee*, request that the Lender does *not* make this fee part of the Lender's closing disbursements schedule. Negotiations between the broker and Borrower can then be resolved following the loan closing. However, if the broker's fee is acceptable, the fee may best be paid out of the loan proceeds—the Lender then knows that the Borrower has satisfied this obligation.

Management: Remember, *the quality and effectiveness of management* is the *first and foremost* concern of the Lender's credit committee. It is usually their feeling that competent management can overcome most all obstacles. Ensure that your Lending Officer transmits such competencies.

Personal Guarantees: Don't quickly agree to provide a personal guarantee to support your business loan. The Borrower *may argue collateral sufficiency,* lack of personal equity, or family members' objections. The Borrower could offer certain business performance benchmarks which, if *not* achieved, could result in providing a personal guarantee. The guarantee would then remain in force until such benchmarks were achieved.

The Borrower should consider replacing a Lender's personal guarantee request with a Borrower's *validity of collateral guarantee*. This action may be an alternative "face saver" for both the Borrower and the Lender. Not all Lenders are aware of this type of guarantee. Read the chapter.

If the Borrower does finally provide a personal guarantee, request a *performance benchmark* that indicates under what circumstances the personal guarantee will be released by the Lender. Have some specific performance targets in mind before approaching the Lender. Of course, even if the Lender agrees verbally—get it in writing.

If providing a personal guarantee, ensure it is limited in nature. Read the chapter.

If a full personal guarantee has been absolutely required by the Lender, make sure it is *not to be collateralized* by your personal residence, other properties, or other personal assets. However, if this additional collateral develops as a "must," again seek a performance target at which point the additional collateral provided to the Lender will be released back to the Borrower. Read the chapter.

Purchase-Money Security Interests: Your regular suppliers(s) could place your Lending relationship in jeopardy—and possibly *cause a loan violation.* Purchase-money security interests can be hazardous for a Borrower. Read up on this one.

On the flip side—purchase money security interests can be *of benefit to the Borrower.* This is especially so if the Borrower has a receivable customer who is unable to pay at this time. Convert this delinquent receivable to a Note Receivable with a payment arrangement in place. Obtain supporting collateral, and perfect (UCC) the Borrower's security interest in collateral. This action should improve your accounts receivable aging. Seek attorney's help on the Note.

Subordinated Debt: Existing business debt, due to officer(s), or other debt required to be subordinated to the Lender's loan is not necessarily bad news. Inasmuch as payments to these select creditors are no longer authorized, subordination may actually improve the Borrower's cash flow (payments deferred). Subordination also enhances a Lender's positive analysis of the Borrower's Balance Sheet. Why would creditors subordinate? See chapter detail.

Chapter 6: Your Worst-Case Scenario

Advantage of an Experienced Commercial Attorney: Engagement of, and effective communication with, a qualified commercial attorney will ensure that the Borrower has a competent advocate on his side. Review some of the functions and advantages such legal counsel brings to the table. Do not attempt to save money by using the Lender's attorney as yours.

Bank Account "Offsets": The Lender makes a move to empty your business bank accounts and *take possession* of all of its collateral to satisfy your delinquent or unsatisfactory loan(s). You think you're going out of business. This can be your "worst-case scenario." Deal with it; read this chapter and work with your attorney.

Even if all checking accounts have been offset by Lender, seek *additional* loan advances to pay all, or a portion, of *payroll, taxes and health benefits* (even management's salary) from the Lender. Many times it is to the benefit of the Lender to do this. Keeping Borrower's taxes current in a difficult situation is especially important leverage when dealing with the Lender. New loan advances could be a symbol of good faith on behalf of the Lender as the Lender seeks the Borrower's cooperation. Frequently these "special" loan advances may be secured by new or other collateral. If there is already an "abundance" of collateral, additional collateral from the Borrower may not be necessary to support these new loan advances.

See the chapter suggestions for *short-term sources of cash flow.*

The 30-Day Letter: The Borrower has received the Lender's 30-day letter; the Lender wants full payment in 30 days. Don't panic. The Lender has gotten your attention—that was his objective. Call your attorney immediately. *Take care of your initial responsibilities* as recommended within the chapter.

Relax—it's going to take between three and four months to obtain a new Lender and close a new loan. Your Lender really knows this. It is the mission of the Borrower to have the Lender's "30-day" letter *reborn* a number of times until the Borrower is successful in obtaining a new Lender.

Follow the chapter's schedule of recommended meetings, which includes *two meetings before the 30-day letter expires and one afterward.* Follow specific and recommended guidelines on attendees, scope of meetings, record keeping, and communications. Stay in *close contact* with your attorney.

Keep copious *notes* throughout the entire process. These can be invaluable later.

The third meeting is the pièce de résistance. All participants are present—at the business site. The Borrower controls this meeting with the objective of Lender reinstatement *or* the gaining of much more time to attract new Lenders.

The objective of the Borrower's meetings and letter guidelines is *to gain time*. The time gained should assist the Borrower in attracting at least *two* satisfactory replacement Lenders.

Always keep in mind: *No deals made, no agreements signed,* without Borrower's attorney confirmation.

Lender's Possession: *All of the Lender's warning letters have expired.* A new level of negotiations may begin, or the Lender may seek to gain physical possession of collateral.

The Lender may alternatively seek a Guarantor loan payment (full or partial), depending upon agreements, *before* addressing collateral liquidation.

The Lender and his representatives arrive at the Borrower's business to execute their rights and remedies. They may seek *to physically remove the business's books and records* along with other pledged assets. Review chapter guidelines and contact your attorney *immediately*. Your attorney should approve all Borrower activities.

The Lender may take possession of the accounts receivable in order to notify customers to pay the Lender, *not* the Borrower. Note that receivables created *after* the Lender's takeover belong to the Borrower and not to the Lender. Your attorney should confirm.

Inform employees and others, *depending on their need to know*, about the gravity of the situation at the time. There have been cases in which the employees never knew there was a problem as the company recovered in the normal course of business. Do not be too quick to tell *everyone* of the current situation. Customers and suppliers alike have their own period of notification as well. Your attorney should approve utilization of chapter suggestions.

Lender Replacements: *Commence activities to qualify and select two possible replacement Lenders.* This should have been commenced as "danger signals" became evident (Chapter 2).

The Borrower does *not* let his current Lender know the identities of the replacement Lenders he is considering. In reality, Lenders being paid off frequently do not know the name of the new Lender until only a day or so before a loan closing and payoff. That is when the new Lender calls up for a loan payoff figure. This is not an absolute rule, but it's relevant in most cases.

The Lenders to be considered as replacement Lenders will want to get the Borrower's deal "off of the street"; that is, to get the deal in their hands so they do not have to worry about competitors. They do not want a Borrower comparison shopping. Be wary of their "stated" deadlines—if they really want your loan relationship they will be there when *you are ready* to make a decision.

Review and compare all proposal letters and term sheets against the evaluation schedule provided within the chapter. Your attorney or accountant may assist.

Lending Officer Change: Need a change of Lending Officers? Follow the guidelines at the end of this chapter.

Loan Workout Department: The Borrower's lending relationship is transferred from the Loan Officer to the Lender's loan workout department, which is also sometimes called "special assets." The Borrower will now work with a very experienced, and usually reasonable, senior lender. When the Borrower receives notice of this transfer, he should inform his attorney and associated professionals.

In all of this, the Borrower must continue to run the business—effectively so if possible. During this time, replacement Lenders may be reviewing the business operations and records to see if this loan could be a "fit" for them.

While the issues and difficulties discussed here are in the process of being resolved—and if it is possible—do not *continue* to violate Lender's financial and non-financial covenants. The Lender is *also* bound by the promises made to the Borrower within the loan agreements. Continuing reporting, as directed, should be on a timely basis. The goodwill of the existing Lender, even if the Borrower is seeking a replacement, can be valuable as special situations present themselves.

Consider Lender suggestions as you and your attorney work with the "Loan Workout Department."

It can happen that the entire loan may not have to be paid back to the Lender. Possibility a limited recovery, which frequently happens, may be satisfactory to the Lender. This is usually processed through the Loan Workout Department.

Chapter 7: Take Charge of Your Banking Destiny

Collateral Additions, Requirements for: Do not *volunteer* to provide additional collateral, business or personal, to the Lender's collateral base. Such assets may be needed at a later time, for either personal or business usage. If collateral additions must be made, work out agreements for benchmarking points at which the newly pledged collateral may be *released* by the Lender. These benchmarking points may be identified in several ways; a company may perform satisfactorily overall, reduce loans to a certain level, or achieve select Balance Sheet ratios.

Collateral Enhancements: There are actions that the Borrower may take which, in the Lender's eyes, can *increase* collateral eligibility and subsequent loan advance rates. While those tactics, mentioned in this chapter, do not have to be implemented prior to attracting a new Lender, it is prudent to understand such opportunities. Then be prepared to request appropriate modifications to a replacement Lender's terms and conditions. Some of these collateral enhancement items may be *of benefit to any business*, whether borrowing or not. Work with your accountant and business consultant(s) in evaluating suggestions.

Collateral & Loan Availability Worksheet: Long title but use it—"Credit Line, Collateral, and Loan & "Availability" Development Worksheet." This worksheet enables the *Borrower* to determine (*before* contacting a Lender) what size loan his business collateral may justify, the credit line potential, and how much in borrowed funds will be available to the Borrower following his loan closing. The worksheet assists the Borrower in making sure he is asking for, and can justify, a large enough line of credit to satisfy his requirements. It may take some time putting it together the worksheet information, but it will be worth it. Your financial adviser may also assist. The worksheet is found within this chapter.

The results achieved by the completion of the this worksheet provide prime information for the development of the Borrower's terms and conditions sheet (T&C). Remember that the *Borrower's* T&C is the *requested* loan structure *prepared by the Borrower*, which will be *presented to prospective Lenders.* The Lender's T&C, later provided to the Borrower, will also be substantially in the same format. The Borrower's job is to provide, through *his* T&C, specific loan elements; those that the Borrower wants the Lender to include in the Lender's T&C. The Borrower's

T&C is a very effective base from which the Lender can extrapolate the Borrower's specific prerequisites. Most Borrowers fail to present their requirements in this time-tested format. See sample of a Borrower's T&C in this chapter.

New Lender Selection (two prime candidates): In your search for a new or replacement Lender, it is fine to review many preliminary candidates, as well as "alternative" Lenders. But, in the final analysis, *consider going forward with two Lenders.* "Going forward" means courting them up to and including the acceptance of *both* Lenders' proposals and/or commitment letters—even up to the time of loan closing. If one Lender attempts to unfavorably change the loan arrangements, or an untenable situation develops at loan closing, the Borrower will not be "left hanging" at the eleventh hour. If only one preferred Lender was pursued, the Borrower has nowhere to go—and third parties are most likely expecting timely payments from a loan closing. If two Lenders have been pursued, the Borrower can leave the (now unfavorable) first transaction (or has the leverage to do so) and close on the other loan within a week. Read up on this—it's quite interesting. Stay close to legal counsel should these deal-saving tactics be employed.

Lender's Vested Interest: In a payoff situation the Lender does *not* want to jeopardize his chances of repayment by alienating a Borrower's *replacement* Lender. The existing Lender has a vested interest for the Borrower to succeed in such a transition; he will be paid off. Accordingly, the former Lender may actually cooperate with the new Lender in the process. The workout situation is one of the few cases in which a Lender will be aware that you are in the process of seeking a new Lender; usually, an existing Lender does not know the potential Lenders that the Borrower is courting.

Leveraging Lenders: If the Borrower is in the process of *leveraging one potential preferred Lender against another,* be careful not to put both deals in jeopardy. While such negotiating tactics are frequently used, and often successfully, caution is recommended. Such negotiations should be accomplished with the assistance of the Borrower's financial consultant and attorney. Suggestions as to using of this tactic are provided within the chapter.

Overview Package for Lender: Create a "Lender's overview package"—a "press kit" for your business. This is *not* a detailed loan presentation or a full business plan—only an overview. This should quickly "weed out" those Lenders that have no real desire to become involved with your business. Once many Lenders have been eliminated, those remaining *choice* Lenders, which the Borrower feels could be effective working partners, are invited to separate half-day meetings at the business site. A *specific agenda* is prepared. See the sample within this chapter.

Following these choice Lender meetings, it is expected that proposal letters, or simply a Lender's terms and conditions sheet, will be received from interested Lenders. The Borrower is expected, following *acceptance* of the Lender's basic and preliminary terms, to provide additional supporting documents. The Lender then continues his due diligence: the credit and approval process. If results are satisfactory, a loan proposal or commitment letter may be issued to the Borrower. Evaluating loan proposals received is an important exercise. A *comparative analysis worksheet* is provided for evaluating many of the key aspects contained with a loan proposal or even a commitment. Remember that the *suggested* loan covenants and terms that were within the Borrower's terms and conditions sheet may be reasonably followed within the Lenders' offerings. This evaluation of opportunities should be accomplished with the assistance of the Borrower's accountant or financial consultant.

Terms and Conditions Sheet ***(Borrower's)***: The Borrower will prepare *his* suggested terms and conditions sheet for prospective *new* Lenders. This is an important exercise that will go a long way in assisting potential Lenders in structuring a loan package that will both work for, and be acceptable to, the Borrower.

The Borrower's terms and conditions sheet will contain, among other things, *Borrower-prepared* financial covenants (with accountant's help). These are formulas that the Lender reviews to determine the Borrower's progress and potential loan violations. They may also include issues of officer salaries and officer loans. This is a chance to develop and support ratio formulas that the Borrower can live with—possibly over a period of years.

There are also *non-financial covenants* which the Borrower may address within his terms and conditions format. These have to do with the types of financial statements required, periodic reporting requirements, insurance requirements, other types of financings that may be needed, capital purchases, business ownership changes, a need for officer loans, extent of appraisal and environmental requirements, and so on. While many of these non-financial covenants may be referred to as a Lender's boilerplate agreements, some may be altered if the Borrower is adamant. The *Borrower must ensure* that important issues are addressed and reflected within the *Borrower's* terms and conditions sheet. The Borrower must also, of course, be prepared to later justify his requests to the Lender.

Relationship Maintenance: Has the Borrower made the decision to leave his current Lender? The Borrower should not send *signals* of his intentions; continue a smooth and cooperative relationship with the current Lender, no matter how tough it is—right to the end.

Timetables: The Borrower *can* manage the important time elements and tactics when leaving a current Lender (work such pre-activities and departures on *his timetable*—not the Lender's). Read this chapter.

Chapter 8: Specialized Lending

Asset-Based Lending: Asset-based lending (ABL) provides the Borrower with a fluctuating availability of borrowed funds. The amount of these funds is dependent upon the *fluctuating and determinable values of selected pledged current assets.* While the advantages are many, there are also disadvantages to consider. Many are detailed within this chapter.

Essentially, asset-based lending enables the Borrower to receive *loan advances against eligible sales* (invoices) created daily. The resulting loan advance will usually be deposited in the Borrower's operating account the next day. Waiting 30-60-90 days for receivable payments may be a thing of the past. Note that customer remittances usually go to a Lender's lockbox. The outstanding loan(s) is gradually reduced by these frequent lockbox proceeds. However, certain businesses may not be candidates for asset-based lending. Check it out.

Advances against invoices are based upon certain lending formulas. As collateral quality improves, Lender advance rates may increase as well.

The satisfactory aging of accounts receivable (frequently within 90 days in age) and the credit quality of the Borrower's customers are major considerations impacting the Lender's determination of loan advance formulas.

Eligible inventory components may also be part of the asset-based Lender's collateral and the revolving financing loan base.

Work in process is generally *not* considered eligible inventory. But there are always exceptions, which may include a modest advance rate against certain components of work in process.

Within asset-based lending there are many other classes of inventory that may be considered *ineligible*. See chapter detail.

The *Borrowing Base Certificate* is the *key worksheet* to calculate collateral eligibility and borrowing formulas, view approved limits, and determine the current borrowing potential. A completed Certificate is provided within this chapter.

Regardless of the amount of eligible collateral a Borrower might have, there will be an approved credit line maximum as well as possible loan "caps" on selected collateral components.

Considering asset-based lending? Your books and records may be subject to periodic Lender audits (one to four times annually) by the Lender or professionals hired by the Lender. The Borrower pays all costs and expenses.

ABL Lender "audits" are *unrelated* to the accountant's preparation of year-end or periodic financial statements. These Lender's audits are primarily focused upon the quality, quantity, and accuracy of reported collateral, and secondarily on company performance.

It can be tough to negotiate these audit costs, as they are usually under contract—but *do* negotiate *audit frequency*—that's the key!

Debtor-in-Possession Financing: Debtor-in-possession (DIP) financing addresses the need for the funding of a Chapter 11 bankruptcy situation. A plan of reorganization, prepared by the bankrupt company and approved by the court, usually addresses the need for financing during the term of the plan. Proceeds are used to address approved creditor repayment programs, working capital needs, and other approved uses. This financing can be attractive to Lenders, as the DIP Lender must be paid out *before* the Borrower can emerge from bankruptcy. Because of their control expertise, larger asset-based lenders handle these opportunities well. DIP Borrowers should rely heavily upon advice from legal counsel and financial advisers as they address and proceed through DIP financing.

Employee Stock Ownership Plans (ESOP): An avenue in purchasing a company is through an Employee Stock Ownership plan, or ESOP. *Employees*, including members of former management, *may participate in* *the purchase and ownership* of the "new" company. An ESOP Trust may borrow funds from a Lender to facilitate the purchase of a business and for ongoing business financing purposes. The larger commercial banks or commercial finance companies are usually veterans of such loan structures. A successful ESOP should be able to reward participating employees by way of growth through their company investment. Such an arrangement may require material negotiations and expenses. Lenders usually seek a comprehensive business plan with realistic expectations, tiered performance forecasts, and reasonable assumptions. A Borrower should consult legal counsel and financial adviser(s) for further direction.

Factoring (of invoices): Possibly the Borrower does not want to, or cannot, finance the entire accounts receivable portfolio through ABL. How about financing only *one customer's sales* or maybe even a *single invoice*? Factoring may be for you.

Like ABL, there are *pluses and minuses* regarding factoring. Read up on these.

Closing an ABL loan may take from one to four months—on average. A factoring arrangement may be concluded in only a few weeks. If timing *and* cash flow are problems, consider *factoring first and then a conversion to ABL.* Sometimes the *same* Lender (larger Lenders) can finance the entire scenario.

Lockboxes: Problems with your accounts receivable payments going to a *Lender's* lockbox? Then ABL or factoring may cause problems for you—or maybe not. There are alternatives discussed within the chapter.

Leverage Buyouts: Looking to *purchase a company, or buy out an existing owner*? Consider the leveraged buyout. Most ABL Lenders address these buyout opportunities. The collateral for the Buyer's loan is usually the eligible collateral that currently exists within the company being purchased. Relatively speaking, the amount of equity that the Buyer must commit may be modest compared to overall funding requirements. Usually the flexibilities of the asset-based loan structure, coupled with additional term and/or real estate loans, may be enough to pull the deal together. Sometimes *more* than one Lender (participants) will pool expertise and funding to make a deal work. One Lender is known as the "lead Lender." If collateral advances are not enough to pull together the funding needed, a "mezzanine Lender" may be invited into the deal as well. Caution—*many* fees and expenses can be involved in this situation.

Also, unique loan structuring, possibly to include seller "take-back" paper, employment contracts, consulting arrangements for the prior owner, and the like, may be material in overall negotiations.

Mezzanine Lending: What would a Borrower do when there is no cash, no credit availability, and the Borrower does not want to give up owner's equity? The Borrower may consider mezzanine lending. For qualified businesses, this quasi-equity lending strategy may provide the funds required for further growth. This is especially so for companies that are, or that have material prospects of, becoming profitable. Mezzanine Lenders typically seek Borrower's requiring over $1,000,000 in funding. Normally, other debt may not be disturbed.

Municipal, State, Regional, and Other Government Financing Programs: The Borrower shouldn't forget the many municipal, state, regional, and other government programs available. Many of these programs may be restrictive as to business size, use of funds, and business locality. Then again, *loan structuring flexibilities can be impressive* and may target exactly what the Borrower needs. Commercial Lenders usually work well with all of these entities. Timing of approvals and loan closings may be of concern; many of these entities meet only once or twice a month, so processing time could be extensive. However, because of loan flexibilities, these may be worth checking out.

Purchase Order Financing: A purchase order comes in. The Borrower does not have the materials to make the product nor does he have the funds, or loan availability, to purchase needed materials or components. Consider purchase order financing. Read of the many advantages to this type of financing product.

Purchase orders (POs) considered for financing must be qualified by distinctive Lender's criteria. Some of these are detailed within this chapter.

State Agencies and Development Corporations: There are a number of state agencies and state and local development corporations that address more localized business financing offerings. A listing of these is provided.

Technology and Export Financing: See the chapter information cited on technology financing and assists in export financing.

U. S. Small Business Administration (SBA): The SBA, working through conventional Lenders (both "Preferred" and "Certified" by SBA criteria), provides a number of lending and loan guarantee programs. Loans (or loan guarantees) may address projects including working capital requirements, business expansion, the purchase of real estate and land, facility renovations, and much more. Some long-term, fixed-rate programs may require equity of no more than 10% from selected Borrowers. There is more on SBA programs and loan qualifiers within the chapter.

Chapter 9: Effective Sourcing of Borrowed Funds

Lenders—Traditional and Alternative: *Traditional* Lenders, such as commercial banks and thrift institutions, have historically been the lead Lenders to business. Many business Borrowers, however, may find it difficult to comply with the credit quality and/or the loan requirements of these established institutions. Also, Borrowers may not seek the magnitude of funds such Lenders are seeking to place. Due to established internal "lending policies," Borrowers are frequently frustrated—but there *are* alternatives. This chapter profiles these "alternative Lenders" and how to find them.

Alternative Lenders: Alternative Lenders are *generally more flexible* regarding loan structuring than are traditional Lenders. While alternative Lenders may sometimes be more expensive than traditional Lenders, the final product may more effectively address the Borrower's needs. Also, alternative Lenders do not seek "AAA" credits, but may specialize in companies with less than stellar credit ratings. An alternative Lender may be in a Borrower's future—and could "make" the future.

Within the spectrum of alternative Lenders, most *all* business financial products are addressed. Some specialize in specific industries, which is a real advantage over many traditional Lenders. There are alternative Lenders of great size, and then there are those that qualify as "boutique shops." Today, alternative Lenders have earned and deserve the same creditability as traditional Lenders. It may be wise for a Borrower to include appropriate alternative Lenders in his quest for a new or replacement business Lender.

To locate these alternative Lenders, read the appropriate portion of this chapter. An excellent source is the membership listing at the Web site of the Commercial Finance Association at *www.cfa.org*.

Credit Unions: In between these "alternative" and "traditional" Lenders are credit unions. In the past, credit unions did not usually seek business loans, nor did they have internal servicing capabilities. Today the larger credit unions, and the multistate credit unions, have established *commercial lending departments* with *full* operational capabilities. Many are staffed with former senior bank and commercial finance company Lenders. They are also able to *address most business borrowers' requirements.* From working capital loans, term loans, commercial real estate loans, and construction loans to investment properties, qualified credit unions can perform. Some of the largest may offer conforming asset-based lending. They do not, at this time, and to the best of this author's knowledge, choose to offer factoring or purchase order financing, nor do they provide the larger leveraged buyout fundings. Inasmuch as credit unions are tax-exempt, they may offer their business Borrowers flexible and competitive interest rate programs.

Credit union loan structuring can be as competitive as that of many conventional Lenders. Businesses are finding more and more receptiveness from credit unions for their financing requirements.

Loan Brokers: Using a loan broker? An experienced loan broker can save the Borrower much time in seeking out the most probable "right" Lender(s) for a situation. A broker will research Lenders, be the Borrower's liaison between the Borrower and many potential Lenders, make and attend appointments, distribute the *Borrower's* terms and conditions only to the appropriate parties, assemble supporting packages, and assist in evaluating offers. For a relatively modest fee, and usually for an *exclusive* performance period, their contracts are by and large straightforward. It is customary that if a satisfactory deal is *not* found for the Borrower, within the specific time frame, no fee is due. The Borrower should have his legal counsel review a broker's contract.

Loan Participations: Don't want to leave your current Lender, but the loan you seek is becoming too large for that institution? Ask the Lender to consider a *loan participation*. Two or more Lenders may share the loan, as well as *share the risk*. The original Lender's loan can be almost half or more of what it was originally. The original Lender can now continue a portion of this desirable relationship. The business accounts and other sundry loans or service functions usually remain with the original Lender.

Chapter 10: Getting Your Share in Difficult Times

Financial Relationship Management: The Borrower must seek to be *more than a risk rating number* to his Lender. The Borrower should favorably stand out from the rest of the loan portfolio—and relationships are *everything*. Go that extra mile to make it so. See *key tactics* discussed within the chapter.

Basics—Of Course: Don't ignore basics. The most basic is to honor your commitments on time! Ensure *timely* and *accurate* financial and business reporting *per the loan agreements. No surprises* for the Lender! If a problem is developing, let your Lender know. Maintain frequent and open communications. Return calls promptly.

Annual Recognition Dinners: Read up on this tactic, which is beneficial both within the company and externally—and fun, too.

Borrower's Self-Analysis: The Borrower should do a portion of the Loan Officer's work for him. Periodically, as required, the Borrower should submit interim financial statements to the Lender, *with the Borrower's analysis* attached. The Borrower may also do some prior period comparisons. Also, in a narrative format, highlight the period's successes, difficulties, and forecasts. If problems exist, indicate solutions. The Loan Officer is receiving valuable information and the Borrower is telling it *his way*. Such reporting is very beneficial to a fruitful relationship. Read about more ideas in this area.

Community Events: Play musical chairs. Attend your Loan Officer's community events and, likewise, invite him to yours. These may be local service, business, or community clubs (chamber of commence, Kiwanis, Lions, Rotary, and so on). Again you are *both* expanding your networking horizons as well as expanding your relationship.

Luncheon for 4: The Borrower should periodically host a Luncheon for 4 with two "outside" business associates, or professionals, and his Lender. The Borrower should not discuss his business concerns, but rather seek to expand the Loan Officer's relations involving these new contacts. Loan Officers are always pressed to further develop their networking potential. The Borrower's help in this area will be valued. See more detail in this chapter.

Open House: It's open house time—*once annually*! This involves much work and planning, but it is well worth it. This can be effective regardless of the size of the business. While additional advantages accrue if the open house is held on the business site, a hotel meeting room (small or large) can be an effective venue. Attendees may include customers, employees, suppliers, Lenders, and other professional associates. Some scenarios invite spouses and families. See the chapter for suggestions on times of year and included activities. There is opportunity for much interaction here, and the event will be long remembered.

Professional Subscriptions: Buy a subscription to *your* industry publication for your Lender. He will become more knowledgeable, which will not only benefit his understanding of your business requirements, but will also allow him to more effectively support your needs before the credit committee. He may become your Lender's resident expert in your industry.

One-on-One: How about some one-on-one activities? Many area "clubs" serve both breakfast and lunch. These may be country clubs, city clubs, and golf courses. These venues are somewhat *out of the mainstream* and could provide a quiet time for periodic meetings.

Stay out of the Lender's cafeteria or local diners—too many interruptions. An exception is the Lender's *executive* dining room—there will be many higher-level contacts there. You also could try a private dinner club.

Tickler File: Prepare a "tickler file" so you can send cards to recognize birthdays, anniversaries, graduations, promotions, and so on. Your efforts will result in an easy and inexpensive recognition factor that showcases *your* thoughtfulness. Follow newspaper notices for promotions, transfers, and the like. Once a year, a small gift to the Lender's secretary or administrative assistant may be appropriate (not to credit personnel). ***Use caution:*** Lenders usually cannot accept gifts over $25 each, and these usually must be perishable in nature.

See more "relationship" specifics within this chapter. Most business Borrowers don't bother—but you should. It can pay off in so many ways.

Chapter 11: Close to Home

Board of Directors: Business management needs to ensure that it has determined, and is utilizing, the suitable strategies and tactics to advance the business. How do business owners address such important challenges? *Additional* professional, and unbiased, opinions can be very beneficial to company management. Senior management should turn to experienced area business leaders and qualified professionals to create a board of directors. Depending on the size of the business and perceived needs, a *formal* board (consult with your attorney) or only an *advisory* board (informal group) may be the choice to make. Area business leaders are usually pleased to accept such positions, even though some liability may be attached. A more *informal* group of business friends and professionals may constitute an effective advisory board. Lenders place additional value on a management team that has a board in place. See more within this chapter.

The Management Team: Never underestimate the value, not only to the business but *also* to a potential Lender, of an *effective* management team. All things being equal, the *quality of management* is the *most important aspect* of a company's identity.

If your company is expanding, ensure that *attracting capable managers* is within your business plan. Have you identified areas where management is lacking, either in experience or manpower?

Even if you are currently close to a "one-man show," such considerations addressed within the plan reflect realistic planning. A Lender will be concerned if an apparent lack of management expertise is not addressed on a timely basis. This is *not* just for show—think *hard* about who this new management member would be, and when and how he would be acquired. Ask questions such as "Why would you like to work for this company?" and "What benefits or inducements should I offer to attract a competent manager?" Always give the new manager a reasonable time on the job to acclimate to the company and to his responsibilities—and time for family relocation as necessary.

Management Profiles: The Borrower should maintain *updated* one-page "profiles" on each officer, owner, and department manager (and possibly consider select loan guarantors as well). These are not to be complete résumés but only a summary recap. Include name, title, and current responsibilities. A brief business experience history with achievements should follow, winding up with an educational summary. Use a good-quality paper and an attractive and uniform format. *Update* annually. These will come in *very* handy for a number of presentations or media venues.

"Contract" Professionals: If a specialized discipline is lacking within your company—accounting, CFO, sales manager, and so on—and a full-time position cannot be financially justified, *consider utilizing those experienced professionals who provide part-time services on a contract basis.* Lenders and accountants usually have a network of these professionals. Activities such as *special projects*, preparing to go public, seeking business financing, information technology challenges, a business expansion or company move, preparation of a business plan, or opening a new sales office may also justify the use of such professionals. *Verify* references. Such management assistance can be extremely effective—even if only employed in the short term. Have your legal counsel review contracts.

Succession Management: What is your plan of succession management? This question, if not answered completely, frequently trips up the business owner. Specific information should be available within supporting company legal documents on file. This information should, of course, be a part of a business plan. But more important, what happens when a senior officer or owner dies (or becomes incapacitated)? What are the provisions and uses of key man insurance? If the company is being financed by a Lender, is it possible that the Lender will get the insurance check? Who will buy out the deceased's business ownership—or will it pass to the family? Who will immediately take up these *vacated* responsibilities? Address these concerns with legal counsel, and document the wishes of those involved.

Chapter 12: Your Winning Financing Package

The "Press Kit": Prepare a company "press kit"—a *preliminary* package reflecting the company identity and *limited* financial information prepared for prospective Lenders. This is really a *business promotional document.* Its contents and presentation should reflect a "bird's-eye view" of where the Borrower has been, where he is now, and where his forecasted strategies and tactics are expected to take him in the future. Once the package is completed, selected elements may be utilized later for a variety of functions. Formats for the cover and contents are suggested within the text.

Executive Summary: The *most important item* within the business plan is the executive summary. Although the plan may be scores of pages, if the two- or three-page executive summary doesn't effectively tell your story, the reader usually will not get much further. Preparing the business plan *first* simplifies preparation of the executive summary. This chapter provides necessary detail.

Business Plan: In situations wherein a *new* Lender is to be sourced, a business plan should usually be part of the financing package. Plans may be complete or abbreviated. The Borrower can spend upward of $5,000 to $10,000 for a professional to prepare a complete plan, or the Borrower can prepare it himself. Detailed sources of help, including the SBA, are provided within Web sites presented in this chapter. Of course, the Borrower has a business to run, and significant management time could be consumed in developing a thorough plan. Consider the best of both worlds: the Borrower prepares the required narrative portions and feeds these to the plan preparer, who edits and formats the plan. The idea behind this approach is to reduce overall costs. See a *suggested business plan flow* within the text. Discuss your requirements and capabilities with your accountant or financial advisers.

A number of *appendices* may complete a plan. While most of the material may already be available within the company, some will require extra effort. It is likely that not all possible appendices would apply to a single business. See the chapter text for appendix suggestions.

About the Author

Kenneth "Ken" Easton brings 38 years of comprehensive and successful business finance expertise. During his business tenure he has worked extensively with lenders and business borrowers of all sizes and within a host of industries.

In creating this book he has drawn upon his hundreds of personal contacts with business owners and associated professionals, as well as the universe of information gleaned from professional associations and responsibilities. Ken's positions included line lending, staff and regional management positions at G. E. Capital, Fleet and Shawmut Banks, Digital Federal Credit Union and Textron Financial Corporation.

Additionally, he has served as a business consultant to individual companies regarding lender mediations as well as funds sourcing. He developed, and was the Seminar Leader, for his small group business seminars, "How to Survive Your Banking Relationship," presented in Maine and Massachusetts during the early 1990s. He has managed his own business, Collateral Controls Corporation, serving commercial banks and commercial finance companies nationally prior to joining G. E. Capital, a former client.

His pro-active approach is critical for businesses challenged by financial survival. His strategies and tactics enable business borrowers to manage tenuous lender relationships. He has been successful in reducing lender demands, extending timing requirements, attracting replacement lenders and creating favorable loan restructurings. Ken has been instrumental in replacing current lenders with ones that are more suitable; even improving the borrower's existing loan terms and conditions. Ken has worked with borrowers, their lenders, involved counsel, loan officers, and borrower's related professionals to resolve difficult situations.

During his 38 years as both a business and lender consultant, seminar leader, speaker and senior lending officer, he has served in a variety of business and credit situations:

Business Financing Expertise	**Organizations Served**
Secured Business Lending	Commercial Banks
Possession / Liquidation Engagements	Alternative Lenders
	Secured Lenders
Funds Sourcing for Business	Corporations, LLC's, Small Business
Asset – Based Lending (Conforming)	Commercial Finance Companies
Leveraged Buyouts	Business Buyers
Factoring	Specialized Industries
New Business Development	De-Novo Loan Production Offices
Risk Management	State Agency Consulting
Real Estate/Investment Properties	Credit Union (Comm. Loans)
Negotiations / Mediations	SBA / Development Corporations
Financial Relationship Management	Business Borrowers

Ken has spoken before the ABA Credit Conference, various industry and credit groups, and business and service organizations. He was also an invited speaker at Bernard M. Baruch College, City University of New York.

Other professional training assignments included General Electric Company's four-week Advanced Sales/Marketing Management School presented in Toronto, Canada. Ken also completed a Strategic Marketing Management program at Boston University (University College). While in the Marines he placed 1st in an Instructors' Orientation Course conducted at the Marine Corps Schools, Quantico, VA.

Prior Professional & Personal Affiliations:

Past President: Kiwanis Club of Portland ME
Commercial Finance Association
Commercial Finance League of Connecticut
Smaller Business Association of New England
Turnaround Management Association

National Association of Credit Management
National Fisheries Institute
Robert Morris Associates

Ken was raised in Syracuse, NY, and attended the New York Military Academy. Following his six years at the military academy he enlisted in the United States Marine Corps. Following basic training at Parris Island, SC, he served with the 1st Marine Division during the Korean conflict. His wife Brenda, of 48 years, is the former Brenda Mellor of Methuen, MA. Along with Brenda, he also served with the Marine Detachment at the United States Naval Academy and at the Marine Corps Air Station at Cherry Point, NC, as well as many other duty stations nationally and overseas. Following his Honorable Discharge from the U. S. Marine Corps he moved to Connecticut where he attended the University of Hartford (Evening College) majoring in accounting.

Index